Sales of this book benefit *Discipline Without Stress, Inc.,*
a public charity assisting schools in the U.S.A.
to promote responsibility and improve education.
www.DisciplineWithoutStress.org

Parenting is a skill and—as with all skills—requires learning.

What Readers in the U.S.A. Are Saying...

"I was thrilled to read your book. It is full of simple, practical, logical advice for parents to guide children into making more thoughtful choices and leading to less stressful family environments."
Donna Rishor
Tucson, Arizona

"I love your parenting book! I have been using your strategies both at home and in the classroom. I can see a significant difference in the behaviors and attitudes of both my daughter and my students."
Monica Mallet
El Segundo, California

"I have been struggling with my five-year-old who knows his own mind. Coercion was not working! I was at a complete loss until I tried your approach. I had never tried anything like it. Your methods have definitely improved our relationships."
Karen McCormick
Norco, California

"I have already tried some things on my three-and-a-half-year-old daughter. The ideas are great."
Cathy Marlow
San Diego, California

"I am delighted that Dr. Marshall has finally written a book specifically for parents. I have been using his approach since my daughter was five years old. His principles are right on the mark."
Jodi Walker
Valencia, California

"Your parenting book gives the antidote to so many challenges. The strategies provide parents and grandparents help to work smarter and more effectively."
Paul Wislocki
Middlebury, Connecticut

"This is a practical, easy to understand, parenting handbook that offers a different way to think about behavior and child rearing. The ideas presented have already proven to be effective in the classroom and are sure to help parents create a happy, effective family unit."
Dr. Gwen Kessell
Lakeland, Florida

"I love this book! It makes so much sense! There are so many big aha moments. It is so helpful and has been magic with my daughter. She finally cleaned up her room! Thank you so much. The book has made a huge difference in my approach to parenting and teaching!"
Patricia Richmond
Port Orange, Florida

"As a former [school] principal, I was a disciple of the *Discipline without Stress* philosophy. As a grandfather, I am also using the excellent strategies in the parenting book. Promoting responsible behavior allows parents to have a life of their own."
Tom Bowers
Venice, Florida

"I have been struggling with my nine-year-old son. He has been consciously making bad decisions. After reading your book, my frame of mind immediately changed to *How can I change my approach?* The wealth of information and how to apply it are overwhelmingly enlightening."
Kehaulani Ah Quin
Hawaii

"This book provides parents with a Global Positioning System for raising responsible children. It is the road map for successful parenting."
James Burns
Winnebago, Illinois

"Powerful in its simplicity, Marshall's approach has the ability to transform relationships and help children see that responsible choices are the key to getting what they want out of life."
Sonya Overman
Goshen, Indiana

"This parenting book is a very easy and quick read. I only wish that they would give out this book at every baby shower or as a gift from the hospital when the baby and new mom go home. If everyone would parent like this, the world would be a much better place."
Lisa Lane
Lafayette, Indiana

"This is the book that parents and others who work with children have been looking for. As I read it, I was able to apply the simple concepts to my situations to see exactly where things went right or wrong. The concepts are universal to human interactions."

Kerry Ketcham
Des Moines, Iowa

"Your parenting book is so timely because responsibility seems a dying character trait—where people are motivated from within to do what is right and accept the responsibility for their choices. Parents need to raise their children to be able to make good decisions. This book lays a great groundwork to help them to do just that."

Elizabeth Finley
Winchester, Kansas

"Knowing what is best and making it happen are two different concepts. Marvin Marshall describes not only what works but also how to make it happen. Elegantly simple to understand, the simple, no-nonsense approaches in this parenting book work as well with young children as they do with teenagers and young adults."

Joy Darden Widmann
Louisburg, North Carolina

"This book shows parents how to teach children to be self-disciplined and to do the right thing simply because it is the right thing to do, rather than relying on obedience."

Sharon Millwood
Monroe, North Carolina

"I am looking forward to recommending this book. It provides fresh and compelling wisdom for parents. It inspires, and the ideas and recommendations will become part of those who read it."

Donna Gawell
Westerville, Ohio

"Your parenting book is exactly what every parent desperately needs because it does what other discipline experts have not done: It retains the authority responsible parents need while creating the respectful relationship parents want. Your sensible strategies show parents how, while your awesome anecdotes, stories, and examples offer practical suggestions. The delightful, well-written, and enjoyable style is an added bonus."

Bill Page
Nashville, Tennessee

"I appreciate the specific steps and suggestions. They are clear and easy to read and therefore easy to apply. I am excited about sharing this work with my adult children who are at the beginning stage of parenting. As a school administrator, mother of five, and grandmother of nine, I wish for all parents to have this book for helping children develop."
Connie Giles
Austin, Texas

"The book gives specific examples of how to help children become more responsible. It is a great asset for parents of any age child."
Diane LaGrone
Austin, Texas

"I have gleaned wonders from this book! There are so many things I have learned and implemented with my children."
Michelle Holbrook
Payson, Utah

"Marvin Marshall speaks with clarity, providing simple and practical steps parents can take to foster responsibility. After reading his book, you will have all you need to parent with confidence and with a predictable outcome."
Brenda Fuller
Charlottesville, Virginia

"As both a parent and a teacher, I strongly believe that in today's world it is more important than ever that we teach children how to make good choices—not through coercion, bribery, or threats, but in a respectful, loving way that inspires and teaches children to do the right thing simply because it is the right thing to do. I have used Dr. Marshall's methods in my classroom for the past several years. Each year I am amazed at how well the students respond to the hierarchy and how much more learning takes place. The *Raise Responsibility System* really works!"
Robin Tzucker
Kirkland, Washington

"My son is oppositionally defiant. I read the entire parenting book manuscript and loved it. Thank you so much for writing it and for addressing the needs of parents."
Alana Newman
Renton, Washington

"Your approach is truly inspiring! I'm using it with my 10- and 12-year-old children. It's awesome!"
Connie Fletcher
Spokane, Washington

"This is a fantastic book! Just learning how to ask reflective questions is worth the entire read."
Joan Brookins
Pine River, Wisconsin

What Readers Are Saying Internationally...

"I am a single parent and my children really test boundaries, but using the techniques and advice in this parenting book I am able to maintain control without screaming or punishing. The approach is fair, predictable and comprehendible, which makes it easy and effective. Best of all, it works!"
Kathy Ferguson
Brisbane, Australia

"This is a goldmine of a book with solid, practical nuggets on every page. Each one is profoundly life enhancing. Implementing the approaches will make you not only a much better parent, but also a much better person."
Jodi Kofsky
Dover Heights, New South Wales, Australia

"Parents will find this book simple, practical, and highly valuable in reducing levels of frustration. It brings a brighter future."
Aaron Grugan
Griffith, New South Wales, Australia

"This is one of the best parenting books I have read. I just wish I would have had it when my children were younger."
Marianna Kulcsar
Cochrane, Alberta, Canada

"Give this book to all of the new and old parents you know."
Helen Watler
Duncan, British Columbia, Canada

"This book is a great reference for parents. The use of empowering contingencies has certainly reduced my stress. The many examples and simple techniques are applicable to young people of all ages."
> Vaidhehi Kumar
> Markham, Ontario, Canada

"This book lays out the principles to affect positive, empowering choice-making change in others."
> Melissa Marsh
> Port Hardy, British Columbia, Canada

"What a timely, intelligent, and useful book! The clear explanation of how to help children make good decisions and be responsible is well stated, easy to implement, and very practical. Thank you, Dr. Marshall, for helping us to raise a responsible next generation."
> Arlene Geres
> Surrey, British Columbia, Canada

"I'm Chinese and a teacher in Beijing, China. It has always been a headache to keep the class in a good order every day before I used your *Hierarchy of Social Development*. After learning the hierarchy, my students have changed a lot. They evaluate their behavior every day. Even the most challenging boy is now trying his best to make progress. Thank you for your great ideas that have brought happiness to me and parents."
> Linda Nan Lee
> Beijing, China

"This book is a magic wand in the hands of parents to transform young people into responsible adults without stress on both either sides. A 'must-read' book for every parent and every adult dealing with adolescents!"
> Dr. S. Dawood Shah
> Vandalur, India

"I loved this book! It's not just another parenting book, and I was pleased to find it was much more than a book for teachers re-worked for parents. I'm passing this book on to my children in hopes that they will not make the same mistakes I made with them. Bravo, Dr. Marshall!"
> Debbie Mills
> Casablanca, Morocco

"I am a member of an educational enterprise that runs five high schools and colleges in Kathmandu, Nepal. I found your thoughts and ideas in your parenting book unique, practical, and effective for parents and educators all over the world who want to make a difference in educating children of all ages."
>
> Joseph Niraula
> Kathmandu, Nepal

"I recommend this book to every parent who wants to assist children to become responsible, self-reliant, independent problem solvers. It offers supportive, excellent advice for difficult situations that arise in parent-child relationships."
>
> Joan Western
> Auckland, New Zealand

"This book is hands down the most practical and resourceful parenting book I have read. It gives hope and down to earth suggestions with the desirable effect of fostering stronger and closer bonds while preparing young people to become responsible and caring adults."
>
> Debbie McFadyen
> Christchurch, New Zealand

"The book makes so much sense. It has long been my belief that children respond best to being given responsibility, which raises their self-esteem. Thank you for your common sense, practical advice."
>
> Judy Lee
> Half Moon Bay, New Zealand

"What good, practical wisdom! I am learning how important it is to acknowledge instead of praise and to communicate in positive ways. The book's advice is practical, clearly written, and has many insights about parenting."
>
> Cheah Yin Mee
> Singapore

"Your approach prompted me to sit back and reflect. Offering my seven-year-old choices rather than decrees showed immediate, positive results!"
>
> Doug Williams
> Seoul, South Korea

"I have been searching for a more human kind of discipline approach. Since reading the book, I've been changing the way I talk to my daughters. By talking to them in a positive way and letting them know how I care, things changed very fast. Dr. Marshall's principles have definitely helped me."

David Henestrosa
Manresa, Spain

"I find many of the things you say in the book help me: avoiding negative language, expect the good to happen, and how to ask reflective questions. A lot of sentences are so good I would like to hang them on the wall. I also like the quotations that you put in to help make your points. Some ideas seem too easy, but they work."

Lena Lilja Hallnissa
Leksand, Sweden

Also by Marvin Marshall

Discipline without Stress® Punishments or Rewards
How Teachers and Parents Promote Responsibility & Learning

Selected Works
Fostering Social Responsibility
Phi Delta Kappa International

Encouraging Responsible Student Behavior
(with Kerry Weisner)
Phi Delta Kappa International

Rethinking Our Thinking on Discipline:
Empower—Rather Than Overpower
Education Week

"Promoting Learning" Articles:
www.marvinmarshall.com/articles/articles_learning.htm

"Promoting Responsibility" Articles:
www.marvinmarshall.com/articles/articles_discipline.htm

"Promoting Responsibility & Learning" Newsletter Archives:
www.marvinmarshall.com/newsletter/index.htm

Parenting
without
STRESS

How to Raise Responsible Kids
While Keeping a Life of Your Own

■ ■ ■

Dr. Marvin Marshall

Piper Press ■ Los Alamitos, California

Published by: Piper Press
P.O. Box 2227
Los Alamitos, California 90720
Distributor's phone number: 800.606.6105
Publisher's phone number: 800.255.3192

DISCOUNTS

Substantial discounts are available to parenting and educational support groups, professional associations, corporations, and other organizations interested in promoting responsibility in youth. For details, contact the special sales department at Piper Press: 800.606.6105.

Publisher's Cataloging-In-Publication Data

Marshall, Marvin.
  Parenting without stress : how to raise responsible kids while keeping a life of your own / Marvin Marshall.

    p. : ill. ; cm.

  Includes bibliographical references and index.
  ISBN: 978-0-9700606-6-2

1. Parenting. 2. Responsibility in children. 3. Parent and child. 4. Child rearing. 5. Discipline of children. I. Title.

HQ755.8 .M37 2010
649/.1
2009936904

Special acknowledgment is given to the following:

Cathcart, Jim. *The Acorn Principle.* New York: St. Martin's Griffin, 1999.

Oakley, Ed, and Doug Krug. *Enlightened Leadership.* New York: Simon & Schuster, 1993.

Printed in the United States of America on acid-free paper.

Book Designer: Pamela Terry *www.opus1design.com*
Cover Designer: Rommel Johnson *www.designbyromjohn.com*
Editor: Brookes Nohlgren *www.booksbybrookes.com*

For parents who want to raise responsible citizens

ACKNOWLEDGMENTS

Brookes Nohlgren, my long-time editor, made this book possible.

I am indebted to Pamela Terry, the book designer whose services were invaluable, and to Rommel Johnson, my long-term friend, technical guru, and graphic artist who created the cover.

I thank the many parents who shared their experiences with me. Kerry Weisner and Darlene Collinson of British Columbia and Joy Widmann of North Carolina were especially helpful.

Evelyn Rochelle Marshall, my wife and partner for decades, has edited all of my writings. Her expertise and support were indispensable.

Our daughter, Hillary Marshall, was the most significant influence in my own growth as a parent.

TABLE OF CONTENTS

FOREWORD

When my elementary school first implemented Dr. Marshall's *Raise Responsibility System,* I was somewhat apprehensive about how such a program would work in my classroom. I have always felt that I created a positive learning environment in my class and, frankly, this system seemed like just one more passing fad to add to our classroom management file.

I realized that if I were going to successfully use this in my classroom, I should first try it at home. As a mother of two teenagers, I found the program's promise of creating a stress-free environment particularly appealing. I talked with my children about how stressful things had become at home and shared with them a little bit about the program I was about to "try out" on them.

Later that day, I heard my daughter slamming doors and screaming at the top of her lungs at her brother. Before, I would have stormed in to intervene and quickly react to the situation without even thinking. Instead, I tried one of the new techniques I was learning. I calmly asked my daughter a few simple questions to get her to reflect on her own behavior: "Is what you are doing something that is beneficial?" My daughter stopped mid-yell, looked at me, and said, "Oh, this is that discipline thing you are using at school, right? Okay, so, no! No, it's not." I asked, "Is what you are doing something that falls in line with the standards of our family?" She sighed, "No." I said, "Would you tell me what our family rule is regarding yelling?" She relayed to me that yelling was not allowed and that if we had anything to say we could say it in a calm manner. Finally, I asked, "Well, what do you think we should do so that this doesn't happen again?"

I told her to go to her room and reflect on what we should do about what had happened between her and her brother. A little while later, she came back and asked to talk to her brother. She apologized for yelling at him and proceeded to give us a list of consequences she had decided on. "I guess I should not use the computer for three weeks, or talk on the phone, or go to the movies with my friends," she began. "I think this will help me remember our family rule the next time I want to yell and slam the door." We were stunned! Honestly, this was the first time she had truly accepted responsibility so calmly.

The next three weeks were very interesting. She answered the phone and we could hear her explain, "I can't talk on the phone right now because my parents . . . I mean, I have restricted myself."

Since we began using this program in our home, life is so much more enjoyable! The truth is that our children do know what is expected of them. Holding them to a higher standard of responsibility has made all of our lives more peaceful.

Thank you!

—Wendi Hall, Vestavia Hills, Alabama

PREFACE

The approach you use helps determine
what the young person becomes.

Getting to a specific destination requires knowing where you want to go and then boarding the train that will take you there.

> As the train conductor made his way down the aisle, the Associate Justice of the United States Supreme Court, Oliver Wendell Holmes, saw him coming. The forgetful Mr. Holmes reached into his pocket, then into a second pocket, then into a third pocket. By the time the conductor approached the then fretful Mr. Holmes, the conductor said, "That's all right, Mr. Holmes, I know who you are. When you get home and find your ticket, just mail it in." Mr. Holmes replied, "You don't understand. It's not the ticket I'm concerned about; it's where I'm going."

Today's parents have two "trains" of discipline from which to choose. The older approach uses rewards and punishments—the same kind used with animals. Its fuel is manipulation in the forms of bribery and force aimed at compliance. Its ultimate goal is *obedience.* This train leads to dependence while the passengers endure stress, resistance, and poor relationships.

Parenting without Stress advocates a more modern approach for the parenting experience. It uses more efficient fuel and travels to a more enlightened destination: *responsibility.* Its passengers experience positive relationships, effective parenting, and joy in the journey.

INTRODUCTION

Situations arise that require parents to discipline.
But discipline need not be negative or stressful.

Parenting should be a joy! Helping to guide and shape the life of another human being from infancy to adulthood offers so many opportunities for positive, meaningful interactions that make life rich, rewarding, and, joyful. Too often, though, parenting becomes frustrating, stressful, disheartening, and in some cases frightening. Increasingly irresponsible and anti-social behavior among today's youth combined with parents' use of outdated and ineffective methods create frequent power struggles that lead to stress and bad feelings for parents and children alike. Everyone loses.

But it doesn't have to be this way—and it shouldn't be. By using three powerful, enduring, and universal practices, you will be amazed at how cooperative your children become. You will reduce your stress and engender responsible behavior in your children the moment you use the *Raise Responsibility System*. Irresponsible behavior diminishes, and distressing and demeaning power struggles become a thing of the past. When disruptions occur, you will be able to handle them swiftly and without conflict or stress.

WHY A NEW APPROACH IS NEEDED

A by-product of the ease of access to information and contact with others in our technological age is that many young people feel more control over their lives than in generations past. Today's young people know and exercise their rights and have an unprecedented level of independence. When a parent tries to change a youth's behavior by forcing obedience—by threatening, punishing, bribing, or using any other coercive or manipulative tactic—the reaction will likely be resistance.

A typical response to this trend might be to blame the youngsters. Think about it for a moment: When we plant flower seeds and if the plant does not blossom, do we blame the flowers? Or is there something the planter *did* or *did not* do? Let us remember that parents are the first contacts and models for children.

If you view young people's misbehavior as a *learning opportunity—a chance to help them grow and develop*—then misbehavior can become the trigger for meaningful and rewarding exchanges. The result is greater responsibility in your children, less stress for you, and improved relationships for all.

Here is my promise to you. Once you implement the strategies in this book, you will become more effective in your parenting, feel less stress, experience more joy, improve your relationships with your children, and have more time for a life of your own. Your children will become more self-disciplined and responsible. Guaranteed! Please note, however, that this doesn't mean you can change their nature—no more than planting an acorn can grow into a giant redwood tree. However, you certainly can influence your children to blossom into responsible and contributing members of society. If you desire these traits, then use the proven methods shown in this book.

ABOUT THIS BOOK

Is this book for you?

If you experience parental stress, this book will help you diminish it while, at the same time, bringing you more satisfaction as a parent.

What areas does this book include?

Although the book offers practical solutions to parental challenges, you will find that it also promotes personal growth by increasing your effectiveness and improving your relationships.

Where can the ideas be used?

The strategies in this book can be used in any home and with any youth or youth group. They also can be used by anyone in a relationship—husband with wife, partner with partner, sibling with sibling, and supervisor with supervised.

When can the strategies be implemented?

Every suggestion can be implemented immediately.

Why this book?

As our daughter grew older, I began to realize that her personality and make-up were unlike ours, her natural parents. I changed my parenting approach—resulting in a significant reduction of stress and a dramatic improvement in our relationship.

Also, when I returned to teaching after 24 years in counseling, guidance, supervision, and school administration, I met with an awakening. Society and youth had changed, but adults were using approaches no longer successful with so many of today's young people. I witnessed an increasing lack of respect for adults, parents who were at their wit's end, and teachers who were leaving the profession—in large part due to discipline problems.

I set out to find a way to have young people WANT to behave more responsibly. After developing the *Raise Responsibility System*, I began sharing it in seminars. "Do you have a book?" became a common question. After publication of *Discipline without Stress® Punishments or Rewards*, I was often asked to write a book specifically for parents.

What is this book about?

The following outlines *Parenting without Stress: How to Raise Responsible Kids While Keeping a Life of Your Own.*

PART I – THE THREE PRACTICES

Chapter 1 Positivity

Our thoughts prompt our feelings, our behavior, and our influence on others. Positivity is the basis of persistence and hope. Positivity is empowering. This chapter shows how to practice positivity and make it a habit for you and your children.

Chapter 2 Choice

Offering choices is a simple approach that parents can use to immediately reduce stress. It also promotes self-discipline and improves relationships. The empowerment of choice is universal; it works with people of all ages. Most importantly, responsible behavior has a direct correlation to the number of decisions young people make. This chapter shows how to employ choice and reduce coercion that works against effectiveness and good relationships.

Chapter 3 Reflection

This chapter shows how to bring about desired changes. It explains the most effective approach to induce people to influence themselves.

PART II – THE RAISE RESPONSIBILITY SYSTEM

Chapter 4 Teaching

The *Hierarchy of Social Development* explains how sharing four concepts has a significant and almost "magical" impact on having young people become more responsible.

Chapter 5 Asking

Recognition that a problem exists is the first step in prompting a voluntary change in behavior. In the vast majority of cases, just this acknowledgment changes the young person's behavior without any other action required by the parent.

Chapter 6 Eliciting

How to handle continual irresponsible behavior is the subject of this chapter. Eliciting a procedure or consequence has dramatic advantages over imposing punishments.

PART III – ADDITIONAL ASSISTANCE

Chapter 7 Promoting Responsibility

A better option than relying on rules, how to control impulses, understanding boys, and additional suggestions are shared in this chapter.

Chapter 8 Increasing Effectiveness & Improving Relationships

Understanding your child's nature, listening to learn, family meetings, and numerous other suggestions are described in this chapter.

Chapter 9 Answers to Questions

Frequently asked questions are answered. They are divided into three categories: general, the young, and older youth.

PART IV – PARENTING PITFALLS

Chapter 10 Rewarding Expected Behavior

Topics include rewards and compensation, rewards as incentives, rewards as acknowledgments, using rewards to promote responsible behavior, rewards and self-esteem, and additional considerations about the use of rewards with young people.

Chapter 11 Imposing Punishments

Some pitfalls of *imposing* punishments on young people are shared along with myths about punishments in general and how they are counterproductive with young people.

Chapter 12 Telling

Topics include the ineffectiveness of telling, problems with telling, and a better alternative.

ABOUT THE AUTHOR

Dr. Marvin Marshall—an American educator, writer, and professional speaker—is widely known for his program on discipline and learning and his landmark book *Discipline Without Stress® Punishments or Rewards: How Teachers and Parents Promote Responsibility & Learning*. The book is described at ***www.DisciplineWithoutStress.com***.

He has founded a public charity to supply this book at no charge to teachers of any school in the U.S.A. Applications are available at ***www.DisciplineWithoutStress.org***.

He has presented in 43 of the United States, in 15 countries, and on 5 continents to parent groups; schools; school districts; universities; local, state, national, and international associations; and government agencies.

He has a worldwide audience of subscribers to his free monthly newsletter, "Promoting Responsibility & Learning." You can subscribe at ***www.ParentingWithoutStress.org***.

His proactive and noncoercive (but not permissive) discipline, learning, and parenting approach stemmed from his acquiring knowledge about young people as a parent; a recreation director and camp counselor; a classroom teacher at the elementary, middle, and high school levels; a middle school counselor; a middle school assistant principal; a high school counselor; a high school guidance department chair; a high school assistant principal of both supervision and control and curriculum and instruction; and as an elementary and high school principal.

He has also been a demonstration teacher, instructional coordinator, athletic coordinator, district director of education, and full-time instructor at California State University, Los Angeles.

He earned his Bachelor's in Language Arts and his Master's in Business Administration at California State University, Los Angeles. His Doctorate in Education was awarded by the University of Southern California.

He is certified with the William Glasser Institute in *Reality Therapy* and *Choice Theory*.

His experiences prompted him to develop a system that employs internal motivation—rather than relying on the external approaches of bribes and manipulation or by employing coercion in the form of threats or punishments. A prime reason for the system's success and the growing number of parents and teachers using it is that internal motivation is significantly more effective in changing behavior than any external approach.

His system is based on the simple fact of life that a person can be controlled by another person but can be changed only by the actual person. This understanding that individuals can only change themselves is critical to successfully influencing young people to become more responsible—while simultaneously reducing parental stress and allowing parents to have a life of their own.

His countless requests to share his approach specifically for parents prompted this book.

Contact Information:
The author can be reached in the U.S.A. at
Marvin Marshall & Associates, Inc.
P.O. Box 2227, Los Alamitos, CA 90720
www.MarvinMarshall.com

PART I
The Three Practices

Positivity

Choice

Reflection

INTRODUCTION
The Three Practices

*Three practices show you
how to reduce your stress.*

Parenting should be a joy. But what do you do when a child defies your request? The usual approach is to get angry and resort to using some type of authority. If you have had this kind of experience and would like a less stressful and more effective approach, then this book is for you.

Even though you may have a wonderful relationship with your own youngster, notice how the following situation illustrates that using authority could have escalated a bad situation into a worse one.

> The young girl was new to a group home where a few other young girls also resided. Various household procedures were explained to her, one of which was to make her bed before coming downstairs for breakfast.
>
> The following morning, the girl refused to make her bed.
>
> The supervisor, rather than falling victim to the usual coercive approach—which would have resulted in anger, stress, and ill will in both parties—went downstairs to the kitchen where the other girls were already gathered for breakfast. She said to them, "We have a new girl who refuses to make her bed. I need a volunteer to help her."
>
> The volunteer approached the new girl and said, "I know exactly how you feel, and making the bed is not a big deal. I'll help you and then we can go to breakfast where the other girls want to meet you."
>
> As soon as the volunteer started to make the bed, the new girl pitched in. The bed was quickly made.

What happened here? The supervisor used a *noncoercive* approach. She knew that trying to coerce the girl would only result in an adversarial relationship—a no-win situation for both parties. The wise adult knew from experience in working with young people that using coercion is the least effective approach for having people *want* to do what you would like them to do.

As you read about the three practices, you will quickly realize that each is based on *creating motivation* to have your child do what you would like your child to do. You will be pleasantly surprised and may conclude, "These are so simple! Why haven't I been using them?" When you start using the practices, you will quickly see how they reduce stress for everyone involved, promote responsible behavior in your child, increase your effectiveness as a parent, and improve your relationship.

1
Positivity

People do better when they feel good—not when they feel bad.

Positivity is like a magnet. People are drawn to the positive and repelled by the negative. This simple truth about human nature is the foundation of our first practice.

WHY POSITIVITY?

Positivity—thinking and communicating in positive terms—works wonders in drawing others toward us and having them do what we would like them to do. By contrast, communicating in negative terms pushes people away. To prove this, take just a moment to recall an incident when you received a compliment or word of encouragement. What kind of feeling did it prompt and what were your feelings toward that other person? Now think about the last time you were criticized or blamed. How did you feel? Did you have negative or positive thoughts about that person?

We are often not aware of the power of our communications. Yet, as the following demonstrates, even subtle gestures can greatly influence how others respond to us:

> A salesgirl in a candy store always had customers lined up waiting while the other salesgirls stood around. Intrigued by the popularity of this one employee, the owner asked for her secret. "It's easy. The other girls scoop up more than a pound of candy and then take some away," she explained. "I always scoop up less than a pound and then *add* to it."

Whether positive or negative, the messages we send trigger emotions in others because *people typically act from their feelings.* This phenomenon is deeply rooted in the interaction between our thoughts and our feelings.

Our Thoughts Affect Our Feelings

What we *think* has a direct impact on how we *feel*. First comes the thinking, followed by the feeling. In other words, *what we feel is the result of what we think*. For example, your youngster fails to arrive home at the usual time. Thinking about the situation prompts feelings of anxiety or fear. Upon returning home, your child explains the reason for being late: Your youngster was chosen as the school's principal for the day. Relieved with this new information, you share your child's joy. Notice that in both instances first came the thought immediately followed by the emotion.

Our Feelings Affect Our Behavior

Imagine for a moment that you are picking up your child after the youngster's very first day of school. Curious about how the day went, you ask questions such as, "How was your day? Did you learn anything? Did you meet any new friends?" But one question inevitably arises: "Do you like your teacher?"

We intuitively know that how a child *feels* toward the teacher will have an influence on the child's effort, behavior, and even personality. If the child has negative feelings about the teacher, it can affect the child's entire school year, and perhaps even the youngster's future education can be affected. *Therefore, it is imperative that adults speak to children in positive ways.*

Our Self-Talk Creates Our Reality

Shifting from negative communications to positive ones starts with our own self-talk. The reason is that our self-talk has a direct bearing on our behavior, our performance, and our influence on others. In fact, *a good case can be made that our self-talk creates our reality.* Think of fear. That is self-talk. Think of anxiety. That is self-talk. Mark Twain in his older years stated, "I am an old man and have known a great many troubles, but most of them never happened."

Our self-talk is filtered. We respond to stimuli (what we hear, see, touch, taste, and smell) based upon current and prior experiences. For example, an adult may consider the concept of *obedience* in positive terms, whereas a teenager trying to cut the umbilical cord who responds negatively to any use of authority may think of the same word in negative terms. It is important to understand that, to the human brain, there is no such thing as immaculate perception: *What we see is what we thought before we looked.* We can develop positive self-talk just by being aware of this nonconscious filtering system.

Many psychologists assert that negative thinking—including labeling something as negative or perceiving something as unmanageable—promotes our own stress. But we have the power to change our thinking—and thereby our emotions. Neuroscientists have discovered that our thoughts alter the physical structure in the gray matter of our brain. In other words, the brain and our physiology change as a result of the thoughts we give it.

For many of us, thinking in negative terms is natural. For example, assume that you are a working parent. One morning your supervisor asks you to stop by the office before leaving for the day. Most people's self-talk would sound something like, "I wonder what I did wrong?" In effect, they would anticipate the meeting as a negative experience. Since you really don't know what the conversation with the supervisor is going to be about, such self-talk can prompt unnecessary stress and anxiety until the actual meeting. Thankfully, self-talk need not be negative. The way you feel about the forthcoming meeting can be changed by just one word. Compare the different feelings aroused from these two thoughts: (1) I *have* to see my supervisor vs. (2) I *get* to see my supervisor.

Performance, too, suffers when we engage in negative or pessimistic self-talk. Our efficiency plummets, and we begin to view ourselves as less capable. This leads us to see our lives as increasingly less manageable and less in control. As a result, our stress increases even more. The greater our stress, the greater our tendency to respond with further negative self-talk. The cycle continues until eventually we have self-talked our way right into a self-fulfilling prophecy.

> A man was driving down a country road in his brother's car when the tire went flat. He looked in the trunk, but there was no jack. He decided he would have to borrow one, so he started to walk down the road looking for a house.
>
> The day was hot and humid, and as he walked along he became more and more negative in his thinking. "They may not have a jack that fits my car. And even if they do,

they may not want to lend it to me. The people around here are probably not very friendly."

When the man finally arrived at a house and knocked on the door, he immediately pronounced to the woman who opened it, "Keep your darn jack!"

We become happier and more effective when we choose thoughts that empower, rather than those that weaken or constrict. A monkey knows to eat only the nourishing part of the banana and throw away the bitter peel. Yet, as humans, we absorb criticism, embarrassment, ridicule, and other negatives—*some of which are our own creation*! We often "chew on the peel" rather than ingest the nutritional part.

Labeling

The topic of labeling arose during a luncheon conversation with William Glasser, M.D.—the eminent psychiatrist, creator of *Reality Therapy,* and author of *Choice Theory.* Dr. Glasser posed to me the following question: "In baseball, when is an *out* an *out?*" He then answered, "Only when the *umpire calls it an out*—and not before."

That conversation had a significant impact on how I began to think and act. First, I soon realized that other people's opinions became "wrong" only when I labeled them as such. The term "diversity" took on a new meaning for me. I started to listen to others with a more open attitude and began to acknowledge others' viewpoints more readily. Since the thinking of my wife and daughter are so different from mine, I began to understand their points of view on various issues. I became more enlightened. Because I was expanding my awareness, I grew. As I became a more open listener by not putting a label on others' thinking, our relationship was the better for it.

The second profound thought I apply daily relates to how I approach situations. I began to realize that a bad situation was indeed *bad* only if I labeled it as such. I could choose to label the same situation as a *challenge.* I found that how I responded to a situation was a direct result of how I labeled it. If I viewed something as negative, it became negative. When I perceived it as a challenge, I was less apt to think as a victim and more likely to view it with a greater feeling of empowerment.

Positivity Is Constructive; Negativity Is Not

What we think and say becomes our habit. When our self-talk is negative, we have a tendency to communicate with others in a negative way. This is particularly true with our children. So often when we want our children to change, we attempt to influence them by using negative communications rather than positive ones that would actually prompt them to *want* to do what we would like. Even the worst salesperson knows enough not to make the customer angry. Yet, because we allow our emotions to direct us, we often ignore this commonsense approach and send negative messages. You can easily tell if your communications are sending negative messages if what you say *blames, complains, criticizes, nags, punishes,* or *threatens.*

Negativity can have long-lasting repercussions. One or two mean words from an adult can stay with a child forever. Think about such scars from your childhood that may still be with you. The adults who spoke negatively to you almost certainly had no idea of the damage they were inflicting. As parents, we must always be *conscious* of the power we wield.

Positive communications elevate the spirit; they offer encouragement and support. They send the message that the other person is capable of handling challenges. Positivity creates hope and prompts feelings of being valued, supported, and respected. Communicating in positive terms triggers enthusiasm, capability, pride, dependability, and responsibility—none of which are triggered by negativity. Because positive communications do not trigger defensiveness in the other person, they are more effective in influencing a person to *want* to change. Therefore, if you want to influence others to do what you would like, *become conscious of phrasing your communications in positive terms.*

See if you can visualize this scenario:

> You were five years old. It was a beautiful spring day. The training wheels had been removed. Your parent steadied the bicycle just a bit as you started to pedal away, and then you were let go. Your parent was running beside the bike, but you were on your own. The wind was in your face; a huge smile developed. You were happy but still nervous. Something inside seemed to remind you that disaster might strike at any time. And then you heard these words,

"Keep going! You're doing it!" They were magical words of encouragement. "Don't worry! I'm here if you need me." Your confidence grew and the negative thoughts seemed to melt away.

There is no empowerment more effective than self-empowerment.

Because being positive is so enabling, it makes sense to stop all thoughts and communications that are negative. Reflecting on the positive can immediately turn around a negative emotion. Continually ask yourself: *"How can I communicate this message in a positive way?"* For example, saying, "You have a bad temper," is disabling, whereas, "It would be in your own self-interest to ease up on your temper," prompts reflection and is enabling.

Use Positivity in Negative Situations

Positivity involves more than just having a positive outlook; it is also about remaining positive *in negative situations.*

Here is an example:

> A mother considered herself a positive person because she was naturally upbeat and smiled a lot, but she hadn't realized that she was only positive and upbeat when things were going well.
>
> She started thinking about her three-year-old son and realized that she often was negative with him when she was feeling stressed. She made a conscious decision to work on her positivity to see if being positive in negative circumstances would be more effective than nagging and getting stern.
>
> One day, just as they were about to leave the house, she noticed that her little boy had dragged all the pillows off the family room couch and put them in piles on the floor. They often put the pillows together to build things for fun, but this time she was angry that there was an unexpected mess on the floor. Because of her son's impromptu pillow-building, they were going to have to spend precious time cleaning up a room that she had already tidied—and just when they were in a hurry to get out the door. She took a deep breath and suppressed her first instinct to bark a series of orders: "Clean this

up now! You made this mess after I had already cleaned and now you need to clean it up yourself—fast—because we have to leave."

Instead, she deliberately searched for a more positive route. She looked for some way to acknowledge her son's efforts and said, "You have really been creative here! Tell Mommy about what you've made." The youngster told her that he had made a butterfly house and then he shared his thinking. He told her about where the butterfly would live and all the different rooms in the butterfly house. It took two minutes to hear and admire his creation. He then happily joined her in putting the pillows back on the couch.

The mother was amazed by this experience. The two minutes she spent listening to her little boy was less time than she normally would have spent demanding he put the cushions back. In the past, the boy's reaction to her scolding was to shut down and become upset and difficult.

The experience was an eye-opener for her. She found that a positive approach took some thinking on her part but that the results were well worth the effort. She had spent less time than she would have otherwise, had preserved a good relationship, and both she and her son left the house in a good mood.

As you will learn in this book, disciplining children using a positive approach is really quite simple and becomes even easy *as you become more positive in your own self-talk.* By making this one basic shift in your parenting, you will immediately see changes in how your children *of any age* respond. Your children will feel better about themselves—and about you. They will become cooperative, you will feel less stress, and the relationship will improve.

How to Practice Positivity
So, how do you do it?

As with all changes to influence others, the first step relates to your own thinking. Do you perceive the youngster as deliberately misbehaving, or do you view the behavior as the child's best attempt to solve a frustration? *Your perception directs how you will react.* If you think your child is deliberately causing problems, your natural reaction will be to respond in a negative way. On the other hand, if you think the child is attempting to resolve some dissatisfaction or frustration, then your approach will be to help the youngster. Thinking of children as *becoming adults but are presently just younger* directs your behavior to help—rather than to hurt.

Avoid Negative Language

If you start a phrase with the word "unfortunately," you immediately create a negative mindset in the person receiving the message. The word conjures up that something bad or unpleasant is about to follow, and whatever you say after "unfortunately" will be viewed negatively. The same holds true with the word "but" because it has a tendency to negate whatever comes before it; for example, "Yes, you can go with your friends *but* you need to be back by nine o'clock." Substituting the word "and" for "but" eliminates the negative connotation: "Sure you can go with your friends *and* be back by nine o'clock." It creates an entirely different feeling.

Your language helps mold your child's thoughts. "No" is a negative word and implies wrongdoing. It almost always provokes resistance. "No" is not meant to be flexible or compromising. Even in a conversational voice, no one reacts well to the word "no"—as in, "What part of 'no' don't you understand?" It has a commanding aspect, is harsh, and builds reluctance. Interestingly, when children are told not to do something, they often want to do it even more. Forbidden fruit always tastes sweeter.

The good news is that parents rarely actually need to say "no" to children. The exception, of course, is when children's behavior puts their own or others' health or safety at risk. Instead of "no," parents can use "not," which does not carry the negative overtones that "no" connotes and therefore does not provoke the same resistance.

Every time you want to say "no," ask yourself what is *not* okay about what your children are doing. Then replace the word "no" with the word "not" and add a phrase that describes the *behavior you want*—rather than one you do not want. This gives children information about what is acceptable. It is easier for children to hear how to do something correctly than to hear that what they are doing is wrong. More often than not, when children are given information respectfully, they comply rather than resist. To a child playing with a ball against the garage door, say, "Please, not against the door; bounce the ball on the sidewalk." You can also empower the child to make a better decision by asking a reflective question, such as, "Can you make a better choice?" These same words can be used in many situations. The approach places the responsibility for coming up with an acceptable decision on the child—where it belongs. This type of communication *starts the child thinking:* "What *would* be an appropriate location for playing with the ball?"

Young people embrace positive words and suggestions; they don't resist them. When you start to think in terms of what you DO want, rather than what you do not want, the practice becomes quite easy, as in, "A shoe is made for walking, rather than for throwing," and "A crayon is made for coloring, rather than for breaking." These verbal guidelines are important. They *teach* children without being negative or using power or control over them. These verbal communications are influential, strong, and effective. *Instead of using power over children, you are helping them to become more responsible.* A parent wrote me:

> Your answer to my question reminded me of a time when my son, Adam, was two. Everything was "No, no, no!" My husband had just had it with him and said, "Adam, don't you say 'No' to me again. I've had enough, young man." Adam looked at him, full of steam, and said, "NOT!" I couldn't help but start laughing. You are right. "Not" doesn't have the same negative effect as "No!"

Paint Positive Pictures

Practicing positivity requires painting positive mental pictures. Let's see how this works. Imagine you have just arrived at a restaurant that does not take reservations. The lobby is full of people waiting to be seated. The host says to you, "I don't have any tables right now. You'll have to wait 30 minutes." Now picture the same situation again, except this time the host says to you, "I'll have a wonderful table for you in half an hour." Notice the difference in how you received the information. The chances that you'll actually wait to eat at the restaurant are greater in hearing the second message.

The brain thinks in pictures, rather than in words. Think for a moment about the last time you had a dream. Did the dream appear in words, or did your dream appear in pictures? Being aware that the brain processes information in pictures can help you become significantly more effective. Success depends upon the *pictures you paint*—both for yourself and for others.

While waiting in an airport, I heard the airline gate agent say to a young boy, "Don't go down the ramp." I knew instantly that the agent had created a problem. Sure enough, within a few minutes I saw the airport official chasing after the youngster—down the ramp! Chances are the agent would have had more success and less stress if he had said to the curious youngster something like, "Passengers wait in this area. Even adults need a special pass to go down the ramp."

The human brain is very susceptible to suggestions. Just for a moment, *don't* think of a pretty white kitten with a red bow around its neck. Now *don't* think of a grey elephant with pink dots. *Don't* visualize the color blue. What did you visualize? Now, try to *visualize* "Don't." Can you? Neither can children. When a child hears, "Don't run in the house," the picture in the child's mind is one of running in the house. If you say, "We walk in the house," *walking* is what the child visualizes. Positive messages encourage the youngster to respond to your request.

Here's another example. Although there is nothing physiologically wrong, a young boy still wets his bed. After tucking the boy in, the parent says, "Now, don't wet your bed tonight." What will the child visualize as he falls asleep? Consider how much more effective a positive picture would be: "Let's see if you can keep the bed dry tonight." Which statement conjures up the image the parent wants? Which is most likely to bring about the desired behavior?

After I shared this scenario with school parents one evening, the following day the superintendent of schools told me about his experience with his three-year-old son who was regularly wetting his bed:

> Before putting my son to bed last night, I first led him to the bathroom as I usually do. Then after I tucked him in and kissed him goodnight, my last words to him were, "Let's see if we can keep the bed dry tonight."
>
> As soon as he got out of bed this morning, he came running to me in the kitchen, calling, "Come, look, Daddy. See, my bed is dry!"

By describing what you *want* rather than what you *don't want,* you can also avoid the problem of stopping one undesirable behavior only to have your youngster engage in a *different* one that is also counterproductive. In response to a positive message, the young person will strive to follow your suggestion, "If you use the fork to tap the rhythm on your knee rather than on the table, you can still enjoy doing it without bothering others."

The story of a banker who often dropped a coin in a beggar's cup further illustrates the point of painting empowering pictures.

> Unlike most people, the banker would insist on taking one of the beggar's pencils. The banker would say, "You are a merchant, and I always expect to receive good value from the merchants with whom I do business." This daily routine went on for some time, but one day the street beggar was gone. Time passed and the banker forgot about him.
>
> Years later, though, the banker walked by a little store and there was the former beggar—now a shopkeeper! The shopkeeper said, "I always hoped you might someday come by. You are largely responsible for my being here. You kept telling me I was a merchant. I started to think of myself in that way, instead of as a beggar looking for handouts. I started selling pencils—lots of them—and today I have a little business. You showed me respect and influenced me to look at myself differently."

Use Contingencies Rather Than Consequences

Although consequences can be either positive or negative, when parents refer to "consequences," these are often in terms of threats or punishments that are *imposed.* An imposed consequence only works when a young person finds value in the relationship or when the person sees value in what he is being asked to do. Otherwise, people perceive an imposed consequence in negative terms because of the inference, "Do this—or else!" It threatens pain or discomfort should the young person fail to comply with the demand. Such is the case when the adult says, "If you continue to do that, then this is what is going to happen to you." Telling a youngster, "You chose to do that and now you must realize the consequence" is a pseudo choice and plays a mind game. It prompts the young person to feel as though he or she brought on the punishment. "If your work is not finished, you're not going" is also perceived negatively. In addition, the adult workload is now greater because the *adult* has the added task of checking that the work is finished before giving the child permission to go. This approach transfers the responsibility away from the young person—where it belongs—to the adult.

A more effective approach than *imposing* consequences is to use contingencies because they paint positive pictures and empower. Contingencies prompt people to *feel better*, not worse. A contingency sounds like, "Yes, you may do that, as long as you first do this." For example, "Yes, you may ride in the boat, as long as you wear a life jacket." Contingencies are very effective because they promise with a positive—rather than threaten with a negative the way imposed consequences do.

Test this on yourself. Reflect on which of the following *you* would rather hear:

A. "If you don't finish, you're not going."
   (negatively stated *consequence*)

B. "Certainly you may go—as soon as your work is completed."
   (positively stated *contingency*)

Suppose your daughter would like to visit her friend on a school night. You would like her to complete her homework first. When she asks, "Can I go to Tracy's house?" your response using a contingency might sound something like, "Certainly, as soon as your homework is finished." Or better yet, "As soon as you are satisfied with the quality of your homework." Two critical components for raising responsibility are at work here. In these contingency statements, the responsibility for completing the homework is clearly with the young person. In addition, the parent has conveyed a message of trust and confidence—not only by allowing the daughter to visit with her friend but also in having *the daughter approve* the quality of her own homework.

Contingencies can be used with young people of any age to encourage cooperation and to build responsibility. For example, saying to a young child, "We're not going to the park until you put away your toys" is not nearly so effective as saying, "As soon as your toys are put away, we can go to the park."

In the preceding examples, the parent's responses are stated using *empowering contingencies*, rather than *disempowering consequences*. The girl is more motivated to complete her homework so she can visit her friend, and the young child is induced to put away the toys in order to go to the park. As Booker T. Washington once said, "Few things help an individual more than to place responsibility upon him and to let him know that you trust him." Contingencies do exactly that.

Joy, a teacher who uses this strategy both at home and at school, related the following experience of using a contingency with her teenage daughter, who, as Joy put it, "always tries to get away with doing the least possible around the house."

> Tonight I told her, "Of course you may go out with your boyfriend—once the dishes are washed and put away." Fifteen minutes later, not only were the dishes put away, but the floor was also swept and the stove and countertops wiped clean!

An example of the difference between a consequence and a contingency was illustrated beautifully on the classic television sitcom *The Cosby Show* featuring Bill Cosby playing the role of Dr. Cliff Huxtable.

> Dr. Huxtable was sitting at the dinner table with Rudy, his youngest daughter. He would not let Rudy leave the table until she had eaten all of her dinner. Rudy refused to finish the food on her plate. The father gave her a choice of finishing her dinner and leaving the table or remaining at the dinner table until she did finish. Still she refused to eat, whereupon the father went on and on about another five-year-old who would not finish her dinner—whose friends all graduated from elementary school, went to middle school, graduated from high school, and then went off to college while the girl remained at the dinner table still refusing to finish her dinner. Rudy was not impressed.
>
> Then Denise, Rudy's older sister, came home. Rudy could hear Denise and her friends move the living room couch, roll up the carpet, start to play music, and begin to dance. Just then, Denise came into the kitchen, and

Rudy asked her older sister, "Can I dance with you and your friends?" Denise responded with, "Sure, as soon as you finish your dinner," whereupon Rudy promptly ate her three Brussels sprouts, placed the plate in the sink, and went out to dance.

Dr. Huxtable had given his daughter what amounted to a *consequence*: Finish your dinner or stay at the table. Denise, on the other hand, offered Rudy a *contingency*. Too often, we say to young people, "Eat your Brussels sprouts or else" and then don't understand why they are not motivated. *Imposed* consequences do not change the way a person *wants* to behave—and thus do nothing to *promote responsibility* or *self-discipline*.

The old adage reminds us, "A person convinced against his will remains of the same opinion still." Each time you threaten with a consequence, you are sending a message of distrust and low expectation. As with other forms of coercion, *imposed* consequences invite resentment. They create stress for both parent and child. They also rob children of opportunities to become more responsible.

In sum, using contingencies is stress reducing and significantly more effective than using consequences—as indicated from a communication I received:

> I already tried some things on my three-and-a-half-year-old daughter. I have quite a strong-willed child who has hit the terrible threes. (The twos were so much easier for my husband and me.) I've always used choices with her for discipline, which makes life simpler, but I didn't use contingencies. I would use a consequence like, "If you don't clean up then you can't go to the park." Saying, "If you clean up, you can go to the park," sounds so much better and works much faster with her. But I have to stop and think a great deal to decide how I'm going to phrase things.
>
> As she sat on the floor with our dog that just wants to be near her, she started complaining that the dog was touching her, being in her way, etc. She started having a fit about him. I just told her very nonchalantly that if she leaves him alone she could stay in her spot. (She had a bed tray with her pizza on it, watching her favorite show.)

She said nothing more and even cradled the dog's head; she has been fine ever since. Before we would have gotten on her about being nice to him, stop pushing him away, and so on.

I told her earlier that when she cleaned up her toys we could go to the park. She's never moved so fast. It's amazing!

Teach Procedures

A major mistaken assumption many parents make is that a youngster knows how to do something without the parent's first modeling, teaching, practicing, and sometimes reinforcing the activity or procedure. A simple example is requesting a youngster to put dirty dishes in the sink. Taking the time to teach the youngster a procedure for how to rinse the dishes and utensils and where to place them can prevent future frustrations.

Another common example is that children often need to take certain items to school each day. To help a child, the parent might typically say, "Remember to take your lunch," or "Remember to take your key." But rather than the parent's having the responsibility of reminding the child, the family could put in place the procedure of making a list. By simply inquiring, "Did you check your list?" the parent puts responsibility on the youngster. Lists can be made for school assignments, special clothing and equipment for sports, or other items that the child might need on a regular basis. Using this approach requires *the youngster, rather than the parent,* to go through the conscious thought process of checking the list. Creating and teaching procedures not only prevents nagging, it also eliminates the negative feelings and stress that accompany such an unpleasant approach while simultaneously promoting responsibility.

If you think about it, you will realize that we run our lives on procedures. Especially with youngsters who have poor impulse control or act randomly and spontaneously, having structure in the form of procedures can be of great assistance to them—as well as to the parents. Each time your child does something you are dissatisfied with—or does not do something you expect of your youngster —ask yourself, *"Does the child have a procedure?"* In fact, anytime your youngster does anything that bothers you, this should be the first question to ask yourself.

Use Creative Solutions

The more frequently we remember to take a positive approach, the greater the chances of reducing stress, building trust, avoiding conflicts, and increasing satisfaction and contentment. Creative thinking, however, may be called for in order to achieve these benefits. This was the case with the two boys and the husband who invariably left their soiled clothes on the floor rather than putting them in the hamper. The sight of the dropped clothes so bothered the wife and mother that she indiscriminately scolded all members of the family. She then asked herself, "How can I turn this into a positive situation for me, as well as for them?" She came up with an idea. She told her family that whenever she found clothes on the floor, she would pick them up but the culprit owed her a two-minute backrub, collectable whenever she wanted it and done lovingly. The result not only freed the air of a lot of negativism, but she received a number of loving backrubs, which her children and husband learned to give with tender devotion. And, much to her delight, fewer clothes were left on the floor, and then eventually, none at all.

Avoid Criticism: Use Feedback

Criticize, and you will often get resistance and hard feelings. This is the case when you are criticizing something over which the youngster *feels* little control. Encouraging in a supportive way is much more effective.

Criticizing is almost always interpreted as, "What you are doing isn't good enough." Such comments stimulate negative feelings. Instead, encourage young people by communicating a higher expectation. For example, if your child is slow to get going in the morning, try this approach: "Yesterday, it took 10 minutes to come to breakfast after I called you. I know you can do better than that. Let's see if today you can come to breakfast in 8 minutes." Using this approach, watch your child rise to the occasion and come to breakfast faster. The success can be explained by the fact that *people enjoy rising to a challenge.*

Criticizing our children stems from a sincere desire to help them. Unfortunately, we focus on what is "wrong," thinking this will motivate them to put more effort into those areas. We want them to become capable and successful in their weaker areas. The problem is that criticism and nagging prompt people to *feel worse,* not better. In most cases these negative approaches don't create the motivation we are hoping for, and they certainly don't build a positive self-image in the recipient.

> After a meeting with teachers, the youngster said to his mother, "Why didn't they talk more about my social studies—what I'm good at—instead of what I'm not good at? All they want to do is fix what's wrong with me." The mother responded, "They are trying to help you." The child retorted, "No, they are trying to fix me."

Criticism is rarely thought of as "feedback," but feedback is essential for encouraging growth and maturity. *Giving guidance is a parental obligation and far more effective than criticism.* The awareness of the *negative effects of criticism* and the *positive effects of empowerment* is one of the most distinguishing marks of superior parenting.

Separate the Behavior from the Person

It is natural to self-defend. If criticized or accused, our instinct is to defend ourselves by justifying our actions. We say to a youngster, "It's not *you* I'm upset with; it's your behavior!" But all of us—regardless of age—have an extremely difficult time separating ourselves from our behavior. You can prove this to yourself by reflecting on any job you have had that required your being evaluated. During your conversation with your supervisor, did your self-talk sound something like, "My supervisor is not evaluating me—*just my job performance*"? Whenever I have posed this question to large groups of people, no one has ever raised a hand to acknowledge this type of self-talk. In reality, however, the supervisor *is* evaluating your job performance—not you as a person. So if you, as an adult, find it almost impossible to separate yourself from your behavior, how do you expect a young person to do it?

Separating the young person from the behavior prevents the tendency to criticize and label. If a child is not acting responsibly, acknowledge the act but do not call the child "irresponsible." *Label the behavior, rather than the person.* "Do you consider this a responsible thing to do?" is far more effective than "You are irresponsible!"

You will find a very simple way to separate the young person from the young person's behavior using the *Raise Responsibility System* discussed in Part II.

Use Acknowledgments More Than Praise

Acknowledgments and praise are not the same. *Praise is judgmental* and infers parental approval. In contrast, *acknowledgments simply recognize.* You may ask, "What's wrong with praise?" Although intended to be a positive reinforcement, praise creates certain pitfalls that acknowledgments do not. For example, praise is conditional upon the judgment of the person giving the praise. It is usually given because the adult feels a desire to approve some behavior. However, *what is truly important is for children to receive self-satisfaction without the need for adult approval.*

Acknowledgments accomplish the intent of praise but *without* praise's disadvantages. Acknowledgments foster feelings of being worthwhile without relying on the approval of others. The long-range effect of acknowledgments is to engender self-confidence and self-reliance, rather than dependence on others for feelings of self-worth.

Understanding the difference between praise and acknowledgment is critical for promoting responsible behavior. After a seminar where I explained the difference, a parent wrote me:

> This hit a chord for me. I've always worried that I may tend to over-praise my 11-year-old daughter, Elena. And recently, she confirmed this in quite a direct manner. She had done something TERRIFIC and I launched into my usual, "Oh, honey, Mommy's so PROUD of you!" Well, Elena stopped me mid-gush, put her hand on her hips, and implored, "Mom, PLEASE STOP! Whenever you do that, you make me feel like you're surprised that I can do things—like I'm not capable!"

The mother was trying to be positive by using praise in an attempt to reward her daughter. Although her intention was honorable, her method was counterproductive. The mother has since started to acknowledge her daughter's actions *without reference to her own motherly pride.*

Notice the difference in these sets of examples:

A. "*I am* so pleased with the way you treated your brother." (praise)

B. "You treated your brother with real consideration." (acknowledgment)

———

A. "*I like* the way you did that." (praise)

B. "How did you do that?" (acknowledgment while reinforcing)

A. "*I'm so pleased that you* washed the dishes." (praise)

B. "Thanks for washing the dishes." (acknowledgment)

Using a phrase that starts with "I like" or "I'm so proud of" encourages the child to behave in order *to please the adult,* but lacks the self-satisfaction that acknowledgments promote. Praise encourages dependence. By contrast, acknowledgments empower.

Three characteristics usually determine whether a comment is one of praise or one of acknowledgment:

1. Praise often starts with a reference to oneself: "*I am* so proud of you for...." or "*I like* the way...." Even "*I noticed that....*" can be a trap because it focuses on what *you* think rather than on simply acknowledging what your child has done.

2. Praise is patronizing. If you would not make the comment to an adult, then think twice before making it to a young person.

3. Praise is often stated as a general comment, such as, "That's good." An acknowledgment, by contrast, calls attention to a *specific behavior:* "You put your toys away!"

If you could have a conversation with a child and ask which would be more personally satisfying, (1) receiving praise or (2) being recognized, more often than not the child would prefer the recognition. Therefore, instead of heaping on praise, simply readjust your thinking and bring attention to things the child does successfully. This approach encourages persistence, which leads to more success.

With older children, praise can be demeaning, as shown above in the comment from the 11-year-old daughter. With young children, praise encourages them to do what parents want them to do in order to make the *adult* happy. This type of communication leaves the child feeling that evaluation depends on *others* to determine when a good job has been done. It implies a lack of acceptance and worth when the youth does *not* behave as the adult wishes. A statement like, "I'm so proud of you because you're such a good boy" implies that the boy is okay *only* when he is good, and that when the boy is not good he is not okay. Praise is also like candy; once you start giving it, stopping is difficult because the child wants it constantly.

If we think of praise as a general statement, "You did a good job" or "I like what you did," we have not given the youngster any feedback or basis to evaluate or improve. We have only given a personal opinion. In contrast to a praising statement, *acknowledging* something gives specific feedback. It promotes encouragement by prompting *reflection* or self-evaluation, a key ingredient for learning and growing. When we give specific feedback, such as, "You ate all of your healthy vegetables," or "You put all of your toys away," then we remove personal opinion. This approach diminishes an action based solely on a desire to please the parents. Notice how the following statements prompt positive feelings: "You seem to be getting the hang of it" and "Would you show me how you did that?" This kind of acknowledgment promotes growth, competence, and confidence and is much more useful than praise, which shows no advancement for self-evaluating any progress.

The reason praise can work in the short run is that young children are hungry for parental approval. But we parents have a responsibility not to exploit that dependence for our own satisfaction. To be sure, not every use of praise is a calculated tactic to control children's behavior. Sometimes we compliment young people just because we're genuinely pleased with what they've done. Even then, however, it's worth looking more closely at the effect it may have, such as turning children into "praise junkies." Also, apart from the issue of dependence, children deserve to take delight in accomplishments—to feel pride in what they have learned and in knowing how to do something.

Every time we give a general praising comment, we're actually suggesting how the child should feel. There are times when our evaluations are appropriate and our guidance is necessary—especially with toddlers and preschoolers. But a constant stream of value judgments is neither necessary nor useful for children's development. Unfortunately, we may not realize that a praising statement, such as, "How nicely done!" is just as much an evaluation as, "How poorly done!" The most notable feature of a positive judgment isn't that it's positive, but that *it's a judgment*. And people, even young ones, don't like being judged.

This doesn't mean that all compliments and expressions of delight are harmful. We need to consider *our motives* for what we say. *A genuine expression of enthusiasm is natural and fine.* But we should reflect whether our reactions are helping the child to feel a sense of control and satisfaction or if they lead the child to constantly look for approval. Are our comments helping the child become more excited about the task itself, or are we turning it into something the youngster wants to do in order to receive a pat on the head?

A prime reason that praise is used is to have people feel good about themselves and, with young children in particular, to increase their self-esteem. However, self-esteem has to do with (internal) feelings of competency. In this sense, people empower themselves. When the focus is on acknowledgments, then reflection and feelings of competency thrive and satisfaction is engendered.

Young children generally want to behave in ways that please parents. However, we really want our children to learn to do the right thing not because someone is dangling a carrot in front of them but because it is the right thing to do. When people do the right thing—when they make good decisions, when they behave in a responsible manner—they feel good. They learn to value themselves. Developing responsibility, rather than obedience in order to please, is more advantageous for both children and parents. The children gain confidence and the parents promote responsibility. Parents who foster this approach give children a precious gift that is treasured for a lifetime. As Ralph Waldo Emerson so aptly put it, "The reward for a thing well done is to have done it."

Build on Success

No child wants to fail or intentionally get into trouble. Henry David Thoreau said, "Men are born to succeed, not fail." Renowned psychologist Abraham Maslow agreed with this concept when he declared that it is a basic human need to strive toward success and self-actualization.

People improve more by building on their strengths than by working on their weaknesses. This does not mean that a weakness should be ignored, but it does mean that the emphasis should be on what the child *can* do, rather than on what the child cannot do. The simple belief that something *can* be done is the spark that ignites action. When a child is first learning a skill, it is the *successes*—not the failures—that encourage perseverance and lead to building character, positive self-talk, and self-esteem.

By building on interests, strengths, and successes, you actuate motivation. In the teacher-parent-youth situation discussed above, where the youngster's belief was that the teacher wanted to "fix" him, the youngster's hard feelings could have been prevented if the teacher had acknowledged the child's skill for analyzing social situations in his history lessons. The teacher then could have challenged the child to bring that same analytical talent to math or English and concluded with an empowering statement such as, "I know you can apply that skill in other subject areas." *It is by focusing on people's strengths that we foster their desire for improvement in weaker areas.*

As a parent, you have a responsibility to find your child's interests, talents, or skills and acknowledge them. "I see that you draw well. I can tell because of the detail in your sketch." (Notice the use of an acknowledgment rather than praise.) Youngsters with low self-esteem require acknowledgments to be repeated a number of times and in different ways. These children *need to believe that someone else believes in them before their own belief in themselves kicks in.*

> Andrew Carnegie, the first great industrialist in America, once was observed as having 43 millionaires working for him. A reporter asked him how he had managed to hire so many millionaires. Carnegie answered that *none* of them were millionaires when he hired them.
>
> The reporter inquired, "Then what did you do to develop them so that they became millionaires?"
>
> "You develop people the same way you mine gold," Carnegie explained. "You go into a gold mine and you expect to remove tons of dirt to find an ounce of gold. But you don't go into the mine looking for the dirt; you go in there looking for the gold."

Go for the Gold

Communicating in positive terms encourages, and encouragement is often the spark that ignites motivation. A phrase such as, "I know you can do this because I have seen how capable you are," encourages people to believe in their own abilities.

Robert Danzig started his career as an office boy and rose to become president of a nationally recognized company. He attributes his motivation to his first office manager who encouraged him by saying, "You are full of promise." This one positive comment prompted Danzig, as he related it to me, to begin seeing possibilities and generated his rise from sweeping floors to becoming the president of the Hearst Newspaper Corporation.

Sometimes *a word of encouragement during a failure is worth more than a whole book of praise after a success.* When a child has not been successful, ask, "What can we learn from this experience?" You can help your child learn to be like the monkey who eats only the healthy part of the banana by teaching the child to focus on the positive in every experience because *every experience can be a learning one.*

Focus on Continuous Improvement

Seeing the positive in situations and experiences becomes easier if the focus is on *continuous improvement.* Success isn't always about winning; it's often about learning, growing, and improving. Although there is a natural tendency to compare ourselves with others, the more this type of thinking is *redirected,* the more successful we will feel. *While having role models is wise, trying to compete with them is not.* We should measure progress by *improvement in ourselves,* rather than in comparison to others. When pleased with our efforts—especially when we see improvement—we invest more effort. Improvement comes through self-evaluation, practice, feedback, and more evaluation. The better the quality of our work, the more we are pleased and the more we want to engage in the activity.

> A woman having lunch at a small café was seated next to a family celebrating their son's basketball game. Their conversation was so lively that the woman joined in. "You must have been on the winning team," she said.
>
> The kid grinned from ear to ear, "No, we lost by 20 points. The other team had a killer defense. We were only able to make one basket."
>
> "Did *you* make the basket?" she asked.
>
> With his mouth filled with cake and ice cream, the boy shook his head, "No." His father reached across the

table to give him a high five. His mother hugged him and said, "You were awesome." The woman at the next table rubbed her chin.

The boy looked at the confused woman and said, "At last week's game, I took nine shots but they all fell short of the basket. This week I took eight shots and three of them hit the rim! Dad says I'm making progress."

When young people try something new and are corrected or criticized before having feelings of success or progress, they become discouraged. When we are tempted to correct our children, *we need to take into consideration where they are in the stages of that learning.* Accuracy and precision should come *after* there has been some sense of success. Periodically, find some improvement your child has made and acknowledge it. Remember, success breeds confidence and further successes.

Avoid Perfectionism

A major dilemma young people face is a desire to be perfect—which hinders them and can have disastrous results.

My son is six years old and is going to be in the second grade. He is developing a very pessimistic attitude toward life. When he has to do homework and does it, he becomes worried that he did not do it right. He is very intelligent and good in his studies. Sometimes he worries so much that he cannot sleep at night. The first thing he needs in the morning is assurance, and even that does not stop him from worrying. He starts to worry over very small things. Do you know how we can help him overcome this?

I responded to this inquiry from a parent, saying: *A person cannot learn and be perfect at the same time.* Teach your child *to implement first, and then aim for continual improvement—but never for perfection.* A focus on perfection interferes with learning and can actually impair performance. When the focus is on perfection, the person always loses because humans are not perfect. In contrast, when the focus is on improvement, you are always a winner and satisfaction and performance increase.

The fear of failure created by a perfectionist attitude can significantly limit a person's success because the person becomes unwilling to take risks. In addition, a focus on perfection has led many young people to adopt the idea that they have to be perfect for people to like them or accept them. The eating disorders of bulimia and anorexia nervosa in teenage girls often originate from this belief. The perception that rejection will follow if a person makes a mistake—the sense that one has to be perfect to be accepted—is an idea that plagues too many young people. Striving for perfection, rather than for continual improvement, also leaves young people reluctant to admit mistakes or apologize when in the wrong.

In extreme cases of perfectionism, children may stop maturing altogether. They simply give up. The belief that they must be perfect can become so tyrannical that these young people develop anxiety attacks, as in the above situation. Aiming at perfection reinforces their counterproductive thinking pattern that they cannot perform or engage in the activity because they will not be good enough. The next stage is total paralysis as in the following incident.

> In the first grade, when I finished my picture of the sun in the sky, I brought it to my teacher. He looked at it and said, "There is no such thing as a green sun. The sun is yellow. Everyone knows that." He said that my picture wasn't realistic, that I should start over. Nightfall came to me in the middle of the afternoon.
>
> The next year, my second-grade teacher said to the class, "Draw something—anything you want." I just stared at my paper and when the teacher came around to my desk, I could only hear the beating of my heart as he looked at my blank page. He touched my shoulder with his hand and whispered, "How big and thick and nice your cloud is."

When our daughter was first learning to speak, she made the sound of "s" in a nonstandard way. We called attention to it—only once. For the next several weeks, every time she spoke any word that contained the "s" sound, she hesitated and tried to make the sound perfectly. We were witnessing the first stage of stuttering. We never again called attention to her speech, and my wife and I were greatly relieved when her natural speech pattern returned.

Learning to speak comes naturally. When attention is called to any activity, the brain begins to focus on it—resulting in an interruption of that natural process. You can experience this the next time you walk down a familiar flight of stairs. You normally do not focus on the activity. However, if you place your attention on the details of stepping one leg down in front of the other, you will start to trip.

When an infant first attempts to walk, we offer encouragement because we know that learning comes by degrees. We do not expect the child to stand up and walk in *one* day. Similarly, we encourage an infant to speak even though the sounds are only approximately right.

When humans are born, we know virtually nothing. If we knew everything, we would not experience one of the great joys of living— learning! To learn anything, we must explore new territory. It is inevitable that mistakes occur when learning to do something new. The process continues throughout life. Making errors is a natural part of living and growing.

MAKING POSITIVITY YOUR HABIT

Making positivity a practice both in your self-talk and in your communications with others begins with awareness. Listen to yourself. Become aware of the number of times you say something negatively that could be phrased positively. Continually ask your-self before speaking, "How can I say this so it will be perceived in a positive way?"

Practice, Practice, and Practice

Using positive phrases can turn what would have been a negative into a positive. The result is dramatic. The more you practice phras-ing communications in the positive, the sooner it will become a new habit. A simple approach is to focus on what you *want* your children to do rather than on what you *don't want* them to do. Eliminate dis-empowering, negative words such as "don't," "shouldn't," "can't," and "have to." Replace them with empowering and enabling communica-tions. "Don't run in the house!" becomes "We walk in the house." "You shouldn't use your fingers when eating cake!" becomes "We use a fork when eating cake." "You can't ride your bicycle without a helmet!" becomes "Wearing your helmet will protect you." You have to go to school!" becomes "You get to go to school."

Positivity becomes a habit. It has been said that *we make our habits and then our habits make us.* This is certainly true of positivity.

As thinking and communicating in positive ways become your new habit, you will notice how good it feels—and how much more effective you become.

Model Positivity

Winston Churchill once commented, "The optimist sees the opportunity in every difficulty. The pessimist sees the difficulty in every opportunity." The pessimist thinks only of problems. But why focus on problems when you can fill your head with solutions? As parents, we have a responsibility to *model* positivity. Hope and optimism can be learned. They are teachable. It bears repeating that *the most influential person you talk with is yourself, and what you tell yourself has a direct bearing on your attitude, your performance, and your influence on others.* So be sure your own self-talk is positive, enabling, and empowering. As is suggested on the airplane announcement before the flight leaves the ground, "Place the oxygen mask on yourself before placing it on someone else!"

Expect the Good

As Henry Ford so aptly stated, "If you think you can, you can; if you think you can't, you can't. Either way you are right." Psychologists call this a "self-fulfilling prophecy."

> An old man was sitting at the gate of a city when a stranger approached.
>
> "Tell me, old man," said the stranger, "how will I find the people in this city?"
>
> The old man thought for a minute and said, "I don't know. How were they where you came from?"
>
> "Biggest bunch of thieves you would ever want to meet—steal the shirt right off your back."
>
> The old man said, "You'll find them the same way here."
>
> A short time later, another stranger approached, and asked the man the same question: "How will I find the people in this city?"
>
> And again the old man thought for a moment and said, "I don't know. How were they where you came from?"

"The nicest bunch of people you would ever want to meet. They will give you the shirt right off their back," he said.

"You'll find them the same way here."

Our attitude is often the paintbrush of our minds. So often we find in life what we think we will find. For three years I traveled on a regular basis to New York City where I worked with schools and parents in Harlem and Upper Manhattan. Before I started to travel to the "Big Apple," I had heard that people there were rude and abrupt. Dealing with this stereotype of New York City, I asked myself, "How can I turn this negative perception into a positive one?" I decided that I would find New Yorkers friendly, conversational, and delightful—and indeed, I did!

> *If you treat someone as he is, he will stay as he is. But if you treat him as if he were what he could and ought to be, he will become what he could and ought to be.*
> —Johann Wolfgang Von Goethe

Why deprive yourself of the power of the positive? It is an attitude that, with practice, you can develop for yourself and with your children. When you do, you will be amazed at how your stress becomes significantly reduced, your effectiveness increased, and your relationships improved.

After a review of the following key points about positivity, we'll turn to the second practice.

POINTS TO REMEMBER

◆ People do better when they feel good, not when they feel bad.

◆ Negative comments provoke negative attitudes. Positive comments prompt positive attitudes.

◆ People are most effective in influencing other people by phrasing their communications in positive terms.

◆ Acknowledgments that simply recognize and validate are more satisfying than praise, which implies an action was done to please someone else.

◆ *Imposed* consequences are usually perceived negatively, which is why they do not change the way a person *wants* to behave.

◆ Contingencies promise with the positive and place the responsibility on the young person—where it belongs.

◆ The pictures people paint in their minds drive their behaviors.

◆ Positivity prompts people to feel valued, supported, respected, capable, and proud.

◆ Positivity brings hope.

2
Choice

Choice ends when life ends.

Chapter 1 discusses why *positivity* is the most successful path to reach a destination. This second chapter demonstrates how keeping in mind two simple words can have an added profound effect on your success as a parent. Those two words are *choice empowers*. Offering choices is a simple and effective approach that parents can use to immediately reduce their stress. It also promotes self-discipline and improves relationships. The empowerment of choice is universal—it works with people of all ages. Most importantly, responsible behavior is directly related to the number of decisions young people make.

THE POWER OF CHOICE

We've been brought up to believe that power corrupts and that absolute power corrupts absolutely. But did you know that *powerlessness* also corrupts? In any relationship—regardless of age—when a person feels a lack of power, that person's mission becomes one of gaining power. Even very young children have a natural desire to feel in control—to be *empowered*. Therefore, you will gain your desired result in a shorter time when you offer choices.

A friend related an incident that illustrates this fact:

> I marvel at what my grandson understands and how he manages to communicate. The other night his parents went out to dinner and he started screaming and crying real tears. I picked him up, gave him a hug, and proceeded

to explain to him that Mommy and Daddy would come back soon.

Then I asked him if he wanted to keep on crying until they returned or if he would like to play with his trains. The tears shut off like a switch! He loves "Thomas the Train."

I realized that I gave him the choice to take responsibility for his behavior in the situation. Pretty cool, huh? He's all of 28 months old!

Consider the rebellious teenager. I believe most theories about the stress and strain of adolescence overlook the main issue. Reasons for such adversarial relationships have focused on physical changes, emerging sexuality, new social demands, struggles between being a child and becoming an adult, delayed development of the neocortex of the brain, and other such suggestions. It is true that teenagers, by virtue of their hormonal changes, are prone to be emotionally volatile, unpredictable, self-absorbed, and hypersensitive. However, upon a closer observation, we can conclude that a major factor in this period of life—which is difficult for both adolescents and parents—has its foundation in *power struggles.*

When a parent picks up a small child who is learning to walk, a struggle erupts. The youngster does not want to be carried when learning to walk. Similarly, a teenager who is struggling for autonomy dislikes being told what to do. In effect, the youth resists "being carried by the parent." Enthusiasm quickly evaporates when there is no sense of choice.

The reason this stage of development is especially stressful for parents and teenagers alike is that in the process of growing up, the teenager has become so physically strong and *mentally independent* that controlling the adolescent becomes a tremendous challenge. A parent who attempts continual control will actually see an increase in the young person's reluctance to do what the parent wishes, and this leads to a power struggle—which results in even more reluctance, resentment, and rebellion on the part of the teenager. Even if the young person complies with the parent's demands, the behavior is temporary.

Many parents assume that adolescent rebellion is inevitable. Although teenagers have an increasing desire for freedom, the main reason for rebellion is simply that teenagers become more able to resist parental power. The typical adolescent believes that he or she has attained enough strength, resources, and personal power to no longer *fear the power of the parents.* An adolescent does not rebel directly against parents; *the rebellion is against parental use of power to control.* Especially with adolescents, the more you use power, the more you lose influence. But, as you will see, you can use parental authority without the pitfall of relying on power.

Aside from the adversarial relationship it creates, using parental power and coercion to try to change young people has severe limitations. If parents were to rely less on *overpowering* and more on *empowering* from infancy on, there would be significantly less for children to rebel against. This is especially the case during the difficult teenage period of life. If you have a challenge with a youngster and you find yourself becoming angry, it may be because you are attempting to overpower your child. You are also prompting feelings in your child of being trapped—of having no options. Simply by offering choices, you can easily eliminate even a very negative situation both for yourself and for the person you are attempting to influence.

USING CHOICES TO BE MORE EFFECTIVE

Change is the result of a decision, but *decisions are possible only when there are choices.* Therefore, offering choices paves the way to changing behavior and is much more effective than giving commands. The paradox is that *the more you give choices, the more effective you become.*

When children of any age resist doing something you ask of them or do something contrary to your instructions, rather than force your request on them, offer them choices; then watch how quickly their resistance weakens. By giving the young person some degree of power, you will get more cooperation. That's because *people do not argue with their own decisions.*

Even when a youngster thinks there are no choices about whether or not to do something, the wise parent will build in some element of choice. Just a small one qualifies because *any* choice allows a person to retain dignity and power. For example, when first learning to walk down a flight of stairs, you cannot give a small child the option to walk down the stairs unassisted; there is a concern for safety. However, by giving a choice of *how* to walk down the stairs, a parent can avoid a confrontation: "Would you like to hold the handrail or hold my hand?" Similarly, children should not have a choice about taking medicine when ill, but parents can give them the choice of *how* to take it. "Would you like to take your medicine from a spoon or from a dropper?" or, "Would you like to take it with water or with juice?" On a very cold day, you would not offer a choice to go outside without a jacket. You can, though, give a choice as to *how* the child will get the jacket on: "Would you like to put your jacket on by yourself, or would you like help?"

Refusing to eat what the parent offers is not an uncommon event for a child. It is an example of a situation in which a youngster can "control" parents simply by observing their reactions. Forcing a child to eat often results in the child's becoming more obstinate. My mother told me that she would simply diffuse the situation by asking, for example, "Which are you going to eat first, your carrots or your peas?" The choice for making the decision was placed on *me*, the child, where decision-making was practiced.

Children are always making choices. Doing nothing can be a powerful choice. We refer to it as "defiance." The most effective way to avoid defiance is to offer *some measure* of choice in any situation where the child is required by an authority figure to do something.

Kerry in British Columbia described how she used the principle of choice with a very challenging young student. The boy often refused to do what he was asked, ripped up papers given to him, and avoided participating by putting his head down in anger. Because he had no control over his negative situation at home, he chose school as the place to act in a way that would give him the feeling of control. In Kerry's own words, here is how she handled one typical situation with this child:

> It was time to go to the gym for an assembly. When we arrived, the youngster saw another opportunity to be uncooperative and said, "I'm not going in. I'm going to stay right out here by the outside door." Rather than get into a power struggle, I said, "I can't make you come in, but I can't leave you out here by yourself either. *I* want to go in because I know the Grade 6's are singing today, and I want to hear them. I'll just ask Mrs. Smith (an aide) to come and stand with you."

The thought of a musical presentation piqued the boy's curiosity and he decided he would come in. But before we walked down the four steps into the gym, he said to me, "I'm not going to sit with the class. I'm going to sit by you."

We stopped right there at the front of the gym. I said, "I can't make you sit with the rest of the kids, but you should know that if you sit beside *me*, away from the other kids in Grade 1, all of the people in the gym are going to be looking at you. They'll wonder why you're sitting with the teacher instead of with your class. Is that what you want?"

He said, "Well, I'm going to sit with the class, but I'm going to curl up in a ball on the floor." It was easy for me to respond, "I can't make you sit up like all of the other kids, but if you curl up in a ball then everyone is *really* going to look at you and wonder what you're doing because that's quite an unusual thing to do."

He didn't say anything more and just sat down with his classmates.

Having the youngster reflect on his choices—*while using a noncoercive approach*—was the way to handle this challenging situation successfully. Notice that the adult acknowledged each of the youngster's decisions, but by having the child *become aware of the consequences of his choices,* he was encouraged to think of other options.

USING CHOICES TO IMPROVE RELATIONSHIPS

Here is an important concept to remember in relationships: *Not losing is more important than winning.* Children's desires will not always be fulfilled, but as long as they are aware that they have a choice as to their responses, they are not put in a position where they feel that they *lose*—which naturally prompts negative feelings.

No one likes being cornered, literally or figuratively. The belief of not having a choice encourages resistance because it prompts a feeling of being trapped. When a child is without options, the result is not only resistance but also resentment. By contrast, offering choices ensures that a child's power and dignity are retained.

As a parent, you are *choosing* a losing situation when you focus on the past and are negative, as in, "You should have been more careful!" or "How could you have done that!" In contrast, you can *choose* to focus on the future by being optimistic, positive, and suggest a procedure, as in, "Next time, you will be sure to hold the glass with both hands," or "What can you do to prevent it from happening again?" So if you *choose* to talk about what a person did wrong—what that youngster *should* have done—the youngster will only resent it because the situation cannot be undone. *Choosing* to focus on the past will only result in your criticizing, blaming, complaining, threatening, or punishing. These will result in stress and negative feelings for all involved. By contrast, you will promote responsible behavior if you *choose* to communicate in terms of, "So, let's talk about what has been learned and how to do it better next time." When you do, you will immediately become a coach instead of a critic or cop.

USING CHOICES TO BUILD RESPONSIBILITY

Offering choices raises responsibility because it is related to the issue of control. A person who makes choices gains control, and having control is a requirement for taking responsibility. *Choice, control, and responsibility are inseparable:*

Make a choice, and control is enhanced.

Fail to choose, and control is diminished.

Deny responsibility, and control is given up.

Choose responsibility, and control increases.

Here is an example shared with me by a friend who understood the basic need of all humans—of any age—to feel some sense of control over their lives.

My elderly mother was recovering from a very difficult surgery. Because of her weakened condition, she had lost her ability to walk and there was doubt about whether she would be able to return to her home of over 50 years; she was losing control of her life. Although the doctors suggested that weeks of physical therapy could help, *she was not willing to cooperate with the hospital staff.* She would not engage in any physical therapy sessions that were offered. As a result, she was being pressured from all directions.

After five days, I was able to see her. As I walked in the room, I realized that she was reacting to the fact that she had so little control over her life. Instead of *telling* her that the exercises were important and that she should do them, I *asked* her what she wanted. She said that she wanted to walk again and go home. I said, "How are we going to make that happen?"

After several minutes she responded, "I have to do the exercises." Within a short time she started therapy, really applied herself, and very soon thereafter returned home.

Offering choices also promotes the most important skill for success in life: *the skill of making responsible decisions.* Responsible behavior is directly related to the number of responsible choices a person makes. Positive discipline approaches—of which offering choices ranks high on the list—motivate children to *want* to act responsibly because it feels good and because children realize it is in their best interests to do so. In contrast, if we deprive people of choices, we deprive them of positive motivation. By giving children opportunities to make decisions starting early in life, we prepare them for greater success as adults living in the 21st century.

In the 19th and 20th centuries, manufacturing led and fed the economy. There were few originators; most people were followers. Obedience, implementation of rules, and top-down management were the order of the day, in part because information was limited to those who were in control. Times have changed. With technology and especially the Internet, information is no longer limited. Few people will stay with only one company all their working years. More people will work as independent contractors or become entrepreneurs. An issue of *Time* magazine's cover stated, "The Future of Work: Throw away the briefcase; you're not going to the office. You can kiss your benefits goodbye, too. And your new boss won't look much like your old one. There's no longer a ladder, and you may never get to retire." Fending for retirement is increasingly becoming an individual responsibility and requires making decisions, rather than relying solely on one's employer.

What drives the 21st century is the creation and distribution of information. Instead of compliance, initiative is required. Today we all need to develop decision-making skills; we can no longer merely follow someone else's plans. And this skill doesn't just happen; it must be developed. *Offering children choices helps develop this necessary skill for responsible living.*

LIMITED VS. UNLIMITED CHOICES

The choices parents offer can be either "limited" or "unlimited." Limited choices allow the child to select from a restricted number of options offered by the parent, whereas in unlimited choices, the child is encouraged to come up with an option of his or her own. Generally, the younger the child, the more limited the choices. For example, "Do you want cereal or an egg for breakfast?" would be a limited choice, while "What do you want for breakfast?" would be unlimited and more appropriate as children mature. However, if the response to an unlimited question is not practical, the choices can again be limited.

In situations when only a few options are acceptable to you, stick to offering limited choices. This will ensure greater success in reducing stress and power struggles. When you are prepared to only accept certain options, offering unlimited choices can result in disagreement, anger, and even resentment if the child continues to come up with alternatives that are not acceptable to you. On the other hand, *expanding the number of choices increases cooperation.* Suppose, for example, a child has household chores. By offering options at the outset, rather than dictating the chores, parents give ownership to the youngster. If the child does not fulfill the selected chores, rather than impose a consequence, simply *add more choices.* If a youngster has two chores to perform and is not doing them, add three more, so that five choices are available. The child then chooses two from the five. *Adding choices* is a positive approach. It saves parents grief and is much more effective than a negative approach, such as threatening to revoke privileges.

A few weeks after one of my presentations in Seoul, South Korea, a father shared the following with me:

> Giving choices has really helped me raise my two daughters.
>
> My youngest daughter seems to be more strong-willed than her older sister, especially when it comes to discipline. I have tried many approaches with her—from

talking, timeouts, taking away privileges, scolding, and even resorting to spanking. Nothing seemed to work. She would turn around and do the very thing she had just gotten punished for—usually acting on emotions. We would remind her and she would say that she was sorry, but again no change.

One time, I decided to try giving choices. Usually, my daughter was so emotionally upset about the entire situation that it was hard for her to answer to why she was getting punished. Her answers usually focused on what upset her and not about what she had done wrong.

This time I gave her a choice that opened an opportunity for dialogue. I told her that she knows that hitting her older sister and lying about it is wrong. She admitted that she hit her sister and that she had lied about it, and we were able to talk about other choices she could make in responding to her older sister and about why lying is so bad.

That day I saw the power of giving choices and how this can lead to a dialogue that facilitates accepting responsibility. I have since broadened the range of choices and have been able to watch my daughter mature as she learns to accept responsibility for her actions.

The Magic of Three

The most effective number of choices to offer is three. With some young people, offering just two choices seems limiting and restrictive. Giving three options eliminates all perceptions of coercion and encourages greater ownership in the choice. Offering three choices is especially useful with young people categorized as "passive-aggressive" or more commonly referred to today as "oppositional-defiant." This type of youngster manipulates by being resistant. It is a way of staying in control. By giving three options, more control is *offered* and the oppositional attitude is reduced.

> "*Would you rather clean up your room* **before dinner, after dinner,** *or* **tomorrow morning** *before you play?*"

The choices need not be limited to the ones offered by the adult. Offering three does not preclude the youngster from volunteering one:

*"Would you rather clean up **before dinner, after dinner,** or when would you suggest?"*

CHOICES IN LIFE

A significant difference between the optimist and the pessimist is related to the *perception of choice.* For example, a school math test is returned with a low score. One student concludes, "Well, I guess I'm not good in math," while another student who receives the exact same score engages in different self-talk: "I guess I'll have to study harder." The difference? The first youngster senses a lack of control—that nothing can be done. "I just have no gift for math," goes the self-talk. The second youngster believes that something *can* be done. The first child's pessimistic self-talk is of resignation— primarily based upon the wrong assumption of a lack of choice and, therefore, a lack of control. The second child, a more optimistic student, resists this victimhood mentality.

Hope is related to optimism and is essential to motivation. Without hope there is no sense in even trying. Both *hope* and *optimism* can be learned, and *both depend on the perception of choice.*

What the pessimist doesn't realize is that we are *constantly* making choices based upon our self-talk. We choose the reactions to our thoughts; we choose what we say, and we choose what we do. Through our perception of choice, we wield power that shapes our lives and makes us our own masters. If you reflect closely, you will soon conclude that so much of life is the result of our decisions made along the way. The reality is that *choice ends when life ends.*

Behavior is always a matter of choice. In the course of a day we make many choices, and although many are made with consciousness (awareness), many of our choices are made nonconsciously (without thinking). Even when awareness is lacking, it doesn't mean that we *aren't making choices.* The more we teach our children that they always have the ability to make choices and that positive self-talk is more empowering than thinking negatively, the more responsible they become.

All of us, *including children,* choose:
   ✓ How to act
   ✓ What to say
   ✓ How to say it

✓ What to focus on
✓ When to go along with others
✓ When to resist
✓ What to say about others

And most importantly,

✓ *What to say to ourselves about ourselves (self-talk)*

Children rarely think about their decisions. One of our most important roles as parents is to help children become aware (conscious) of the decisions they make. This is how we promote responsible decision-making. Responsibility, persistence, consideration, honesty, and integrity cannot be mandated. Behaviors for these values are *chosen*; therefore, the concept of choice is essential to the teaching and learning of values and characteristics that contribute to successful and satisfying lives.

HOBSON'S CHOICE

> A man drove on a long and lonely unpaved road in Arizona on his way to watch Hopi Indian ceremonial dances. Afterward, he returned to his car only to find that it had a flat tire. He replaced the flat with the spare tire and drove to the only service station on the Hopi reservation.
>
> As he stepped out of his car, he heard the hissing of another tire going flat.
>
> "Do you fix flats?" he inquired of the attendant.
>
> "Yes," came the answer.
>
> "How much do you charge?" he asked.
>
> With a twinkle in his eye, the man replied, "What difference does it make?"

This is what is called a "Hobson's choice," named after Thomas Hobson (1544-1631) of Cambridge, England. Hobson kept a livery stable and required every customer to take either the horse nearest the stable door or none at all. In essence, a Hobson's choice is a situation that forces a person to accept whatever is offered—or do without. Perhaps the most famous of Hobson's choices was made in 1914 when Henry Ford offered the very popular Model T, making it available in any color so long as it was black. Fortunately, most situations in life offer more than a Hobson's choice. Most of the time we really do have choices—*even when we think we don't.* We may say that we "have to" do something. However, in thinking about it more carefully, we realize that we do it because we *choose* to. In a sense, there is very little in life we truly *have* to do. The way we spend our time is a choice. *We* set the priorities. *We* have control. By recognizing that most of what we do is by choice, we begin to make our choices more consciously and carefully.

Being aware that options are always available puts us in control, and it makes our life happier and more fulfilling. We become more responsible when we recognize that very rarely are our choices limited to a Hobson's choice. As the sage stated, "Destiny is as much a matter of choice as one of chance." Here is an experiment: For the next 48 hours, eliminate "I have to" from your vocabulary and replace it with the phrase *"I choose to."* Instead of saying, "I *have* to get out of bed," make your self-talk more accurate: Say, "I *choose* to get out of bed." Try this experiment and almost immediately you will feel more in charge of your life. Since you will be taking responsibility—both the blame and credit for your choices—you may find yourself acting in different and more positive ways. The reason is that choice promotes self-confidence and self-reliance. Most importantly, you will find your world more manageable, which will reduce your stress. Knowing that we have choices fosters a sense of independence and empowerment.

THE ABILITY TO CHOOSE OUR RESPONSES

Victor Frankl, the famed psychiatrist who survived Nazi death camps and wrote about his experiences, taught that even in the direst of circumstances we still have choices. He demonstrated that, even in the most horrendous conditions of psychic and physical stress, *a person still has the power to choose one's thinking.* He taught that even when the body is a prisoner, a person still has independence of mind. In his groundbreaking work, *Man's Search for Meaning,* Frankl notes:

> Even though conditions such as lack of sleep, insufficient food, and various mental stresses may suggest that the inmates were bound to react in certain ways, in the final analysis it becomes clear that the sort of person the prisoner became was the result of an inner decision and not the result of camp influences alone.

As Frankl explained, even under such extreme circumstances a person still has the freedom to choose one's attitude. Being aware of one's choice of attitudes relates closely to other choices. For example, teaching young people that they can choose their responses—that they need not be victims—is one of the most valuable thinking patterns we can provide them. I refer to this approach as *"choice-response thinking."* Young people become more responsible when they learn that *regardless of* the situation, stimulus, impulse, or urge, they still have a choice as to how they respond. *Responsibility* is literally *"response-ability"—the ability to choose a response* in any set of circumstances.

Choosing a Response to a Situation

None of us should ever be tested with situations as horrendous as those Victor Frankl experienced. For the most part, our challenges will be in choosing how best to respond to everyday normal situations. The decisions made in living day by day actually create the very fabric of life. When viewed from this perspective, everyday choices deserve our *awareness.*

Here is an example that gave me new insight into choosing a response to a situation I could not change or control. I was comfortably seated in an airplane ready for takeoff on a flight from Chicago to Los Angeles. I had just started reading a book when the pilot announced that there would be a two-hour delay; Los Angeles International Airport was fogged in. Even with a good read, adding two hours to the three-hour flight seemed a bit long to remain seated. I left my materials in the overhead storage compartment of the plane and returned to the airport's passenger area. After a half hour of strolling, the thought suddenly occurred to me that if the fog in Los Angeles lifted, the plane might take off sooner than the two-hour announced time. I quickly headed for the loading area, just in time to watch the plane depart from the gate—with my coat, seminar materials, and luggage.

Certainly, had I not gone strolling, this situation would have been avoided. However, at that moment, though I was powerless to change the circumstances, I did have the power to *choose my response.* Getting angry would have been useless. I calmly checked the departure schedule, arranged for a later flight, and told an official in Chicago that my belongings were on the departed plane. When I arrived in

Los Angeles, my coat, seminar materials, and luggage were securely waiting for me. I felt pleased that, when in Chicago, I immediately accepted the situation and then calmly had *chosen my response.* I was proud of my decision; I did not allow the situation to become distressful. *I chose to direct my attention to choices I could control,* rather than to those that were beyond my control.

Either momentarily or regularly, we experience circumstances that are beyond our control. Be it with family members, weather or other natural forces, inconveniences, unpleasant assignments, or unrewarding relationships, we all encounter situations we cannot change. However, we can *choose our responses* to these situations. How we choose to handle life's challenges largely determines how we feel about ourselves. As Oseola McCarty, a washerwoman who donated $150,000 to the University of Southern Mississippi, once said, "If you want to be proud of yourself, you've got to do things you can be proud of." Choosing to respond positively in any situation improves the feelings we have about ourselves.

A friend describes the feeling this way:

> I like to talk about self-pride. I will tell a child that you can't eat self-pride or spend it. You can't use it up. No one can take it away from you. You can feel it any time you want, and you can nourish it. It even grows. It never hurts anyone and it makes you feel good.

Choosing a Response to a Stimulus

As with situations that we cannot change, life also brings us experiences that *stimulate* or *provoke* us. When a parent smiles at the infant, the infant smiles back. Such a stimulus becomes less "automatic" with growth—as when the parent smiles at the teenager who does not reciprocate.

Some responses *seem automatic,* but really aren't. For example, imagine that you are watching a climactic scene in a television drama. The telephone rings. You may *choose* to answer the phone, or you may *choose* instead to let it ring, or you may *choose* to let your answering machine respond. If your doorbell rings, you will probably see who is at the door. As you approach a red light in a busy intersection, you *choose* to stop. Answering a ringing phone, responding to the sound of the doorbell, or stopping at a red light are learned responses. None of these stimuli *makes* a person do anything. They enter our brain as information, and we respond to them. There are innumerable examples of such reactions in daily living. In practical application, when it comes to answering the phone, or seeing who is at our door, or stopping at a red light, it doesn't make any difference if our reactions are conscious or nonconscious. A misconception in thinking arises, however, when we perceive that these stimuli *cause* our behavior or *make* us react to them.

> During surgery, a very competent nurse was asked for a specific instrument and handed it to the surgeon a moment later than the surgeon expected. The surgeon, who possessed brilliant surgical skills but lacked people skills, berated the nurse in front of all of the other professionals in the operating room.
>
> Throughout the day, the nurse frequently replayed the scenario in her mind—her anger at the surgeon building each time she did so. At dinner that night, she related the disheartening experience to her husband who asked her what time the event had occurred. She responded that it had taken place around nine o'clock that morning. The husband inquired, "What time is it now?" The wife answered, "Seven o'clock." Her husband then said, "You're telling me that this incident took place ten hours ago and that the surgeon is *still* making you angry?"
>
> The nurse decided to never again give that man control to ruin her day, allow him into her car, or invite him to her dinner table.

The nurse originally believed that the surgeon *made* her angry. Eleanor Roosevelt succinctly addressed the same issue when she commented, "No one can make you feel inferior without your consent."

After you receive a stimulus, there is an instant during which you have the ability to consider possible choices. The ability to make a *reflective (thoughtful)*—rather than a *reflexive (without conscious thought)*—decision is a fundamental characteristic that differentiates humans from all other species. Assume, for example, that John bullies Eddie. Young Eddie may choose to strike back, or run away, or tell an adult. We know that Eddie *chooses* what he does because of his actions. He runs home and *only* when he is in front of a parent—only then—does he begin to cry. The crying may be a natural reflex, but nevertheless Eddie chose his course of how to react at the time of the bullying.

We all experience reflex actions—automatic responses to stimulations. When a door slams or someone shouts and we jump in response to the sudden noise, we are experiencing *reflex actions.* All humans inherit a certain level of reactivity to external stimuli. Some of us are highly reactive, while others can shut out certain amounts of incoming stimuli.

Of course, reflexive responses are very important; without them we would not function normally. The most basic of these—the so-called "fight, flight, or freeze" reflex—saves our lives. Think of what it was like when a friend who was watering the garden suddenly turned the hose on you. When we lived in a less protected environment, this startle reflex was caused not by the threat of getting soaked, but by the possibility of a very real danger in the form of a tiger or a spear. In order to survive against predators, we had to make an instant decision whether to stay and fight, to run away, or in some cases just to freeze. The situation triggered a reflex action, but even then it involved some choice. However, since most problems humans face today do not require instant *reflexive* responses, the challenge is to help young people develop *reflective* responses—where conscious thought is given to their choices.

When provoked or stimulated, we should realize that there is always a choice of responses. Imagine that you see one of your children hitting another. You did not see the first child do the instigating; you only saw the retaliation of the second child and called him on it. The youngster exclaims, "He made me do it!" Even though *stimulated* to act, the child still made the decision to hit his younger brother back. No one else made that choice for him. The child had the freedom to choose a response, and his choice was to retaliate by hitting back. Children need to learn that regardless of the stimulus, they still have the power to choose their response.

Choosing a Response to an Impulse or Urge

We also have the freedom to choose our response to an impulse or urge. Infants are given diapers to wear because they are not able to control their natural urges and impulses. As children grow, diapers are no longer needed. We learn to respond to our physiological urges. The same holds true for emotional impulses. When we become angry, there is a moment of awareness before the emotion takes over and we become "emotionally hijacked." As normal, healthy individuals, we can—at any moment—exercise some choice of response. A response will occur, but *how, when,* and *where* are *decisions we control.*

Regardless of the *situation,* the *stimulus,* or the *impulse,* people choose their responses. To do otherwise would be to operate from compulsion. This is the beauty of being human. Unlike animals, we humans need not succumb to our reflexes or emotions. Furthermore, the less we succumb, the less we are driven by tyrannical obsessions. One of our most important tasks as parents is to teach and model *choice-response thinking*—that even young people can be in control of their choices.

So as not to fall back on previous habits and approaches, it is necessary to become *aware* of our options. You can do this very simply by teaching your child a procedure. Have the youngsters say, "I am choosing to...." before taking an action. For best results, this should be said out loud the first few times. Teaching young people to use this self-talk is one of the most effective lessons we can share.

As Harry Potter's mentor, Albus Dumbledore, advised the youth, *"It is not our abilities that say who we are. It is our choices."* It's not only the circumstances in which we find ourselves—but also our choices that make us who we are. Because we always have the freedom to choose, we are therefore responsible for our own behaviors. When we teach young people that they choose their own behaviors, they begin to become conscious that no one else chooses their behaviors for them.

Choice-response thinking encourages self-control and responsibility and is fundamental for a civil society. Our litigious society today is more victim-oriented than ever. If something bad happens, it becomes someone else's fault. As one cartoon has the plaintiff state, "The cigarette that I was forced to smoke dropped ashes on the silicon breasts I was forced to implant, and they melted all over the hamburger I hadn't cooked, so that's why I deserve $32.5 million." In another cartoon, this same type of thinking may prompt a sad smile. The parent is talking to the school principal, saying, "When we found out that our little son was flunking out of school, we first thought that it might be due to the fact that we never took an interest in his education, never talked to his teachers, never checked to see if he was doing his homework, and never encouraged him to do well. But then it dawned on us: It was the school's fault."

It is no kindness to treat young people as helpless, inadequate, or as victims—regardless of what has happened to them. Kindness is having faith in people and treating them in a way that encourages and empowers them to handle their situations, stimuli, impulses, and urges in positive and constructive ways. In addition, having young people become aware of *choice-response thinking* can have a liberating effect, especially with those who feel they are helpless or victims.

THE VICTIM TRAP

Although there are things in life that are out of our control, it is how we perceive them that is critical. This understanding is not new; it's just not common. Centuries ago, the Greek philosopher Epictetus (55-135) proposed that we are disturbed not by events but by the views we take of them. In other words, it is not the event itself that is the problem; it is our *perception* of the event that creates our suffering. Is it a problem or a challenge? "Victimhood thinking" is a perception and the opposite of *choice-response thinking.*

Besides creating unhappiness, victimhood thinking is also counterproductive to developing responsibility. A cartoon shows a young boy explaining his report card to his parents, as he says, "No use debating environment versus genetic causes. Either way, it's your fault."

People stuck in the victim trap do not perceive themselves as being in control of their lives and often see the world as unfair to them. *Their focus is on the event, rather than on their reaction to the event.* They perceive that whatever occurs happens *to* them, as if they are not responsible for their responses. These people are often angry. They cannot allow themselves to be happy because doing so would challenge their perceptions of themselves as victims. Much antisocial behavior by young people is the result of feeling powerless and without choices in life—of feeling like a victim.

Too often, irresponsible behavior is viewed as a "condition" and results in parents' excusing young people's irresponsible choices. Thus viewed through the prism of "special handicaps," these youngsters are often not held accountable for choosing their behavior. *This approach does them a disservice.* Growing into adulthood claiming, "I couldn't help it" or "I have ADD" will not satisfy law enforcement or society's expectations. All young people need to learn that they have the freedom to choose their responses and that they are accountable for their choices.

Our language itself shapes how we communicate. "He made me do it," "I couldn't control myself," and "I had no choice" are phrases one hears—and all are indications of victimhood thinking. Becoming aware that these are examples of not accepting responsibility—of giving up control—can be enough to empower a young person to make a more responsible choice the next time. *We increase our control by the language we use.* Notice the difference in the sense of power when an emotion-related adjective is turned into a verb, as in, "I am angering," rather than the usual, "I am angry."

Because language shapes our thinking—particularly when it comes to self-talk—a victimhood mentality is the result of thinking about outside forces rather than about *internal responses.* Common thinking patterns are: "Someone else is at fault," "Something else caused my behavior; I'm not responsible for it," and "I'm a victim." Taking conscious control of inner chat can act like a magic wand to help us shift to more positive and empowering mental states.

As parents, we need to teach our children to be *victors*, not victims. If we are not happy, we have the choice to make ourselves happy. As Abraham Lincoln said, "Most folks are about as happy as they make up their minds to be." In fact, not demonstrating negative (unhappy) emotions to other members of the family can be considered a moral obligation. Why should one member of the family's unhappiness be allowed to contaminate other members of the family?

No one can give happiness to another. We can assist our children in learning this life lesson by teaching them to self-talk in enabling and empowering ways. Phrases such as "prompts me" and "stimulates me" can be substituted for the powerless "made me" and "caused me."

Research on the value of choice is solid. The chemicals that our brains generate when we feel optimistic and in control are different from those created when we feel pessimistic and without control. Therefore, *teaching young people that they always have a choice and need not be victims is truly one of the most valuable insights parents can share.*

USING CHOICES TO RESOLVE CONFLICTS

In our complex society, few people work or live in total isolation. We are continually involved in social relationships. Interactions between people inevitably bring some disagreement and even conflict. Conflict itself is neither positive nor negative. Rather, it is the *response* to conflict that transforms it into either a destructive or constructive experience. Conflicts challenge but at the same time offer opportunities for growth. When conflict arises, there are essentially two operational choices: (1) continue the conflict or (2) resolve the problem.

The ability to handle conflicts in a constructive way rests on the choices *we* make first—not on the choices others make first. The following illustrates the point:

> A father was seeking advice because he felt that he could not communicate with his 17-year-old son. The counselor asked, "Whose fault is it? Do you expect your son to communicate with you if you don't successfully communicate with him?" The counselor suggested that when the father arrived home he should approach his son and say, "I realize that I have not communicated the best I can. Is it possible that you could be doing the same?" The counselor then challenged the man, "But I don't think you will have the courage to do it."
>
> Although believing that he was already doing what he thought he could to reach out to his son, the father acknowledged that his attempts were unsuccessful. Then on a Sunday morning, when the son was in the kitchen chewing on a sandwich (and the father was in the bedroom chewing on his nails), the father decided to follow the advice of the counselor. He walked into the kitchen and said, "Son, I realize that I have not communicated with you the best that I could. Is it possible that you could be doing the same?" The son, suddenly overwhelmed with emotion, joyously lifted his father up and hugged him.

As is so often the case, reaching out with compassion and dignity, as this father finally did, is an option that any individual can initiate to resolve a conflict. This is a point to be emphasized again and again: *If you want to change someone else, the change always starts with yourself.*

Solving Circles

Solving circles is a simple technique for resolving conflicts between any two people—without the involvement of a third party. It is easiest to understand as a visual. First, draw two interlocking circles. The left circle represents Person A; the right circle represents Person B. The overlapping area between the circles represents the problem, a conflict to resolve.

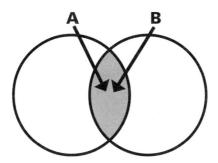

The natural tendency during a conflict is for each person to tell the *other person* what that person should do or stop doing. Basically, the message sent is that the *other person* needs to change. *Solving circles* uses a different strategy. Instead of pointing to the other person, Person A describes what *he himself* or *she herself* will do. Person B is then naturally drawn into the same procedure to also state what he or she will do to resolve the problem. By focusing on one's *own* behavior, even difficult conflicts are resolved. The reason is that each person reflects and takes responsibility for one's own action. This approach is so successful because it is not accusatory or coercive. *Solving circles* allows participants to retain dignity, resolve situations quickly, and immediately improve relationships.

A good way to teach this strategy to young children is to draw two large overlapping circles or place two hula-hoops in an overlapping position. Begin by asking each child to stand in one of the circles. Then have each describe a problem previously encountered with another person. Have each use *solving circles* for the situation described. They will quickly see how any situation can be resolved. The technique need not be limited to young people; it can be used by people of any age.

I successfully employed this technique with two four-year-old boys. Using words they could understand, I simply explained that neither could change the other—that the only person each could account for was himself. I then challenged the two youngsters to come up with a resolution to their conflict within four minutes. They resolved their dispute in two.

A key to the success of this strategy is to avoid "recycling the past." Too often, disputants focus on the past and simply revisit *memories*. But the more we stay in the past, the more we avoid facing the present. The past cannot be changed; it is useless to water last year's crops. Since we can only plan for the future, when we want to resolve a conflict our discussions must be *future-oriented*. Two key ingredients—(1) keeping the conversation focused on the future and (2) realizing that people can change *only themselves*—make *solving circles* a winning recipe for resolving conflicts in a simple and effective way. As long as people psychologically "stay in their circle," they can negotiate almost anything. Each person sends the message, "I want to improve the situation. Here is what I am willing to do."

If the young people in conflict are angry, first have a cooling-off period. An effective and simple procedure is to have both parties extend their arms outward as if holding a large box and then *slowly* count backward from 10 as their outstretched arms slowly come together until the palms touch when they reach the count of 1. Since emotions follow what we think about, the anger disappears because attention has been redirected. With older children and adults, first call a short timeout period. Stepping away from the situation allows everyone to cool down. When angry, we rarely focus on a solution. As soon as tempers have cooled, resume *solving circles*.

CHOOSING "CHOICE" AS YOUR NEW HABIT

Simply stated, *the more you empower others, the more effective you become.* This is a true and universal paradox that requires some experience to fully understand. The following comment given to me after a presentation in Australia may assist:

> If we want kids to be caring, honest, generous, and responsible, we have to be caring, honest, generous, and responsible ourselves. As has been said, "Modeling is not just a way to teach; it is the only way to teach."

Choice is essential to the teaching and learning of values. You cannot mandate generosity, caring, responsibility, honesty, and so on. These values can only be promoted in an environment of choice. You can only show honesty, caring, responsibility, and so on when you can choose not to behave in irresponsible ways. Many kids these days have huge amounts of freedom, but they do not choose responsible behaviors to handle their freedom.

In schools we often believe that these kids know how to behave appropriately and are choosing not to. Maybe many of these children have never been taught the behaviors necessary to be responsible, caring, honest, and so on. Or they have been taught the skills and behavior but have never been given the choice to choose to behave in these ways. Choice is the basic ingredient for the promotion of pro-social values.

—Nancy Snow, District Guidance Officer
Newcastle, New South Wales, Australia

Offering choices can be the easiest of the three practices to initiate. Giving options eliminates coercion simply and easily. By implementing this practice, you will enable your children to make wiser decisions, become more responsible, increase their cooperation, reduce stress on all concerned, and increase your joy of parenting.

CHANGE, CHOICE, AND OWNERSHIP

Chances are that you are reading this book because you would like to bring about some change(s). Two requirements are necessary for change. The first is the *awareness* that a change is necessary. The second is *ownership*. Choice brings ownership because, as mentioned, *people do not argue with their own choices.* Lasting change only occurs if the person *owns the change.*

A discussion of choice would not be complete without mentioning the trap parents can easily fall into of thinking that if choices are given, parental power is compromised. This is a false assumption. A common and erroneous approach is to think in terms of one *or* the other, "this" *or* "that." Such thinking can lead to power and ego struggles. The reality is that a third alternative is almost always available. When the parties first share their desires and then agree to try to satisfy all parties, the situation becomes *transformative* because no one loses and everyone wins. You will soon find that such situations result in positive and empowering feelings for all involved.

Having learned the power of positivity and the empowerment of choice, we next turn to the third practice.

POINTS TO REMEMBER

◆ Young people move toward confidence and competence by making decisions.

◆ Choice empowers, and offering choices not only significantly reduces stress but it also is remarkably more effective than the use of coercion.

◆ Young people can learn to choose their responses to any situation, stimulus, impulse, or urge.

◆ Young people should be taught that they are products of their choices as well as of their circumstances.

◆ Teaching young people about *choice-response thinking—that they need not be victims*—is one of the most valuable thinking patterns we can bestow on them.

◆ The critical difference between optimistic thinking and pessimistic thinking involves the perception of control—which, in turn, depends upon the perception of choice.

◆ Choice, control, and responsibility are so interwoven that one significantly affects the others.

◆ Young people can be taught to self-talk in enabling and self-powering ways by focusing on options available to them.

◆ Using *solving circles* to focus on one's own choices—rather than on what the *other person* should do—is a very successful conflict resolution strategy.

◆ As parents we can choose to focus on the past, which results in stress and negative feelings, or to focus on the future, which is less stressful and more effective.

◆ Choice brings ownership, and lasting changes only occur if the person *owns the choice.*

———————————————————

3
Reflection

Asking reflective questions is a skill anyone can learn.

One of the joys of parenting is the pride we experience in watching our children grow and become responsible. When we see them act irresponsibly, we want to change them. But our desire for change and the youngster's desire to change often come into conflict. How to bring about change is one of the greatest challenges of parenting and is the subject of this chapter.

CHANGING OTHERS

To quickly review, Chapter 1 demonstrates the power of *positivity* to alter behavior. We become more effective when we think and communicate in positive ways. If you are committed to reducing your stress and to becoming more effective, you will already have started to change negative self-talk and negative communications to be more positive.

Chapter 2 introduces the concept that *offering choices* significantly reduces stress and is remarkably more effective than attempting to force change. If a parent coerces or forces a decision upon a child that the youngster does not like—and if the child does not respond as the parent desires—the youngster is making a choice. Call it defiance, but nevertheless a choice has been made. Conversely, if the youngster does comply, a choice also has been made. So, since the child has choices anyway, providing options diminishes stress and is more effective than not offering them.

This chapter focuses on *reflection*, the third practice for parenting without stress and for raising responsible children. In order to understand the power and significance of reflection, you need a clear understanding of two basic facts of life: The first is that *any control of another person is temporary*. The second is that *attempting to control another person is really an attempt to change that person*. As long as we believe that we can change another person, there is a natural tendency for a parent to employ force or coercion, especially when the young person doesn't do what we want.

Just for a moment, think of *one* person with whom you have had a personal relationship—a child, spouse, significant other, parent, fellow worker, or friend. Now, answer the following two questions to yourself: (1) Have *you* ever changed that person? (2) And if the person did change, did *you* do the changing or did *that person* actually make the change? *A fact of life is that no one can change another person; we can only change ourselves.* A prime reason that *solving circles*, described in the last chapter, is so effective in resolving conflicts is that the technique is based on this simple truth.

Certainly, a parent can control a young child by using authority—as, for example, when a parent "grounds" a son or daughter or sends the child to a "timeout" area. But temporary *compliance* does not mean that we have *changed* the way the other person *wants* to behave or might behave in the future, especially when we are not present. People may be *controlled* by others, but they are not *changed* by others.

Please note that the point I am making here is not whether a parent should exercise authority. There are times when using authority is not only appropriate but necessary. My point is that attempts to control and/or change someone else by using authority is temporary, prompts stress and poor relations, and is the least effective approach for actuating change in another person.

COUNTERWILL

"Counterwill" is the name for the natural human resistance to being controlled. Although adults experience this phenomenon, we seem to be surprised when we encounter it in children. Counterwill is the most misunderstood and misinterpreted dynamic in adult-child relations.

This instinctive resistance can take many forms—the reactive "No!" of the toddler, resistance when hurried, disobedience or defiance, and lack of motivation. Counterwill can manifest itself in procrastination or in doing the opposite of what is expected. It can be expressed as passivity, negativity, or argumentativeness and is such a universal phenomenon at certain stages of development that it has given rise to the terms "terrible twos" and "rebellious teens." Despite the myriad of manifestations, the underlying dynamic is deceptively simple: a defensive reaction to felt coercion.

Counterwill is normal in the toddler and preschooler and explains why in older youngsters praise sometimes backfires, why some youth are preoccupied with taboos, and why some children do the opposite of what is expected. Adults misinterpret counterwill in a child as a manifestation of being strong willed, as being manipulative, as trying to get one's way, or as intentionally pushing the adult's buttons. Trying to deal with this dynamic with traditional coercive techniques is a recipe for disaster because no one likes to be pushed around—including children. The antidote to counterwill is to avoid prompting feelings of being coerced. The key is to focus on influence—rather than on coercion. *The art of influence is to induce people to influence themselves.* Parents who aim at influencing rather than dominating have more success, less stress, and greater joy in their relationships with their children.

INFLUENCE AND REFLECTION

Reflection is basically self-evaluation. Reflection engenders self-correction, which is the most effective route to improvement and growth. It is the way that adults learn and grow. This same approach applies to young people—who are *in the process* of becoming adults.

Prompting reflection is the most effective approach for influencing another person to accept an idea. And the most effective way to prompt reflection is to *ask reflective questions.* During my seminars I ask: "For those of you who are or were married, was the marriage proposal *told* to you? That is, were you told that you were going to marry the person proposing to you?" Rarely are any hands raised.

Then I ask, "How many who are or were married were *asked* to be married?" Everyone raises a hand.

When we really want something, we intuitively know to *ask* for it—rather than to tell.

Following is an example where asking was the key to a more effective resolution to a problem.

Two sisters lived together and got along rather well, but on this particular day they locked horns. The older sister was washing some dishes. The younger sister walked into the kitchen and took the last orange out of the basket. The older sister said, "Hold it. That's my orange." The younger sister said, "Sorry, I have it now." They argued back and forth and forth and back—typically as occurs in many homes.

Instead of continuing the argument, however, they put together a relatively creative solution. The older sister cut the orange in half, and to ensure fairness, the younger sister took first choice of which half of the orange she wanted.

That was a practical, creative, and, what most people would think, a fairly good solution—but *not the best* solution. The older sister asked the younger sister for what purpose she wanted the orange. The younger sister replied, "I want to squeeze it to make orange juice." The younger sister then asked the older sister, "What do you want it for?" "I want to scrape it and use the rind for baking."

By inquiring, by *asking*, the sisters each obtained double what they would have received from the original agreement.

Although, as in this story, asking questions seems simple, the types of questions that foster self-evaluation and change are of a particular kind. The word "question" originates from the Latin root *quaestio*, which means "to seek." Inside the word "question" is the root word "quest," suggesting that the question is an adventure. Therefore, think of questions as an adventure to find the other person's thinking, and you will enjoy the process!

THE ART OF REFLECTION

Change—in contrast to *control*—is always the result of an *inner decision*. In the final analysis, we do what we do because we want to do it. To have another person *want* to do what we would like the person to do rests with the skill of *creating desire*. The most effective approach for achieving long-lasting changes in behavior will invariably be a result of *reflection*—thinking about one's own actions and choices and then *desiring* to do something differently. When specific *reflective questions* are asked, people are prompted to think, reconsider, change their minds, and grow. By *asking reflective questions*, you will accomplish what you want more effectively, with less resistance, and with less stress. By having the youngster reflect, you instantly avoid the child's natural resistance to being controlled.

Benjamin Franklin said, "You cannot coerce people into changing their minds." Once you clearly understand this simple fact of life, the inevitable question arises, "If I cannot change another person, then what is the most effective approach for getting them to change?" As Franklin and other great influencers learned, it is never through criticism or coercion; these approaches are negative, rather than positive. As with practicing *positivity* and *choice*, this third practice of *reflection* will significantly increase your effectiveness in achieving your goals of influencing others to change.

Reflective Questions

Reflective questions are noncoercive. They *guide*, rather than *force*.

Here's an example. I was seated on an airplane next to an active four-year-old boy whose mother was having a challenging time with him. During the course of the flight, the young boy took the phone out of its security case from the back of the seat in front of him and started to play with it. I leaned over to him and asked, "What would happen if you broke that?" He immediately put the phone back. My question simply prompted him to think, to reflect. It's worth noting that the first two principles were also in play—the question was positive in nature (in contrast to a negative one, which would have prompted his counterwill), and the question elicited a choice. Rather than aiming at obedience by telling the youngster what to do, I asked a reflective question. If the mother would have *told* her son to put the phone back, my guess is that she would have had a challenge.

One reason this technique is so successful in influencing others to change is that such questions direct a person's thinking in a *positive* way. Two critical factors are involved here: (1) the youngster acknowledges that a change is necessary, and (2) the youngster owns the answer, ownership being a critical component for change. The point is reemphasized: *People do not argue with their own decisions.*

Questions Are a Gift

When you use reflective questions, you are directing the other person's thinking. *It is this questioning process that starts the thinking process*, both for you and for the other person. This kind of question is a gift to the person being asked because it induces clarity of thought. Similarly, the answer can be a gift to the person asking because it is a quick way to obtain and understand the other person's viewpoint.

Asking reflective questions increases the parent's awareness of a child's perceptions, thereby significantly increasing the parent's understanding of the child. This clarification leads to both increased effectiveness and improved relationships. *A key purpose of all communications is to gain understanding, to get clarity of the other person's thinking, and not necessarily to achieve agreement.* Clarity takes precedence over agreement. Experience has shown time and time again that aiming at understanding and clarity is the most effective route to resolving differences.

> When my wife and I were visiting my cousins, we went with them to pick up their daughters after school. On the drive, the parents described the six-year-old as a parent's dream, whereas the three-and-a-half-year-old was a real challenge. The parents told us that the younger daughter had difficulty sharing. In preschool, if she did not get what she wanted, she would express her unhappiness by screaming. Her parents described her as very manipulative.
>
> When the two daughters got in the car, my wife and I announced that we had a gift for them—a game that could be played by only one person at a time. I asked the girls if they would mind taking turns and they assured me that this wouldn't be a problem. After showing the girls how the game worked, it was agreed that the younger daughter would have the first turn. It was also agreed that each would have two turns before passing the game on to the other. Predictably, after her two allotted turns, the younger sister did not want to give the game up. I reminded her of her agreement to share with her sister. She ignored my comment.

I asked myself, "What can I *ask*, not *tell*, to have her reflect on the agreement—on the agreed-upon procedure—and have her take responsibility?" As she was playing the game for the third time, I simply asked, "Is this your second try at your second game?" The youngster looked at me and then handed the game to her sister. Asking a reflective question was more successful than attempting to use coercive persuasion.

This example brings up an important point. *Sometimes we parents need to be satisfied with only a single step in the right direction.* A single is not a home run, but it gets the baseball player to first base and moving in the desired direction. In the situation with my cousin's daughter, the child was obviously not pleased to give up the game when she still wanted to play with it. I was not pleased that she did not keep her agreement to share after her second turn. However, progress was made, and so I was satisfied with a step in the right direction.

As soon as you start asking reflective questions, you will immediately realize the effectiveness and power of this strategy. Questions such as the following are designed to promote deep and reflective thinking:

"Are you willing to try something different?"

"What would you do if you could not fail?"

"What can you do to accomplish that?"

Guidelines

Effective questions elicit a *thinking* response and are framed to fit the situation and to clarify.

1. They focus on the *present* or *future*—as opposed to the past.

2. They often start with "What?" or "How?"

3. They are usually open-ended in that they require more than a "yes" or "no" answer.

Questions that can be answered with a simple "yes" or "no" are referred to as "closed-ended" because they often close the conversation. Ask closed-ended questions *only* if they lead to self-inquiry or self-evaluation. For example:

"Did you do your best?"

"Are you pleased with what you have done?"

In other situations, "yes" or "no" questions can be effective if followed up with further questions that call for an explanation. Examples are:

"Are you taking the responsible approach? How so?"

"Are you satisfied with your results? If not, what could you do?"

In some instances, just asking the question is sufficient. For example,

"Are you going to let this (situation, person, problem) hold you back?"

"Can you picture yourself doing (a specific procedure)?"

In contrast to closed-ended questions, open-ended questions invite children to engage in a dialogue with you. They prompt more thoughtful responses. Examples are:

"What was your favorite part of your day?"

"What did you learn today?"

The more we encourage children to do things for themselves, the more strongly we communicate the message, "I believe in your ability and skills." As you get into the habit of using the language of responsibility, you will be able to see tangible evidence of your children's growth. When we ask young people for their ideas and suggestions, we are often pleasantly surprised by their creative and practical solutions. People of any age are more likely to follow through with the solutions when they have helped create them.

Questions need not end with a question mark. For example, the following are effective statements that promote reflection and clarification:

"Please describe it to me."

"Explain to me what you mean when you say...."

Some questions prompt reflection without requiring a response. Tag questions are an example. A tag question is simply a question offered quickly and nonchalantly at the end of a statement or observation that encourages review of the previous communication, such as, "So you think that will help the situation, do you?" When using tag questions, you make a statement and then leave it up to the person with whom you are talking to think about. Tag questions in particular give parents a tool to help a young person review what has been said or done. They prompt an opportunity to have the young person reflect—without requiring an accounting to the adult. Here are more examples of tag questions:

"You meant that you could go to your friend's house when you finish your homework, didn't you?"

"That's quite an achievement, isn't it?"

"You didn't really mean that, did you?"

"Do you really think that will get you what you want? No reply needed!"

It is extremely challenging to parent without criticizing. One way to reduce such negative communications is to turn criticism into a question. Asking, "If you were to do that over again, what would you do differently?" will get the message across without bringing aggravation to the parent and negative feelings to the child. There is a big difference between a parent's rejection *of the child* and the parent's lack of support *for an action by the child*. Children can easily see and understand the difference. Having a youngster reflect is an excellent way to separate the act from the actor.

A Personal Example

My wife has been chatting with the same cashier at our neighborhood grocery store for many years. At the beginning of their interchanges, the cashier commented how her strong-willed five-year-old granddaughter was such a challenge and that the mother was at a loss in how to handle her child. My wife gave the cashier some suggestions emphasizing choice and reflection. When the grandmother started to use these practices, her conversations with her granddaughter were like the following:

The five-year-old was crying. The grandmother asked, "Do you want to act like a big girl or a baby?"

Reply: "I want to cry, so I want to act like a baby."

Shortly thereafter, the youngster said, "Now I want to act like a big girl."

In another incident, the grandmother asked, "Why are you crying?"

The granddaughter replied, "I don't' know," and then stopped crying.

In the most recent conversation my wife had with the cashier, she mentioned what a joy her now 10-year-old granddaughter has become.

There's an old saying, usually attributed to Confucius, which goes something like, "Give a man a fish, and you'll feed him for a day. Teach a man to fish, and you've fed him for a lifetime." This simply means that if you give a person the answer, the person will only have a temporary solution. But teach the person the principles that led to that answer, and the person will be able to create solutions in the future. The cashier's granddaughter learned the mechanism for reflection that will last her a lifetime.

A First Nation's Example
Standing Bear does not recall his father saying, "You have to do this," but instead his father would often create expectations by saying something like, "Son, some day when you are a man you will do this."

An Example for Dealing with Complaining
A parent related the following story to me about how she used reflective questioning to stop her son's complaining:

During a search for a more effective approach to discipline, I began reading Dr. Marshall's book, *Discipline without Stress.*

After attending my son's hockey game in a city about two hours from home, I continued my reading in the car while my husband drove. My son, who was 11 at the time, announced that he had been invited to a friend's house and wanted to go when we arrived home. This is how the conversation went:

Son: "Can I go to Greg's house when we get home?"

Mom: "No. It's already late and we still have quite a
    drive ahead."
Son: "I really want to go. Can I go?"
Mom: "No. Not tonight."
Son: "But Greg asked me. Can I go?"

At this point, as I was beginning to get irritated, I
suddenly remembered one section in the book that had
questions to ask a child at a time like this. I quickly turned
to the part on "Complaining." When my son asked again
if he could go to his friend's house, I was ready:

Mom: "How long are you going to do this?"
Son (with a hint of humor in his voice): "Forever!"
Mom: "Is this getting you what you want?"
Son (pleasantly): "No."

And that was the end of it. He didn't ask again.

Ineffective Questions

Generally, be cautious of asking "why" questions. "Why?" is one of
the most frequently used and yet most *ineffective* questions you can
ask. Not only does it have an accusatory overtone, but it also blocks
communications because it prompts negative feelings. Try this
experiment out loud so you can hear for yourself.

Ask: "Why are you doing that?"
Then ask: "What just happened?"

Notice that in the first question, your voice pitch goes up and, if
you were speaking to someone else, your volume also would have
increased. Did you notice the difference in your emotions by asking
the "why" question in contrast to the "what" question?

In addition, asking "Why?" aims at a person's motivation, and
articulating one's motivation can be difficult. Even if the motivation could be articulated, the young person may not want to reveal
it. Therefore, when used with some youngsters, "why" questions
prompt giving an excuse, being a victim, and leads to avoiding
responsibility. This is particularly the case with youth who have been
"labeled." Although the classification is meant to help, the label can
become a crutch. Saying or thinking, "I can't help it. I have attention deficit disorder" is an example of the harm labeling can do.

Besides, young people often *do not know why* they do what they do. Even if they were able to articulate the reason, it is demeaning to have to do so. No one enjoys admitting a poor decision. If you are really curious about the reason, then ask in a non-judgmental way. "Out of curiosity, why did you choose that rather than this?" Changing the structure of the question eliminates any negative inference. *Most importantly, asking a "why" question has little effect on changing behavior.*

Additional kinds of questions other than those beginning with "why" can have a negative implication. Notice the unspoken demand and negative undertone of, "When are you going to stop doing that?" In contrast, "How long do you believe you'll be continuing that?" is inquisitive when asked in a non-accusatory manner.

Compare the two questions below. The intention behind each is the same; yet notice the subtle differences. The first question has a negative overtone and comes across as an unspoken demand. The second is inquisitive—not accusatory.

> A. "When are you going to start your homework?" (accusatory)

> B. "Do you have a plan in mind for your homework?" (inquisitive)

If you were the young person, which question would you rather hear? Which would be more effective in prompting you to act?

An important feedback mechanism for developing your skill of asking effective questions is to notice the quality of the responses you are getting, for *the quality of the answers largely depends on the quality of the questions.*

Here's an example. The parents spend $300 to send their child to summer camp. When picking up the child, the parents inquire, "How was camp?" and the youngster replies, "Okay." The parents are rather disappointed when they receive only an "okay" for their investment. In contrast, if the parents were to ask a more specific *reflective* question, the outcome would be completely different. "What was the most interesting experience you had at camp?" prompts reflection that, in turn, would give parents the pleasure of hearing about their youngster's experience.

Effective Questions

The following sample questions are particularly effective and will help you get started. They can be even more effective when young people begin to ask the same types of questions to themselves.

"What would an extraordinary person do now?"

"What would be the best way to respond in this situation?"

"What's getting in your way to prevent you from doing it?"

"What can be done to prevent that urge from dictating future behavior?"

"What is your body telling you?"

"What can you do to get what you want?"

"What will you do to rise above this?"

"Some people choose to _____. What do you think about that?"

"How can you repair what happened?"

"How is what you are doing helping you?"

"What can you do to change the situation?"

"How can you do that without bothering your sister?"

"What could be a better choice to make everybody happy?"

"How would you describe the way you want it to turn out?"

"It's okay to make a mistake. Now, how are you going to correct it?"

"When you do that, what kind of a relationship are you creating?"

"On a scale of 1 to 10, what would it take to make it a 10?"

"What did you learn that you could apply to other areas?"

Additional Questions for Specific Purposes

A Four-Step Question Series to Change Behavior:

1. "What do you *want?*"

2. "What are you *choosing to do* to get what you want?"

3. "If what you are choosing is not getting you what you want, then what is your *plan?*"

4. "What are your *procedures* to implement the plan?"

For Reducing Complaining:

"How much more time do you think you will need to continue this?"

"Is what you are doing helping you to get what you want?"

"What do you notice about the experience you are having?"

For Getting on Task:

"Is what you are doing helping you to get your task done?"

"If you would like to get your task done, what would be your first step?"

"What do you like to do that you can apply to this task?"

For Commitment:

"In the realm of all things possible, could you have kept your commitment?"

"What can you do to make it happen?"

For Improving Quality:

"How does that look to you?"

"What could you do to make even more progress?"

"What limitations can we remove that would allow you to do it even better?"

For Starting Conversations:

> "What was most pleasing for you today?"
>
> "What bothered you the most today? How did you deal with it?"
>
> "What was your biggest challenge today? How did you deal with it?"
>
> "If the situation comes up again, what will you do?"

The Golden Question: "What do you think?"

If I were limited to offering one question that would have a positive undertone by acknowledging the person, that requires choice, and that would prompt reflection, that question would be: *"What do you think?"*

PRACTICE IS THE MOTHER OF SKILL

When we first learned how to walk, we wobbled, were unsteady, and fell down. When learning to ride a bicycle or drive a car, most of us went through hesitant and uncomfortable stages. We go through such stages whenever we are learning a new skill.

Reflect on a time like this in your own life. Perhaps it was when you learned to swim, play a musical instrument, skate, or type. Remember how awkward it felt at first? Remember too that the hesitation, discomfort, and awkwardness faded away once you "got the hang of it." Learning even a simple skill is not always easy *until the skill is regularly practiced.* As Ralph Waldo Emerson said, "That which we persist in doing becomes easier—not that the nature of the task has changed, but our ability to do it has increased."

The concept bears repeating: *You cannot learn a skill and be perfect at the same time.* We should not expect perfection of our youngsters, and we should not expect it of ourselves. Expecting to be perfect at a strategy we are learning is unrealistic. Give yourself permission to be a learner. It helps to think of developing a skill as a *direction*, rather than a *destination.* Just as an athlete, musician, or any professional does, we can continually learn and hone the skill. *Continuous improvement*—rather than perfection—must be our motto.

As you will discover, the skill of reflective questioning improves with use. Each question is a learning experience. After starting to ask reflective questions, you will learn which ones bring desired outcomes and which do not. Creativity and confidence come with practice. Be a person who taps into creativity. Two guiding thoughts will help: (1) Be committed to the strategy of guiding children to self-evaluate, and (2) rather than putting a child on the defensive, frame your questions in an attitude of helping, not hurting—guiding, not punishing—*acting as a counselor and coach rather than as a cop.*

Forming New Habits

As with any skill, asking effective questions needs to become a conscious strategy and requires patience and continual practice to become proficient. The following experience, told to me by Alan, illustrates this reality.

> Alan grew up in New York City and drove a taxicab to put himself through college. Obviously, he was an experienced driver in all kinds of weather. Years later, when driving to work in Upper State New York on a winter day, he encountered black ice (a nearly invisible coating of ice that forms on asphalt), and his car started to skid. The more the car skidded to the right, the more he desperately turned the steering wheel to the left against the skid, and the more the car kept skidding until finally it hit a tree. Alan said that during the accident he felt as if he were experiencing slow motion. Fortunately, Alan was not injured and the car was not too badly damaged.
>
> When the tow truck driver arrived, he said to Alan, "You know, you should have turned *with* the skid—in the direction of the skid—in order for the car's tires to regain traction with the road." Alan thought, "I knew that." When he described his experience to the mechanic, the mechanic also said, "You know, you should have turned with the skid." Alan started to become quite uncomfortable as again he said to himself, "I *knew* that." The next day, Alan related the story about the accident to a friend, explaining that it seemed as if time slowed down just before he hit the tree. His friend said, "If you had so much time, why didn't you turn with the skid?" This time Alan became angry. As he told me the story, he ascertained that the reason he felt anger was that he

knew what to do in a skid—but didn't do it. Why didn't he do what he knew? The answer was that he did what "came naturally."

Alan lived by a lake, and in the winter the lake could be 30 inches thick with ice. Sometime after his accident, still disappointed about how he handled the situation, he put his car on the ice, revved it up to 15 miles per hour, and then slammed on the brakes. Naturally, the car went into a skid. Much to his dismay, Alan turned the steering wheel as he had during his accident—in the opposite direction of the skid, instead of with or in the same direction of the skid. He made a second attempt, again turning the steering wheel the wrong way. Alan told me it took him three tries before he actually turned the steering wheel in the direction he knew he should—*with* the skid, instead of against it. When he did finally turn the steering wheel in the same direction as the skid, he regained control of his car.

As with Alan's experience, consciously developing a new habit can have you feeling uncomfortable at first. *You need to be aware of this.* Just for a moment, interlock your fingers with one thumb over the other. Now pull your fingers apart and interlock them with the other thumb on top. Does it feel a little odd? Cross your arms. Now cross them in the opposite way. Feel funny? Similarly, when you start asking self-evaluative, reflective-type questions, you are going to feel slightly strange. Knowing this ahead of time will assist you until your brain makes new neural connections so that your habitual inclination will be to ask, rather than to tell. It is necessary to ask reflective questions a minimum of seven (7) times until the brain has made new neural connections so that the *skill of asking*—instead of telling—feels comfortable and becomes natural.

POSITION YOURSELF

With learning any new skill, putting yourself in proper position always precedes any action. This is as true when asking evaluative-type questions as it is when holding a golf club before the swing, grasping a baseball bat before the pitch, sitting properly at the piano bench, or positioning your mouth before breathing into a flute.

When asking reflective questions, the first step is to place yourself in the position—both mental and physical—of being *inquisitive*.

TONE OF VOICE

You do not shout questions. The adage, "What you are doing speaks so loudly that I can't hear what you are saying" rings true here. The *tone of voice* communicates almost as much as the words.

> It's not only what you say
> But the manner in which you say it.
> It's not only the language you use
> But the tone in which you convey it.
>
> "Come here!" I sharply said,
> And the child cowered and wept.
> "Come here," I gently said. He looked and smiled
> And straight to my lap he crept.
>
> Words may be mild and fair
> But the tone can pierce like a dart.
> Words may be soft as the summer air
> But the tone can break my heart.
>
> Words come from the mind
> And grow by study and art.
> But tone leaps from the inner self,
> Revealing the state of the heart.
>
> For if you want behavior to change,
> Of this you must remain aware:
> As much as the words you use, it is the tone of your voice
> That communicates how much you care.
>
> (Author Unknown)

Only the actual asking of reflective questions in a *caring tone* will improve your effectiveness. Success comes—especially with adolescents—with persistence and perseverance, as indicated by the following experience:

> The parent knew about asking reflective questions, so instead of the normal evening greeting, "How was your day?" the parent asked, "What was the best thing that happened to you today?"

The youngster replied, "Nothing."

The parent did not give up. The same question was asked day after day—getting the same negative response.

Weeks later, the daughter came in for breakfast and said, "I already know what is the best thing that will happen to me today."

The parent was startled by this uncharacteristic expression but asked, "What is it?"

The teenager replied with a big smile, "I woke up this morning looking for the best thing that will happen to me today."

Although simple, asking questions—as is the case with communicating in positive terms and offering choices—only becomes easy with constant awareness and use.

With this in mind, the question is asked,

"How do you develop the skill?"
Answered the sage, "With experience."
"But," asked the disciple, "how do you get the experience?"
Came the answer, "By asking poor questions."

Keep in mind that each question asked is a learning experience and, if the desired result is not obtained, it should be thought of as feedback, not as failure.

CONTROLLING THE CONVERSATION

When you enter a store and the salesperson asks the common greeting, "How are you today?" do you ignore the person—or is there a natural tendency to give a response? During a conversation where you are explaining something and your friend suddenly asks you a question, do you continue talking and ignore the question or do you respond to it? Notice that in each of these scenarios, there is a natural tendency to respond to a question. And herein lies the most important and effective key to remember if you want to reduce your stress and promote responsible behavior: *The person who asks the question controls the conversation.*

A national magazine ran a cover article about frustrated parents who were exhausted from answering their young daughter's constant questioning, "Why?" The parents would have been less frustrated if, instead of always attempting to answer her every question, they would have asked the golden question, "Why do *you* think?" This simple approach would have reduced the parents' stress, prompted the youngster's imagination, and helped to develop the young girl's reflective skills.

The point to remember is that when conversing with your child, *you* need to be the one doing the asking. Your questions will direct the situation and prompt your child to think in the direction you would like. Even when your child recognizes what you are doing, the approach is still successful because (1) it is noncoercive, (2) your child understands that what you are doing is in her or his best interests, and (3) the process is empowering for the child.

CAUTION: Your communications should not be a continual series of questions. Talk, share, offer suggestions, and when you desire to *redirect* the conversation or attention, *then* rely on your questioning skills.

A final point to ponder: As parents, we can also reflect on the questions we ask ourselves, such as, "Am I proud of the way I interacted with my child?" and "Would I be offended if someone interacted with me as I interacted with my child?"

CONCLUDING REFLECTIONS

Think of the questioning strategy as a car: It is a means to get to your destination. How you get there depends on the roads you take and how you drive. You may want to get to your destination as fast as you can and, thereby, take the risk of a ticket or an accident—and perhaps deprive yourself of the joy in the drive. This speedy approach can be compared to *telling*, the subject of the last chapter of this book. In contrast, *asking* will take you on a road that eliminates stress and has you enjoying your journey.

The following question is one you may want to ask yourself on a periodic basis:

"If I were a child, would I want me as a parent?"

POINTS TO REMEMBER

◆ Control over another person is always temporary.

◆ No one changes another person; people change themselves.

◆ The least effective approach for long-term change is trying to control and coerce.

◆ Influencing another person to change usually starts with changing one's own approach.

◆ Reflective questions are noncoercive.

◆ Reflective questions help clarify.

◆ Reflective questions lead to self-inquiry and self-evaluation.

◆ Reflective questioning is a skill that can be developed and is made easier through practice.

◆ Asking reflective questions is helpful for parents to better understand their children.

◆ The person who asks the question controls the conversation.

◆ Asking reflective questions reduces stress.

PART I
The Three Practices
Summary and Conclusion

One evening, an old tribal chief told his grandson about a battle that goes on inside people. He said, "The battle is between two wolves inside us all. One is bad. It has anger, regret, greed, self-pity, resentment, inferiority, lies, and selfishness. The other is good. It has joy, peace, love, hope, kindness, empathy, generosity, and truth." The grandson thought for a minute and then asked, "Which wolf wins?" The old sage replied, "The one you feed."

SUMMARY

Positivity, choice, and *reflection* are to be fed. They reduce stress, increase parental effectiveness, and improve relationships.

Negative comments prompt negative feelings. Positive comments engender positive feelings and responsible behavior. Parents who are effective in influencing their children to positive actions phrase their communications in positive terms. Positivity creates an atmosphere in which children feel valued, supported, respected, motivated, capable, and proud.

Either consciously or nonconsciously, people are always choosing how to respond to any situation, stimulus, or impulse. Teaching young people about *choice-response thinking*—that they never need think of themselves as victims—is one of the most valuable thinking patterns we can give them. This type of thinking teaches the difference between optimistic and pessimistic thinking, empowers young people, and continually fosters hope—the greatest of motivators.

Reflection is the most powerful strategy for prompting change because reflection engenders self-evaluation. This is particularly important for parents to understand because parents cannot change children. Although a parent can control a child, no one can change another person. A person can only change oneself. The key to actuating a change in behavior is asking *reflective* questions. Asking these types of questions is a skill that is developed through practice and that any parent can learn in order to prompt young people to make responsible decisions.

CONCLUSION

In most discipline situations, especially if your child is extremely independent, you will have more success—and reduce stress on everyone's part—if you aim at *empowering*, rather than *overpowering your child*. When a young person feels overpowered by a demand for obedience, then defensive behavior often results in both resistance and resentment. In contrast, when you *aim at promoting responsibility, obedience follows as a natural by-product*.

How to do this is explained in Part II, which describes the *Raise Responsibility System*, a simple system that prompts young people to *want* to behave responsibly.

PART II
The Raise Responsibility System

Teaching

Asking

Eliciting

INTRODUCTION
The Raise Responsibility System

The best discipline is the kind nobody notices
—not even the one being disciplined.

The first section of this book describes three motivational practices that are both universal and effective with any age group. This section describes a discipline and learning system that is being used around the world. However, your success with even the most successful of systems will depend on your using the three practices. Specifically, you will find the greatest success with the *Raise Responsibility System* when you communicate in positive terms, when you reduce coercion by the use of choice, and when you ask reflective questions.

As the name states, the *Raise Responsibility System* aims at promoting *responsibility*. This is in contrast to approaches that aim at fostering *obedience*. When parents aim toward obedience with young people today, they often get resistance, resentment, and even rebellion. The result is stress for both parent and child. As children grow, the more we try to force obedience the more they resist. However, *when responsibility is promoted, obedience becomes a natural by-product.*

The *Raise Responsibility System* is *proactive* rather than *reactive*. Instead of waiting until an undesirable behavior occurs and then reacting to it, this approach starts by having young people learn four words referred to as the *Hierarchy of Social Development*. In this way, they continually have something specific (the four words and their meanings) as their base.

We parents are constantly teaching and influencing. As a matter of fact, we cannot help but influence our children. We are often unaware of our constant role-modeling. This is especially the case when we react to what children do that does not please us. Reacting to irresponsible behavior by aiming at obedience is a primary cause of stress in parent-child relationships—whether we are *telling* them to do something, using *threats* and *punishments*, or attempting to manipulate their behavior with *rewards*. But what if you could influence your children to make better choices because they WANT to? And what if, when challenges do occur, you have an approach of placing the responsibility for *self*-correction on the youngster?

When using the *Raise Responsibility System*, you will learn to handle disruptive and irresponsible behavior simply and easily. Use the system and you will find your children developing self-discipline, developing respect for self and others, and becoming more responsible. As you implement the system, you will quickly see how stress and adversarial relationships are significantly reduced. Young people really *want* to behave appropriately, and the system induces them to do so. The reason is that the A, B, C, D hierarchy promotes responsibility.

4
Teaching

When I first came upon the system, it was the hierarchy and its concept of motivation that initially grabbed my attention. It was the first time I had ever seen anyone explain that high-level behaviour is actually all about personal motivation. The contrast between the higher levels points this out perfectly. To me, the hierarchy is absolutely brilliant, especially because of its simplicity. When something is simple enough that even children can understand it and yet so striking that many adults are stopped in their tracks by it, it's got to be worthwhile.

—Kerry Weisner, Teacher and Parent
British Columbia, Canada

The foundation of the *Raise Responsibility System* is for young people to understand four basic concepts that are *descriptions* of social and personal development. You may find success with every approach discussed in this book, but you will find that your child's greatest growth and one of your greatest reductions in stress come from the use of these four concepts.

Just in case you feel a reluctance to use the concepts, think of a rocket about to pull away from the earth on a space mission. Most of the thrust has to do with surging past the earth's gravitational pull. Similarly, once you overcome any reluctance to use the concepts, you will soon find them easy to use and will even enjoy referring to them. *Trust the process.* As thousands of others have already done, you and your children will grow as you both refer to them.

How young people mature after learning the hierarchy is what makes sharing it so valuable. Youngsters starting at about age four can understand the concepts referred to as Levels A, B, C, and D. Here is an example of how Kerry Weisner used the hierarchy, which is just as applicable in the home as it is in a school:

I recently had a situation in which I was able to use the hierarchy to help a child feel better about her dealings with a difficult desk partner. I think it's helpful to know about experiences because I want to encourage people to use the hierarchy to help children acknowledge not only misbehaviour, but also to become aware of higher levels.

Sarah was waiting for me at the door. A very sweet child who is always smiling, she seemed near tears and was obviously worried. She explained that another student was going to "tell on her" and that she "hadn't done it!"

I didn't bother to find out any more details because I believed Sarah; she had never given me one moment of trouble and I knew I could trust that she was telling me the truth. If she told me that she "hadn't done it," I knew that she hadn't—whatever it was!

I took her over to our social development hierarchy chart and asked her to show me where she generally operated. She pointed to D, and I said, "Sarah, you're right. You are always operating at C or D." Then I went on to ask her about what kind of relationships students who operate at the higher levels build with their teachers? She was able to answer, "Good," which doesn't really say it all, but I knew she understood what I was talking about.

Then I explained further, "You're right, Sarah. When people operate at the higher levels, it means that other people come to trust them. If, day in and day out, you are behaving yourself and being honest, teachers know they can count on you to do the right thing and to tell the truth.

"Now, what do you think, Sarah, if someone does come up and tattles on you, and you tell me that you didn't do it, will I be able to believe you?" She said, "Yes," and I said, "That's right, Sarah. You have shown me day after day that I can trust you, so if you tell me you didn't do it, I can easily believe you. That's one of the great things about operating on a high level; other people trust you and you don't need to worry that someone is getting you in trouble for something you didn't do." And with that, the look of worry disappeared; she seemed quite relieved as she went off to her seat.

I love that hierarchy!

A hierarchy is a series of stages, like steps on a ladder, in which the higher the level the better. Two of the better-known hierarchies are Abraham Maslow's *Hierarchy of Needs* and Jean Piaget's *Hierarchy of Cognitive Development.* Maslow's hierarchy has *survival* at the *lowest* level and *self-actualization* at the *highest* level. Piaget's hierarchy indicates level of brain development so that, for example, a 13-year-old is more capable of performing skills than a 3-year-old. His hierarchy helps adults understand what is appropriate at various ages.

As a side note, unfortunately many adults misinterpret what Piaget taught. The essence of his hierarchy is that children's brains develop at different ages but they have *similar feelings as adults.* Smile at an infant and you receive a smile back. Smiles prompt good feelings. But infants also experience negative feelings of pain, anger, and fear—just as adults do. Unfortunately, however, often an adult will deal with a child in the reverse way, that is, as if the youngster has the same *cognitive development as an adult* but does not have the same feelings as adults.

WHY A HIERARCHY?

A hierarchy was chosen because it engenders a natural desire to reach the top level. It is a simple way to motivate young people. The hierarchy used in this system describes levels of social development. Having young people learn the levels is significant because of *what young people become* when exposed to it; they grow and mature.

Before the concepts of the hierarchy are described, it helps for you to understand some of the benefits of the *Hierarchy of Social Development:*

1. It completely bypasses the natural tendency for a youngster to self-defend. It separates the deed from the doer and encourages reflection of the *situation,* rather than of the *person.* If the hierarchy did nothing else, it would be worth teaching for this fact alone.

2. It brings attention to young people that they are constantly making choices (responses to situations, stimuli, or urges).

3. It engenders understanding and empowerment to deal with both bullying and the influence of negative peer pressure.

4. It promotes motivation to *want* to do the right thing.

5. It fosters taking responsibility, the bedrock of all character development.

A unique feature of the hierarchy is that the same vocabulary is used with *any age* and for *any situation*. However, the examples and understandings differ depending upon the age of the young person.

THE VOCABULARY

The vocabulary of the hierarchy describes four concepts of social (and personal) development. The concepts serve as a simple tool for categorizing *behavior* and *motivation*. After you have explained the concepts, you will then only refer to the *letter* of the levels—rather than to the actual vocabulary. For example, the highest level in the hierarchy, *Democracy*, is referred to simply as *Level D*.

THE HIERARCHY OF SOCIAL DEVELOPMENT
The two higher levels refer to *motivation*.
Both are acceptable.

LEVEL D – Democracy: *(Highest level)*
- Develops self-discipline
- Demonstrates initiative
- Displays responsibility
- *Democracy and responsibility are inseparable.*

The MOTIVATION is *internal*.

At this level the person does the right thing because it is the right thing to do.

LEVEL C – Cooperation/Conformity
- Considerate
- Cooperates

- Complies
- Conforms

The MOTIVATION is <u>external</u>.

This level is characterized by cooperation and complying with requests, as with Level D, but the motivation is *external*. Action at Level C is often prompted by *motivation* to please others, receive some external reward, or to avoid something negative, such as threats or punishments. A danger exists at this level, however, when young people conform to irresponsible peer influence.

It is critical to understand that the difference between Level C and Level D is in the *motivation*, rather than in the *action* itself. For example, the parent requests that the teenager make the bed before leaving for the day, and the youth does as requested (Level C). However, if the youth knows the expectation in the home is to make the bed before leaving and takes the *initiative* to make the bed *without being asked*, then the *motivation* is on Level D. In both cases the youngster has shown responsibility—the bed has been made; only the *motivation* is different.

Critical concept: The hierarchy is a tool for *self-assessment*. A person cannot know another person's motivation with complete certainty. Level C is expected. Level D is an *option*.

**The two lower levels describe <u>behaviors</u>.
<u>Neither</u> is acceptable.**

LEVEL B – Boss<u>ing</u>/Bully<u>ing</u>
- Bosses others
- Bullies others
- Bothers others
- Breaks laws and makes own standards

Must be bossed to behave

This level is characterized by a lack of impulse control, a lack of consideration for others, and by displaying inappropriate behaviors. When a child behaves at this level, the message being sent to the parent is, *"Control me because I am not capable of controlling myself."*

LEVEL A – Anarchy *(Lowest level)*
- Absence of order
- Aimless and chaotic
- Absence of government

This level is characterized by chaos, being out of control, or unsafe.

Anarchy is the fundamental enemy of civilization.

Behaviors at the two lower levels are the kinds that prompt stress. The approach for effectively handling behaviors at these unacceptable levels is provided in the following two chapters.

AN ANALOGY

Here is how one person explains the four levels:

I begin with the four stages of the *life cycle of a butterfly: egg, caterpillar, pupa, and butterfly.* We talk about how all butterflies are in some stage of this process, but they have no control over their movement through this process.

We then move on to comparing the butterfly's life cycle to that of humans. We decide that humans go through four basic stages as well. We call them *baby/infant, child/youth, adolescent/teen,* and *adult/grown-up.* We agree that humans have little control over the stage of *physical development* in which they find themselves.

Then we begin to look at the four stages of *social development* in which one human and/or a society could operate. We talk about what a human and a society in anarchy would look like and how such a situation would be so hopeless. Then we talk about what would likely occur to remedy the problems of an anarchy-based society. We conclude that someone would rise up and take control of the situation (thereby becoming a boss) and that this may or may not be a good thing. We look at countries around the world where we thought this might have happened.

Next we move on to looking at the level of control or power in a group of friends. We decide that a group of friends works together and that group control is not ever discussed; it is more or less just understood among the group members. From here a discussion of blind conformity develops and how this type of cooperation is not necessarily good. We then look at how being considerate of others and cooperating for the right reasons results in a civil society.

We conclude that doing what is right because we know it is the best thing to do is a much higher level of social development than doing what is right because of peer pressure. Finally, we talk about how we have more control over our stages of *social* development than we do over our stages of *physical* development. The thought of being in control always heightens interest in the *Raise Responsibility System.*

SIGNIFICANT POINTS ABOUT THE HIERARCHY

What young people become and how they mature after being exposed to the four concepts makes sharing the hierarchy so valuable. Think of the hierarchy as an *opportunity* for young people to have a *reference for making decisions in life.* Notice that *the term "discipline" is never used.* Refer to the hierarchy for what it is, namely, levels of social (and personal) development.

1. At first, you may feel uncomfortable using the vocabulary, but these specific terms have been found to be the most effective in empowering young people to *resist bullying, resist negative peer influence,* and *actuate responsible behavior.* Also, remember that after you have explained the concepts, you only refer the *letter* of the level—rather than to the words themselves. For example, for the lowest level, *Anarchy,* you would simply say "Level A."

2. The words can be taught to very young children, who absorb new words quite readily. They have no context for deciding whether any particular word is more advanced or difficult. For them, it is just a new word. It may be helpful to remember that young children are constantly coming across new words and concepts. They already know many abstract concepts like "empty," "blue," and "nothing." The only reason that the

vocabulary seems advanced to adults is that we were much older when we were first introduced to such terms. Perhaps just as important is that children enjoy learning advanced words. Of course, as a child matures, the concepts behind the vocabulary take on more complex meanings. For very young children, you can teach the levels by referring to them as *high* levels (D or C) and *low* levels (A or B).

3. Occasionally, an adult thinks that youngsters may confuse letters of a grading scale in school with letters of the hierarchy. Since language has meaning only in context (for example, when to spell *to, too,* or *two*), even young children do not confuse the hierarchy of D, C, B, and A with the reverse order of these letters in a grading system.

4. A significant advantage in referring to the hierarchy occurs immediately because the *act* is separated from the *actor,* an irresponsible behavior is differentiated from a good kid. The young person never has the need or the desire to self-defend, which is the natural response when criticized. By referring to something separate from or outside of the person, the hierarchy completely skirts this natural tendency and avoids confrontations, which so often arise when referring directly to a person's behavior.

5. The hierarchy is *not* an assessment tool for someone on the outside looking in. The motivation of some young people during an activity will be at Level C while others will be at Level D. Only the individuals themselves can assess their own level of motivation.

6. As we live our lives, we all experience the various levels. If you have experienced great anger, chances are that your concern was about yourself—with little concern for the effect that your behavior had on others (Level A). If you ever drove faster than the speed limit, you made your own rules of the road (Level B). If you were courteous and considerate of others, your motivation could have been to do what others were doing (Level C), or your motivation could have been to be courteous and considerate of others because that was the right thing to do (Level D).

7. Motivation at Level C is essential for a civil society. This is the motivational level at which most of us live our lives most of the time. However, when working with young people, the goal is to promote motivation at Level D. Doing what is right *feels* good and promotes responsible behavior.

8. Since rewards change motivation, once you give a child a reward for behaving appropriately, the reward becomes the child's focus. Therefore, rewarding Level D is both counterproductive and guesswork—since no one can know the motivation of someone else with complete certainty.

9. When referring to motivation, this book intentionally employs the terms "external" and "internal," rather than "extrinsic" and "intrinsic." The reason is that this book is devoted to raising responsibility in young people, and responsibility is not a characteristic that we associate with "intrinsic" motivation—something that naturally arises within us. The motivation to be responsible is more cognitive and rooted in ethics and values. In a technical sense, however, all motivation comes from within. For example, a "motivational speaker" stimulates the audience, but we don't usually refer to people as "stimulators."

10. The hierarchy becomes significantly more effective when *the focus is on the difference between the motivational levels of C and D.* The more you encourage reflection on the *motivational* level, the more effectively the hierarchy serves both you and your children.

UNDERSTANDING THE LEVELS

Level A – Anarchy

At the lowest level, people are motivated solely by their own self-interests. If everyone behaved with little if any consideration for others, society would constantly be in chaos. There would be no order, no stability, security, or government. The situation could be described in one word, *anarchy*. The word comes from Greek and literally means "without rule." Under anarchy, everyone is free to do whatever he or she wants—without rules, regulations, or responsibilities. Alan Bennett poked fun at this level with his statement,

"We started off trying to set up a small anarchist community, but people wouldn't obey the rules."

To older youth, who are naturally striving toward autonomy and therefore instinctively tend to resist authority, anarchy may initially seem attractive. To offset this mistaken belief, simply bring your explanation down to a *personal level*. For example, present a situation in which someone stole the youth's prized possession—let's say, a new bike. Under anarchy, there would be no police to enforce laws to return the bike. In fact, there would be no government and therefore no laws at all. Each person would be left to fend for oneself or to get help from others, thereby pitting one small group against another. *When anarchy becomes personal, it quickly loses its attractiveness.*

For young children, anarchy can be explained as being unruly, harming others, and unsafe. To make this personal for the very young, ask, "How would you like it if someone hit you?" This kind of reflection immediately registers negative thoughts and feelings. Follow up by using phrases the child will be able to understand, such as "being hurt," "feeling bad," and "wanting to cry." Explain that under anarchy there would be no one to provide protection from harmful acts.

On occasion, someone will confuse anarchy with anarchism, which is the political theory that all forms of government interfere unjustly with individual liberty and should be replaced by voluntary association of cooperative groups. In contrast to the theory of anarchism, *anarchy* is not a theory. It is very real and can be found in current situations around the world—in some societies, families, and individual lives.

Countless historical events can be cited that, when anarchy prevailed, someone or some group rose up, took control, and began making the rules. All too often leadership that came from this type of situation led to "bossing" and "bullying" others. This brings us to the next step on the ladder of the hierarchy.

Level B – Boss*ing*/Bully*ing*

Bossing or *bullying* is one level above anarchy. "Anarchy is the stepping-stone to absolute power," stated Napoleon Bonaparte in his maxims. When chaos exists, some person or group exerts enough influence to become the leader or ruler.

Since we generally do not live in anarchy (Level A), it is Level B that typically identifies irresponsible behavior arising in everyday situations—the making of one's own rules and standards. Notice that only Level B on the hierarchy uses the verb ending in "*ing*." Level B uses the action word "bully*ing*" rather than the noun "bully" for important reasons:

- Using the term "bully_ing_" rather than the term "bully" eliminates any tendency to label a child a bully.

- Bullying behavior is separated from the person doing the bullying.

- Using this verb form indicates that the person is choosing, consciously or not, to behave at this level.

A person behaving at Level B violates the courtesies and accepted standards of the home and of civil society. A bully attempts to become ruler by making the rules and standards; bullies boss by violating the rights of others. With boys, bullying is most commonly acted out as physical aggression: hitting, punching, kicking, or the destruction of another's property. (This is not to be confused with the tendency for young boys who are friends to be physical with each other.) With girls, bullying often occurs in the form of name-calling, backstabbing, humiliating, and isolating. *All forms of bullying can be devastating to the young psyche.*

We make our biggest mistake in not understanding the nature of a bully. Accommodating a bully only encourages more bullying behavior. If allowed to prevail, a bully's irresponsible behavior will be repeated. The sooner a person stands up to bullying, the easier it will be to handle—and the sooner the bullying behavior will stop. One way to accomplish this is to teach a lesson such as the following:

> Use a ruler to demonstrate a teeter-totter (see-saw). Hold it horizontally and describe that this is how it looks when the teeter-totter is balanced. People who are getting along and making responsible choices are in balance. However, when one person starts to pick on or bully someone else, the teeter-totter gets out of balance. (Tilt one end of the ruler.)
>
> The person who is picked on usually starts to feel "lower" than the other person. This is a normal reaction.

However, upon reflection, it becomes obvious that it is the *bully who initially feels unbalanced* because of a desire for attention or for power. Otherwise, there would be no reason to bully.

So, it is the *bully who really has a problem* (pointing to the lower end of the ruler). So it is the *bully who is really lower.* The bullying behavior is actually an attempt to pull the other person down to the bully's level—to try to bring things back into balance from the bully's perspective.

People should see the bully as someone who is having a bad day or feeling a desire to do wrong for some reason. *Challenge young people to keep this in mind as they decide how to respond to bullying behavior.*

With younger children, prompt them to say, "Sorry you are having a bad day." The usual result is that the bully is left speechless. Many times the choice is simply to recognize what is going on and walk away, realizing that the person with the problem is the bully.

Having youngsters understand that bullying behavior indicates that the bully is "out of balance" with life is empowering and very liberating. The discussion also opens the eyes of the bully. No one wants to be known as someone who has problems. Young people usually have never thought about their own behavior in this way.

When one sibling continually pesters another, the action is on Level B. Viewed from this perspective, and not quite so obvious, is the teenager who misses curfew. The youth is bullying the parents by establishing a new timeline, rather than following the standards already set. When this concept of bullying is first introduced to young people, it is an awakening; youngsters do not think of irresponsible behavior as bullying others—especially in situations involving their parents.

Level C – Cooperation/Conformity

When first introducing this level to young people, two characteristics need to be made clear: (1) *cooperation is the expected and acceptable norm,* and (2) *the motivation is external.*

Society cannot exist without norms, standards, and laws under which its citizens function. By their very nature, laws are external. Level C describes this reality. It refers to the accommodations and compromises people make when they accept the values and mores of society. A society becomes *civil* when its people cooperate and conform to these influences willingly. If *everyone* always lived according to society's mores, there would be no need for laws.

Like the larger society, a family also needs to cooperate in order to function smoothly and for its members to live together in harmony. When each member of the family conforms to established standards, people are cooperating. It is very important to note that conformity at Level C does not mean or imply *regimentation*—trying to make everyone the same. Rather, it means to be connected and involved with others in cooperative ways. *In this context, the external motivation for conformity has a positive value.*

Another aspect of this level also needs to be recognized. It is referred to as peer pressure, or more properly, *peer influence.*

> A woman was interviewed and was asked, "And what do you think is the best thing about being your age?" Without any hesitation, the 103-year-old responded, "No peer pressure!"

The following example from a mother who shared her story with me illustrates how peer influence has an effect even with those as young as three years of age.

> I just discovered the *Raise Responsibility System*, but I can definitely relate it to my experiences trying to potty train my daughter. I started working with Emma and her potty skills when she was 12 months old. She was very interested in her potty chair and loved to sit on it and play. When she finally realized that there was a certain feeling when she needed to go, I started using stickers as a reward for using the potty instead of her diaper. She would use the potty sometimes, but more often she would just rely on her trusty old diaper. This went on for two years! I was really at my wit's end.
>
> We worked intensively on this all summer. I was home and felt this was the perfect time to get the concept down. Unfortunately, Emma didn't agree. She was perfectly content to stay in those pull-ups for as long as she lived. When summer was over, I took her to a babysitter, apologizing profusely. I mean, really, Emma was almost

THREE YEARS OLD! Peggy, my new sitter, had been watching kids for 40 years and had much experience in this area. When I told her that Emma still wasn't out of the pull-ups she said, "Oh, I can train her for you." (Had I not had so much pride, I would have fallen sniveling at her feet, thanking her profusely.) Instead, I said casually, "Yeah, that would be great!"

My sitter's advice was, "Throw away the diapers and pull-ups. Buy her some old-fashioned training pants and let her wear those. The kids will do the rest."

It took Peggy TWO DAYS and Emma was completely potty trained. All she needed to see was that all the other kids used the "big potty." She was in no mood to be left behind. There were no stickers, or candy, or even extra praise involved. Emma just realized that this is what her peer group expected, and she fell in line.

Teenagers are greatly influenced by their peers, and they have a strong desire to conform. You see this as adolescents dress the same way, use their own language, and possess a strong desire to fit in—to be liked. What is the easiest way to be liked? The answer, of course, is to *be like* those whom you want to like you. We can see this in young people who start to smoke. An adolescent wants to be liked by members of a group whose members smoke. No one from the group approaches the outsider and says, "You want to be like us? Here is a cigarette; smoke it." It simply doesn't work that way. The person starts to smoke to impress, to be accepted, and to be like the group. *The motivation is external.* Parents should be aware that around this age, *adolescents shift their reference group. The strong desire for approval—to be liked and to fit in—is largely influenced by their peers.*

Here is my concern and, as a parent, it should be yours. Parents are not present when adolescents get pressured from their peers to smoke, get high on alcohol or drugs, or do something else that is destructive to themselves or to society. One way to counter this type of negative peer influence is for young people to *learn the difference* between the *external* motivation of Level C and the *internal* motivation of Level D. People, even young ones, do not like to be controlled—not even by their peers.

Level D – Democracy

Level D is the highest level of personal and social development. At this level, people take the initiative to *do the right thing*—not because they have been told or asked or to please an adult or peer—*but simply because it is the right thing to do.* People operating on Level D *display initiative.* As with the highest level in Abraham Maslow's famous *Hierarchy of Needs,* people at this level are autonomous or "self-actualized." Their motivation to be responsible is *internal.*

This level is referred to as *Democracy* because taking the initiative to be responsible is essential for self-rule. As people grow, mature, cultivate manners, and develop values of right and wrong, their motivation for civility—originally external—becomes more and more internal.

When referring to the *Declaration of Independence*—written by Thomas Jefferson, with editing from John Adams and Benjamin Franklin—people often omit the critical phrase that changed human history. That significant sentence is the last one cited below:

> *We hold these truths to be self-evident, that all men are created equal, that they are endowed by their Creator with certain unalienable rights, that among these are life, liberty and the pursuit of happiness.* ***That to secure these rights, governments are instituted among men, deriving their just powers from the consent of the governed.***

Before these words were penned, societies operated on the belief that people's rights emanated from the king, the feudal lord, or whoever held power. The founders of the United States of America turned this approach on its head. Power in this newly created society would be vested in the people—and then delegated—*from the people* to those who govern. This foundational principle of people governing themselves can only function when the citizens take responsibility. As stated in the hierarchy, *democracy and responsibility are inseparable.*

Level D is associated with qualities of good character, such as the four classical virtues of prudence, temperance, justice, and fortitude. *Prudence* refers to practical wisdom—recognizing and making the right choices. *Temperance* involves much more than moderation in all things; it is the control of human passions and emotions, especially anger and frustration. *Fortitude* is courage in pursuit of the right path, despite the risks. It is the strength of mind and heart to persevere in the face of adversity. *Justice*, in this classical sense, includes fairness, honesty, and keeping promises.

When at Level D, people demonstrate compassion, consideration, helpfulness, and understanding. They exhibit civic virtue, accepting the rights and duties of citizenship and acting for the common good. Justice and fairness are fundamental to them. They show respect for themselves, others, property, and the environment. They display responsibility, *holding themselves accountable* for their actions. And, finally, they are trustworthy, reliable, and honest.

The *Hierarchy of Social Development* acts as a prompt for young people to aspire to this level. By discussing Level D with children, they understand that this is our *expectation* for them. John F. Kennedy, 35th President of the United States, articulated this in his Pulitzer Prize–winning book, *Profiles in Courage*:

> *In a democracy, every citizen, regardless of his interest in politics, "holds office"; every one of us is in a position of responsibility.*

"Every citizen" includes *children.* Just as "location, location, and location" are the three prime factors for success in real estate sales, so "expectation, expectation, and expectation" are the prime factors for helping young people fulfill their potential as successful citizens. *Explaining the four levels of social development is a proactive approach to instill expectations and help young people become responsible and live successful lives.*

ADDITIONAL NOTES ABOUT THE LEVELS

Operating at Various Levels

It is important to understand that there is no such thing as a Level D, C, B, or A *person.* As we go through our daily lives, we operate on various levels. At any given point in time, we choose the level on which we operate. As we learn to make our choices more consciously—rather than nonconsciously or by habit—we become more successful in *reflecting* before acting, thereby assuring more positive and responsible outcomes.

This type of valuable self-awareness is facilitated when we refer to the hierarchy as a regular practice. By knowing about and reflecting on the levels, people are more apt to strive for the higher ones. In fact, this understanding that we operate on different levels from situation to situation is what makes using the hierarchy so effective. As we proceed through the day we can be uplifted by the knowledge that *choices can be made to aim for the highest level in each new situation,* regardless of what was done earlier in the day.

Even if a child is accustomed to acting at Level B, it does not mean that the youngster need be stuck at that level for very long. Level C and Level D are always within reach with the very next decision. By teaching this concept to children, we are offering valuable information that can help them develop optimistic and positive mindsets.

It is also important to realize that if a child is accustomed to acting on Level B, then the immediate goal is to help the child raise the level by just one jump—from Level B to Level C. Encouraging the child to aim for an immediate and ambitious two-level jump, from Level B to Level D, is most often not realistic and could leave both parent and child feeling unnecessarily discouraged. In almost all cases, children require much experience and success at Level C before they can be at Level D. Additionally, we must keep in mind that Level D is characterized by motivation on an *internal* level. Internal motivation can never be forced; it is *voluntary.* An interesting paradox—especially with young people—is that when something is presented as a voluntary option, it often becomes more attractive.

Motivation as the Focus

More examples will help you and your children grasp the difference in motivation between Level C and Level D. *Having a clear understanding of how these two levels differ is critical for making the most effective use of the hierarchy.* Assume a child completes daily homework or regularly does the household chores. Is this Level C or Level D? In order to answer this question, we would need to know the child's motivation—something almost impossible for an outsider to determine. Since we don't have access to other people's motivation, it is not obvious which of the levels is at play at this *higher end* of the hierarchy. Fortunately, adults need not think about making this distinction but should realize that it is *empowering for youth to understand the difference.*

If the youngster does homework or chores at the parent's direction, this would be categorized as Level C. Even if the parent doesn't remind the youngster, but the youth does so *for the purpose of gaining parental approval,* it would still be at Level C. Although the motivation is certainly at an acceptable level, contrast this situation to one where the youth completes the assignment or chores by taking the *initiative* to do what is expected *because it would be the right thing to do.* In this second scenario, the child is operating at a higher level of personal and social development. Because the *motivation is internal, rather than external,* this would be categorized as Level D.

When explaining the difference between *being asked to do something* versus *doing something because it is the right thing to do,* we can make this concept clear even to very young children by providing examples from daily life such as cleaning up one's toys, helping a sibling, or following daily routines. Understanding the difference between internal and external motivation promotes young people's maturity.

When Conformity Becomes Negative

The desire to fit in and be like members of their age group becomes a major factor in the lives of young people. As mentioned, the easiest way to be liked by others is to *be like* them. This brings to mind the cartoon showing a group of girls dressed in school uniforms. Their blouses, skirts, socks, and shoes are identical. The girls are talking with a group of boys whose school doesn't require uniforms, but the boys are also dressed alike—wearing the same style of caps, shirts, pants, and shoes. One boy says to the girls, "Ha! At our school, we don't have to wear uniforms." Of course, the humor of the cartoon is obvious; the boys *are* wearing a uniform—that of their peer group. What they wear is motivated by a desire to fit in, to conform.

The danger with this type of "herd" or "join the gang" mentality is that it can draw young people toward actions that are not good for them or for society, such as participating in school subcultures that put down academic learning. So compelling is this pressure to "fit in" that many young people lack the strength of character to resist.

Motivation on Level C can be to cooperate *or* to conform. In both, the motivation has to do with *other* people or *other* things—outside of the person. As children grow, the desire to be like their peers becomes of overriding importance to them. This understanding about *conformity* becomes of increasing value. *Just knowing the difference between external and internal motivation is empowering and greatly assists in rejecting conforming to irresponsible behaviors.* Once young people become aware of the effect that external influences have on them—especially in this area of peer influence—they begin to feel empowered. This awareness assists adolescents in resisting negative group temptations of anti-social behaviors.

SHARING IMAGES AND STORIES

People remember best in pictures, images, and visions; therefore, creating examples of the levels is a far better technique than just memorizing definitions. Sharing examples at each level is the most effective approach to both remember and gain understanding. Experiences and stories are a wonderful way to learn. The classic storyteller's tale makes the point:

> TRUTH walked around naked, and everyone shunned Truth.

> STORY walked around in colored clothes, and everyone liked Story.

> TRUTH inquired of STORY, "What is it that you do that people love you?"

> STORY lent TRUTH some colorful garb and interesting clothing.

> Everyone began loving TRUTH.

Personal experiences of young people themselves are an excellent means for understanding the concepts. The more that young people are actively engaged in constructing examples, the greater will be their understanding. An effective approach is to use paper to draw examples of each level. Both you and your child can participate.

1. Start with "Anarchy" by explaining that at this level there is no law or order. At the level of anarchy anyone can do anything without consideration for anyone else. Now, have the young person draw any scene that comes to mind representing anarchy—that is, any situation that shows chaos. The scene can be from home, school, the neighborhood, or even a current or historical event. Stick figure drawings will do. After the child finishes sketching, ask for a description of what the child drew and add the title "Anarchy."

2. Make another drawing labeled "Bullying." Following the same guidelines as above, have the youngster draw a picture showing someone being bullied and then describe what was drawn.

3. Depict "Cooperation/Conformity" with a third drawing and description that conjures up people behaving in an expected manner, cooperating or conforming to do what is expected.

4. One more sketch needs to be made representing "Democracy." Create a scene that illustrates the idea of someone taking the initiative to do a good deed or something responsible without being asked. As before, write a caption.

5. Share the examples. If more than one child is involved, simply take turns sharing.

The reason this activity helps people grasp the concepts so quickly and easily is that it uses very powerful learning strategies. For each of the four concepts, the person *visualizes, draws, writes, describes* and then *listens* to the other's descriptions. The four concepts are made meaningful because of the involvement and perceptions. Bullying to a 6-year-old will be different from bullying to a 16-year-old, and so their own sketches will be genuinely meaningful to each of them.

For further practice, and especially to reinforce the desired higher levels for a youngster, pose questions such as, "What would Level C look like when playing a game with others?" For older youth, "What would Level C look like when shopping in a mall with some friends?" Then, to stimulate *a desire* to voluntarily operate at the highest level, you can pose the question, "What's an example of Level D in the same situation?"

As young people become more familiar with the levels of personal and social development, they will recognize examples in stories they read and in behaviors they witness or experience in their own lives. Here is one little story a friend shared with me that demonstrates how examples of the levels are everywhere.

While riding bikes in our neighborhood on a hot day, my family came upon a container of fresh-looking water at the edge of a flowerbed on the side of the road. A little message on the side of the container said, "For thirsty dogs."

I felt a little glow in my heart as I recognized that someone at this house was operating from Level D—taking the
initiative to do a kind thing. It gave me an opportunity to
help my children connect the hierarchy to real life.

In order to be sure that the levels are understood and to make the
most effective use of the hierarchy, explore the *results* of acting on
each level. You might ask, "What would be the result if you plan what
you will wear tomorrow before going to bed tonight?" or "How did
you feel when you helped your younger sister?"

By now you should see that teaching the four levels is a lot easier
than you may have originally thought. And it is astonishing to see
how quickly young people start applying the concepts to their own
lives *once they are exposed to them.*

VARIATIONS OF THE LEVELS FOR YOUNG CHILDREN

One practical benefit of the hierarchy is that the levels can be tailored
for use with young people at various ages and for specific purposes.
The hierarchy can be used with children as young as three years old.
These youngsters can say the words and discuss simple examples of
what each level would look like at home, at daycare, or at preschool.
As the levels are applied to everyday situations, the understanding
and use of them continue to take on new meanings.

As with any hierarchy, the most desired level is placed at the top;
however, it is better to *start an explanation with the lowest level and then
move upward.* Following is an example of how the four concepts can
be shared with young children. Remember, start with Level A and
work your way up.

> **D – Democracy** *(Highest level)*
> * Completes a task *without* being asked.
>   Example: Cleans up when bedtime is announced.
>
> **C – Cooperation**
> * Completes a task *after* being asked.
>   Example: Cleans up after being reminded.
>
> **B – Bossing/Bullying**
> * Knows what should be done but does not do it.
>   Example: Cleans up only when parent uses
>   authority.

A – Anarchy *(Lowest level)*
- Resists and gets angry when being informed what needs to be done.

  Example: Refuses to clean up.

Young children can also be taught about the levels in a meaningful way simply through discussion. Here is an example. Toys are all over the floor in a young boy's room. When asked by his mother to pick up the toys, the boy, whose behavior is at the lowest level, starts to *kick* the toys. Moving up the ladder, the boy operating at Level B also would not feel compelled to pick up the toys but instead might scatter them around the room. At an acceptable Level C, the boy would pick up the toys at his mother's request and place them where they belong. At Level D, the boy would take the *initiative* to pick up the toys and put them away after playing with them—without being asked and whether or not anyone was watching.

Stories are an excellent approach to teaching the levels to the young. The children's book *Miss Nelson Is Missing* beautifully illustrates the lesson that, when primary students in a classroom behave on Level A, an authoritarian teacher will take control. The reason is that someone operating on this level will only follow a greater authority. *The Three Little Pigs*—where the wolf acts out bullying/bothering/bossing behavior—is a good illustration for Level B. *The Little Red Hen* can be used to demonstrate motivation at Level C. The characters in this story were willing to "help" only with something they wanted—*eating* the bread, but they would not do any necessary work to *make* the bread. They might be willing to help the Little Red Hen because they would anticipate the reward of getting something good to eat—but not because it was the right thing to do. Level C is acceptable; so even if the characters would join in the work next time in hopes of getting bread, it would be okay. But this would not be the highest level, and they would miss the satisfaction that could come from their efforts. *The Hole in the Dike*—where Peter, the young Dutch boy, kept his finger in the dike all night and saved his town from being flooded—illustrates Level D for taking the initiative to be responsible. Peter was motivated to action not because someone asked or told him what to do but because he cared about the good of the entire community.

He persevered even though it was at great discomfort because he chose to be that kind of a person. He took responsibility because it was the right thing to do. Motivation at Level D is the most satisfying and rewarding of all feelings.

The following poster can also be made to help youngsters understand the concepts:

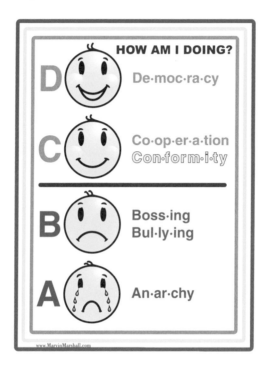

You and your child can create your own poster. Draw the faces and write the letter "D" on top with a big smiling face in GREEN. Under the "D," draw another smiley face but with the smile smaller than the smile in the "D" face. Mark the face and the letter "C" in YELLOW (cooperation and *caution for conformity—following others when you shouldn't*). Draw a line below the "C" to separate the acceptable levels (C and D) from the unacceptable levels (B and A). Below the line draw a sad face. Color the face and letter "B" in RED. Below the "B," draw another sad face with a downward smile and tears coming from the eyes. Also label the face and letter "A" in RED.

VARIATIONS OF THE LEVELS FOR OLDER CHILDREN

Using the Levels to Teach How to Play with Others
Following is an example for playing a sport:

Level D
- Displays sportsmanship whether or not an adult is present
- Encourages others to participate and feel welcome
- Is a good sport when either losing or winning

Level C
- Plays by the rules when an adult is present
- Cooperates with others

Level B
- Doesn't follow the rules of the game; makes own rules
- Leaves clean-up for others
- Shows poor sportsmanship

Level A
- Refuses to listen to the coach or referee
- Acts in a way that endangers the safety of others

Using the Levels for Getting to School on Time
This example pertains to responsibility:

Level D
- You set your alarm clock, wake up, and get to school on time.

Level C
- You depend on your parents to wake you up so you can get to school on time.

Level B
- You ignore the alarm clock and come to school late.

Level A
- You don't even set your alarm clock because you are only interested in what you want and do not consider how your actions affect others.

BENEFITS OF TEACHING THE HIERARCHY

Oliver Wendell Holmes said, "The human mind, once stretched by a new idea, never regains its original dimensions." When young people learn about the levels of development, they become more aware of social responsibilities and their relationships with others. Yet, evaluating one's own behavior can be so challenging and threatening that it is often avoided. As has been continually noted, however, influencing change in another person starts first with oneself. Reflecting on the different levels involves engaging in self-evaluation—the type of activity that prompts motivation to change in a *non-threatening* way, which is a major reason for its effectiveness.

As parents, we too can reflect on the hierarchy. For instance, asking, "In this situation, what level am I modeling for my children?" can prompt a valuable change. Also, taking the initiative by admitting a mistake (to yourself *and* to your child) can be a powerful agent for positive change.

Raises Awareness

Awareness comes before acknowledgment. When a person can recognize that a behavior is on an unacceptable level, that person has taken the first step in moving to more responsible behavior. You cultivate awareness by having your children learn the levels. Awareness and acknowledgment are both necessary to change behavior. This is clearly visible in the following:

> Shortly after my presentation to an elementary school, the school counselor called me to share a remarkable happening in a first-grade classroom. She had walked into the classroom and heard the teacher give an assignment. The teacher then announced that as soon as the students completed the assignment they were free to go to one of the learning centers.
>
> A few minutes passed, and the noise level in the room began to grow louder and louder. One first grader stood up and exclaimed, "Anarchy! This is anarchy!" Immediately, the noise level subsided. The teacher had not said a word. The youngsters controlled their own learning environment. *Awareness of the concept of anarchy* prompted the young students to manage themselves.

A teacher whose school also implemented the approach related the following story:

> A mother called me the other day to tell me that Dr. Marshall's levels are working even at home. Her first grade son is very tired at the end of each day. On the previous evening, he had soccer practice after school and at about 6:30 she was trying to get him to take a bath. He was lying naked on the bathroom floor, crying, "I am not going to take a bath and I am not getting my picture taken tomorrow!" His mother calmly responded by saying, "I guess I will have to call Mrs. O'Donnell (his teacher) and tell her you are at Level A." He immediately got off the floor and took his bath without another complaint!

Promotes Morals and Ethics

Awareness as it relates to moral development has an emotional component. Often when young people perform an inappropriate action, the only emotion is the negative feeling associated with getting caught. Of course, the negative feeling *should* be related to the inappropriate action itself. Young people need to be helped to see that the negative emotion *should be the result of what they do, rather than the result of being found out.* Understanding the four levels serves as an excellent introduction to moral and ethical development.

While learning the concepts, young people are also learning the underlying value system. For example, "Bullying," which implies selfishness, is at a lower level of social development than "Cooperation/Conformity." Cooperation, which implies order and fairness, must prevail in order for democracy to succeed. Democracy calls for acting responsibly and with self-discipline.

Opens the Doors for Easy Communications

The hierarchy provides a shared vocabulary and thus offers a means of easy communications between children and parents. Behavioral issues and expectations can be discussed in a way everyone can understand *without being defensive.*

Promotes Independence and Self-Reliance

The hierarchy encourages youngsters to look to themselves to solve problems, rather than relying on others. This is of critical importance because parents, desiring to help their children, too often do things for them that they could and should be doing themselves. In these situations, parents not only create more work and more stress for themselves, but, more importantly, *they deprive young people of opportunities for growth and developing responsibility.* As it has been aptly said, "If you want children to keep their feet on the ground, put some responsibility on their shoulders." If your children are to learn how to become responsible, they must *experience* responsibility.

As a school administrator, I often experienced teachers bringing their "monkey" (problem) into the office, wanting to give it to me to handle. In the forefront of my mind was, "What can I say or ask so they don't leave me their monkey?" (I had enough of my own!) I learned to ask, "What do you suggest?" and "Do you want me to do it, or can you handle it yourself?" Invariably, the complainer came up with a solution—that a desired result could be achieved without me. My suggestion for you is not to accept "monkeys" from a child if the child is capable of meeting the challenge. The reason is that every time you solve a problem for a child who is capable of solving the problem without you, you are depriving the youngster of an opportunity to become more responsible. The youngster also misses the satisfaction that arises from the effort. In such situations, start with empathy *before* referring to the youngster's handling the situation. It can sound something like this: "I know it is hard; the same thing happened to me when I was younger. But what would an extraordinary person do in this situation?" In other words, *elicit* a possible solution from the youngster.

> I was at a preschool when Mary, the teacher, asked a group of three-year-olds to come inside. Jerry, a shy redhead, came up to ask for help in taking off his jacket, saying, "I can't get the zipper undone." Mary started the zipper and he pulled it down the rest of the way. Then Jerry stood there waiting for her to take off the jacket. Mary encouraged him to do it himself. As he struggled to get his arms out of the elastic sleeves, she said, "That's not easy to do, but you can do it. Keep pulling." He tugged and struggled, and finally the jacket came flying off. Jerry ran to his cubby to put his jacket away, shouting, "I did it! I did it all by myself!"

If Mary would have done the job herself, she would have robbed Jerry of the experience of struggling and therefore of the success that the struggle produced. As a result of this seemingly insignificant experience, Jerry's self-esteem increased.

After being introduced to the concept of Level D, children often *want* to attain this higher level of independence and self-reliance, as illustrated by the following communication sent to me from a teacher in Phoenix, Arizona:

We recently had a guest speaker visit our fourth grade. Dressed as Wyatt Earp, he performed a monologue based on the life experiences of the famous man. After the hour-long performance, "Wyatt" commented that in the past three years of traveling the world doing this show, he had not come across a group of better-behaved children. He was very surprised at how well the students listened—no interruptions, respectful, and so on. He said that he really enjoyed the experience because of the children.

I passed along the comments to the students. They were thrilled with themselves. One student even commented that the best feeling was that a teacher didn't even remind them what the expectations were—they just did it on their own. "We did it because it was the right thing to do. This man gave us his time, and we should be respectful." I felt so good about the situation. It was nice to see 62 fourth graders at Level D!

Raises Social Responsibility

The hierarchy raises awareness for responsible citizenship. Our society is based on great autonomy for its citizens. However, citizenship *assumes* values such as responsibility, respect, caring, fairness, and trustworthiness—the values that transcend divisions of race, creed, politics, gender, and wealth. These values are fostered in the hierarchy and are reinforced in the examples created for Level C and for Level D.

Combats Negative Peer Influence

By helping young people become aware of their natural desire to belong, and by showing them specific examples of what conforming to peer influence looks like, the hierarchy helps them take the first step in resisting inappropriate influences and behavior. Peer influence is so compelling that it often prompts young people to do things that are personally and/or socially irresponsible. Just knowing the levels of social and personal development can have a liberating and empowering responsibility-producing effect. After all, no one likes to be manipulated. When young people are negatively influenced by others to do things that are inappropriate or damaging to themselves and/or to the larger community, familiarity with the hierarchy can influence them to summon the necessary strength to resist the temptation to go along with the group engaging in such activities.

Empowers and Reduces Victimhood Thinking

Using the hierarchy calls attention to the fact that people are constantly making choices and choosing their own level of behavior, whether consciously or not. Youngsters learn that their behaviors are self-chosen, a product of their decisions. They learn that they have a choice as to how they respond to a situation, to a stimulus, and even to an impulse or urge.

Sets High Expectations for Behavior

As emphasized, the hierarchy encourages young people to achieve the highest level. The very nature of a hierarchy serves as an inspiration. Young people have a natural desire to be as competent and successful as they can be—to reach for the highest level available to them. *We deprive them of opportunities if we do not expose them to possibilities.* Having the *choice between two acceptable levels* encourages such motivation.

Encourages Mature Decision-Making

Adolescents are looking for roles—more than goals. Exposing young people to the levels has a natural effect of encouraging them to think about long-term decisions. This is important because so much advertising, peer influence, and behavior of young people is aimed at instant gratification, rather than at development of responsible character traits.

Improves Relationships

An advantage to labeling a level rather than referring directly to a person's behavior is that relationships improve. Labeling people often creates negative overtones that damage relationships. In contrast, labeling a behavior as Level B, for example, is far less antagonizing than calling someone a bully.

> One summer day on a long drive, my wife was describing a story she was writing. She was, in effect, thinking aloud. After what I thought was a somewhat lengthy pause, I turned on an audiotape that was already in position to be played. After listening to it for a minute I realized that something was wrong. I ejected the tape, turned to my wife and asked, "Is everything okay?"
>
> "Sure, you're from Mars!" she answered, alluding to John Gray's book *Men Are from Mars, Women Are from Venus.*

We had often discussed the natural differences between males (action-oriented) and females (relations-oriented) and were familiar with Gray's metaphors of men being from Mars and women from Venus. By labeling my action as "Martian," she dispersed in a matter of seconds what might otherwise have created great tension. Communicating the understanding by labeling the behavior allowed us to continue on a pleasant ride. The important learning from this episode is that my wife and I shared a common vocabulary; we were both familiar with the Mars and Venus metaphors. My wife did not tell me I was rude, and I did not feel attacked; she merely referred to my actions as being Martian. We understood that her reference was made to a type of behavior and was not intended as a personal attack. Labeling the behavior was non-confrontational, aided communication, assisted understanding, and encouraged readjustment.

Promotes Autonomous Behavior

Understanding the difference between an external and an internal incentive can have a significant impact on motivation. It is common practice these days for parents to offer rewards to children for behaving well, thus *conditioning them to expect something in exchange for their behavior.* Therefore, when these children are asked to do something by another adult, it is not unusual or surprising for some to ask what they will receive in return. For them, the incentive has become getting the reward, rather than doing what is responsible. In this process, children have fallen under the control of the external reward—at the expense of responsibility and autonomy.

The paradox here is that we want to assist our children in becoming self-disciplined, independent problem-solvers, yet external incentives set them up to be dependent. After exposure to the hierarchy levels, even young children quickly understand that external incentives are really bribes to influence their behavior. People of all ages would rather be autonomous than manipulated.

Raises Self-Esteem

Once young people understand the difference between external rewards and internal satisfaction, the stage is set for understanding *self-esteem*. Parents may give rewards and praise in attempts to build self-esteem. However, the building blocks of self-esteem are *skills* and *perceptions of competency*—not some external manipulative, such as rewards. The more people realize that self-esteem is related to motivation, the reason behind what they are doing, the greater is the tendency to act on Level D, taking initiative.

A person satisfied with an accomplishment has a tendency to repeat it. The more often we complete a task successfully, the more proficient we become. This reinforcement builds feelings of competency and self-worth—critical elements of self-esteem. In short, self-esteem is the result of *feelings of competency,* rather than of something external.

Teaches Young People That They Play a Role in How Adults Treat Them

The hierarchy helps children learn that their behavior plays a role in determining how their parents and other adults relate to them. Since neither Level A nor Level B is an appropriate or acceptable behavioral level, behavior at either of these levels encourages a controlling reaction from the adult. It can be explained to children that when they operate on these levels, they are in effect telling adults, "Use authority on me because I am not capable of directing myself."

One father I know has taught his children that they can choose the type of parent they want:

CHILD		DAD
Anarchic (A)	➡	Angry
Bullying (B)	➡	Bossing
Cooperative (C)	➡	Contented
Democratic (D)	➡	Delighted

When youngsters understand the levels, a parent can stop an unpleasant situation with a simple inquisitive question, "Do you want me to become a Level B mommy/daddy today?" Prompted to reflect, children invariably say, "No, we will be on Level C." What a simple way to resolve the situation!

WORTH THE EFFORT

Regardless of how troublesome doing the right thing may be, the satisfaction gained is well worth the effort. The following communication from a subscriber to my monthly electronic newsletter illustrates this:

> I purchased some items at the grocery store. When I took the bags out of my cart and prepared to leave the store for my car, I noticed I had a small lime clutched in my hand that I had forgotten to put on the conveyor belt; so I hadn't paid for it. At 10 for $1, it would have cost 10 cents. My first thought was, I don't want to walk all the way back to a cashier to return 10 cents. The store won't miss that meager amount. Nevertheless, I pulled a dime from my wallet and walked back to the nearest cashier and handed it to her, explaining the reason. She replied by saying, "God bless you for your honesty."
>
> Well, I have to admit; I did feel better than I would have if I had simply walked to my car without paying the 10 cents.

ADDITIONAL CONSIDERATIONS ABOUT THE HIERARCHY

The following question was asked about the levels:

> I had a thought on adding another level to the hierarchy: Level "E" for excellence—Level E being the daily

consistent habit of being on Level D. Your thoughts when you can. Thanks.

I responded that there have been many suggestions about the levels. However, they all detract from the power of using the letters A, B, C, and D because of the perceptions behind these terms.

The hierarchy offers a choice between two unacceptable levels and two acceptable levels. In this regard, the choices are clear. When first starting to use the hierarchy, there is a tendency to refer to the level at which the person is "*acting*" or "*behaving.*" The distinction needs to be reinforced: Levels C and D refer to *motivation*, rather than to behavior. The action may be identical on both levels even though the motivation may be different. For example, some children will do household chores to please a parent (Level C). Others will do their chores because they realize that a family is a unit where all should assist and do chores because it is the right thing to do (Level D).

No one operates on Level D all the time. *A major point about thinking about the hierarchy is to be continually aware of the level one chooses.* It is like sitting up straight. You choose it, and then in a few minutes you realize that you are slouching again. Pull in your stomach for girth control (a conscious activity), and in a few minutes you realize that you are no longer "pulling it in." *Once an activity becomes habitual, awareness is lost.* Hence, although the idea of a "Level E" may seem like a good one, it would lose the significant step of *always being aware of one's choices*—a key to empowerment that so many young people need.

By the way, the same "awareness" is necessary for the *three practices*: positivity, choice, and reflection. Are you aware when your own self-talk and/or communications to others is negative? Are you offering choices to reduce coercion? Are you asking reflective questions, such as, "What can I learn from this experience?" These practices will only be implemented when we are *consciously aware of them.*

POINTS TO REMEMBER

◆ The hierarchy eliminates the natural tendency to self-defend because it separates the youngster as a person from her or his behavior.

◆ The hierarchy is proactive and positive by setting expectations, prompting awareness of choice, and promoting reflection.

◆ Using a hierarchy promotes a desire to get to the higher levels.

◆ Creating examples for each level makes the hierarchy relevant and easy to understand.

◆ After the concepts are taught, reference is made only to the *letter* of the levels—Level A, B, C, or D.

◆ The vocabulary can be used with any age group.

◆ Levels A and B behaviors are always unacceptable. The use of authority by the parent is required at both of these levels.

◆ Level C motivation is acceptable, but the motivation is external—to gain approval, receive a reward, or avoid punishment.

◆ Levels C and D differ in motivation but not necessarily in their behaviors.

◆ Level D motivation promotes the most rewarding of positive feelings.

5
Asking

*This second phase is used
when Level A or Level B behavior is exhibited.*

Now that you are practicing positivity, offering choices, asking reflective questions, and have shared the hierarchy, you are in a position to successfully deal with Level A and Level B behaviors.

The last chapter was devoted to the foundation of the system, learning the levels of development. This chapter explains the procedure, which is simply *checking for understanding* to determine if the youngster can identify the chosen level. Often, this is all that is necessary to prompt reflection and change an unacceptable behavior.

DEALING WITH LOWER LEVEL BEHAVIOR (LEVELS B AND A)

The procedure starts by the parent's viewing the situation as one of *guiding* or *coaching*. When a youngster acts on an inappropriate level, the adult views this as an opportunity to *help* the youngster readjust. This positive mindset prevents stress and has a significant and positive effect. The youngster perceives that the adult is attempting to help and does not feel any parental attempt to control or coerce.

Questions as Inquiry
When the adult is doing the talking, the adult is doing the thinking. Because the objective is to have the young person change, *it is the young person who needs to do the thinking and the talking.* An inquiring approach assists in setting a positive mental frame in the adult because people do not normally feel anger or become stressed while asking a reflective question.

Questioning for Levels A and B

The purpose of the questioning is simply to see whether the child recognizes the level of the unacceptable behavior. If the youngster appears not to know, then the adult guides or coaches the child to acknowledge that the behavior was on an unacceptable level. The behavior could be at Level B—making one's own standards, rather than following the standards set by the adult. Or the behavior could be on Level A, such as showing no regard for others or hurting someone else. Don't quibble with a child over determining whether an unacceptable action was on Level A or Level B. It doesn't matter; *both levels are unacceptable and that should be the focus*, rather than fitting the behavior into one of these two categories.

The questioning process is very short. You simply *ask* in order to determine whether the youngster understands that Level A or Level B—the youngster's chosen level—is unacceptable. Notice that the two sample dialogues between a parent (**P**) and a challenging youth *(Y)* below demonstrate the strategy. The parent **asks** and the youth *reflects*.

P: On what level is that behavior?
Y: He was doing it, too.

P: That was not the question. Let's try it again.
On what level is that behavior?
Y: I don't know.

P: What level is it when someone bullies others?
Y: I don't know.

P: The letter comes right after A in the alphabet.
What letter comes after A?

◆   ◆   ◆   ◆

P: On what level is that behavior?
Y: I don't know.

P: Tell me what the other children are doing.
Y: They're playing together.
P: Were you doing your best to play together with them?
(Closed-ended question calling for a "yes" or "no" response but involving reflection)

Y: No.

**P: What level is it when someone makes his own
rules?**
Y: Level B

P: What can be done about it?
(You will be eliciting a procedure, the topic of the
next chapter.)

Asking Is the Key

Notice that in the first illustration, the youngster was evasive in
answering. The parent persevered. Remember, the question directs
the dialogue. Remain in control by continuing to *ask* until an answer
is satisfactory. *You will find it hard to believe how simple and effective this
strategy is* and even wonder why you have not used it sooner.

When the youngster acknowledges a level of inappropriate behavior, you will find that the misconduct usually stops. The reason is
that you have prompted reflection, thereby inducing the youngster
to change through self-influence.

You may find that the child apologizes. This is a natural by-product
of accepting responsibility. However, if an apology is in order but
is not forthcoming, a parent may suggest, "If you don't plan to hit
her again and she is still feeling bad, now might be a good time to
say something."

For Older Youth

Asking is the usual procedure when a youngster is behaving on an
unacceptable level. However, with older youth asking may seem coercive to them. In such cases, just substitute asking with a comment
such as, *"Please take a moment and reflect on the level you are choosing."*

Cautions

Since the quality of the answer depends on the quality of the question, asking, "What are you doing?" will lead to a potential frustration. The
reason is that the youngster will most likely respond, "Nothing," in
which case, the parent would have been better off not asking that
question. The strategy is made simple, however, by *always* starting
the questioning process with, *"On what level is that behavior?"* The
beauty and magic of the strategy is that by referring to the level—
rather than to the behavior directly—the youngster's ego is not

engaged. To reiterate: *Referring to a level eliminates the natural tendency to defend oneself.* This is a critical point and a prime reason that the *Raise Responsibility System* is so effective.

EFFECTIVELY ACKNOWLEDGING LEVEL D

When parents witness a young person's taking the initiative to be responsible, they are often so moved that they want to reinforce it. How does an adult encourage repetition of such admirable motivation? This is best accomplished by the asking approach—a rhetorical question (one not requiring an answer), such as, "I wonder what level that was on?" The parent may catch the child's eye, smile, and even walk away. This leaves the child to *reflect* on the higher levels and inwardly experience the positive and powerful feelings *inherently* associated with the internal motivation of Level D.

For parents who are used to reinforcing desirable behavior by using external manipulatives of praise and rewarding, reflective questioning may not seem like enough. Yet, parents who are effective in encouraging more consistent higher-level motivation and resulting behavior will *start* by reflecting on their own goal: Is it Level C, *obtaining obedience*—or Level D, *promoting responsibility?*

WHAT NEXT?

Teaching the levels and then *checking for understanding* handles the great majority of irresponsible behaviors. However, when a youngster has *already acknowledged behavior at an unacceptable level* and then *continues* to act irresponsibly, we employ *guided choices*, discussed in the next chapter.

POINTS TO REMEMBER

◆ *Checking for understanding* starts by setting the mental frame that irresponsible behavior is viewed as an opportunity for the parent to promote responsibility.

◆ An *asking* approach is employed because this is the most effective strategy for encouraging self-evaluation.

◆ The youngster is asked to identify the *level* of chosen behavior, not the behavior itself.

◆ With older youth, simply prompt the person to reflect on the level chosen.

6
Eliciting

People don't argue with their own decisions.

The situation is that the youth understands the levels, has acknowledged irresponsible behavior, and still acts on an unacceptable level. You now employ *guided choices.*

Since behavior on the two unacceptable levels sends the message, "I'm not mature enough to act responsibly, so you need to control me," the strategy complies with the young person's request. *You use authority—but without being authoritarian.* The key procedure is to *elicit* from the youngster what should be done.

A CHALLENGING CASE

A teenage girl often slammed the door when she entered her bedroom. The father told his daughter that her slamming the door really bothered him. She agreed not to slam the door, but the behavior continued.

The father informed his daughter that if she were to develop a procedure for closing the door gently, it would be easier for her to redirect her impulse of slamming the door. He also communicated that he had confidence she could do this. He attempted to assist: "When walking into the bedroom," he said, "pause, then close the door." The daughter visualized the procedure. The father invited her to suggest a better procedure or perhaps to alter his.

The father knew, however, that breaking habits could be challenging, and he wanted to be prepared just in case the situation were to be repeated. So the father asked, "What should be done if the slamming occurs again?"

The *daughter* suggested that, if the slamming were to continue, the door would then be removed.

The slamming continued. The father calmly removed the door hinge pins and put the door in the garage. He informed his daughter that he knew how much she desired her privacy and that he preferred to leave the door on its hinges. He told his daughter that the door would be returned to its place as soon as she came up with a more effective plan for closing the door properly.

The daughter created the procedure (plan) of entering the room, turning around, and then closing the door. She demonstrated this to her father and then asked that the door be replaced.

It is clear from his methods that the father was interested in helping his daughter *develop impulse control* so that she might become more *reflective*, rather than *reflexive*, in her actions.

A Useful Model

This example provides a useful model that can be applied in any situation. It is effective with both youngsters and adolescents. Let's review the strategy the father used to approach the situation:

1. He was *positive*, showing faith in his daughter by helping her to establish a procedure.

2. He helped her to become aware of her *choices*.

3. He encouraged *reflection*.

4. He proactively elicited a *procedure* to help the daughter with her impulses and a consequence, should the inappropriate behavior continue.

5. He *followed through* but still invited his daughter to make a new plan.

USING AUTHORITY WITHOUT BEING PUNITIVE

When a young person operates on an unacceptable level, the parent explains that the message being sent is, "Please use authority so that I can become more responsible." As indicated, the parent grants the youngster's request. *Guided choices* uses authority without being punitive. The key is to *elicit*—rather than the more common and less effective approach of *imposing*. Eliciting refers to the young person's choosing a *consequence* or choosing a *procedure* that will help redirect any similar unacceptable behaviors in the future.

Here is an example of how simply this approach can work.

> My six-year-old son and two other boys got into a tussle on the playground and were disobedient. My son knew that if we ever got a call from school about his behavior, it would be met with our disapproval. When I went to pick him up, he said right away, "What is my punishment going to be?" I said to him that he knew what he had done wrong, and that his behavior was inappropriate; he had to decide for himself what his punishment would be. He thought about it and decided that six days of being "grounded" should be his punishment—no electronic games, no friends over, no extra activities, no dinner out. This happened on a Monday, and he told me that he picked six days because if he were good for those six days, he would be un-grounded by Sunday and would still have one day to play on the weekend. It was a long six days for him, but he made it and actually had a friend over to play on Sunday. When I went to pick him up on Monday from school, he was very excited, and as he left the building, he yelled out to one of his friends, "It's good not to be grounded!"
>
> By the way, my son started putting himself in time-outs probably because that's what I did with myself. If I got frustrated, or angry or impatient with him, I would excuse myself, "I am going to go sit on the porch and take a break; I'll come back and talk with you when I'm calm." He usually came to look for me to apologize for his behavior or to see if I was all right.

As we learned from Chapter 2, choices are a critical component for fostering responsibility and influencing behavior. The reason that choice is so effective is that it brings ownership, and lasting changes only occur if the person *owns the change*. Two points need to be reinforced here: (1) No one actually *changes* another person, and (2) people do not argue with their own decisions. Offering options by *eliciting* engages a youngster in the decision and is much more effective than giving commands or imposing consequences.

Not Losing

The strategy of *guided choices* is to acknowledge the youngster's unacceptable chosen level and then to ask a question that commits future action. Authority is used because *the person who asks the questions controls the situation*. However, as long as the youngster can make a decision, regardless of how minor it may be, dignity is preserved and confrontation is avoided. Generally, a youth who loses dignity becomes reluctant and resists the person who instigated the loss of dignity. The point needs to be kept in mind: *Not losing is more important than winning*. This does not mean that the young person will feel like a "winner," but it is essential not to feel like a "loser." Besides, no one really wins in a confrontational relationship. Solving a problem is much more difficult when people are in conflict because their egos and emotions interfere. Referring to the levels negates such interferences.

Employing *guided choices* is a "win/win" strategy. In "I win/you lose" situations (from the parent's point of view), the parent only wins a form of satisfaction, but the child is left with feelings of anger and victimhood. In "lose/lose" situations, neither wins; the parent gets aggravated and the child again takes the brunt. In "I lose/you win" situations (from the parent's point of view), the child has outsmarted the parent. In contrast, when using *guided choices,* the parent wins by using a non-confrontational guidance approach that gains cooperation and avoids stress. The child wins because dignity has been left intact, and the child grows by controlling or redirecting impulsive behaviors. In addition, the relationship wins because it is not fractured.

HOW *GUIDED CHOICES* WORK

The keys to success in using authority without coercion are the three practices of positivity, choice, and reflection. These methods instill the mindset that the goal is to raise responsibility and promote self-discipline, rather than to punish. Punishment pushes children farther away from taking responsibility as well as increases the emotional distance between parents and children. A far more effective approach is to treat the situation as a teaching and learning opportunity.

The Procedure

You first ask the child to identify the *level* of the unacceptable behavior—Level A or B. This is followed with, *"As you know, that behavior is at a level that is not acceptable and cannot continue."* Then pose another question, *"What do you suggest we do about it?"* If you think that the *procedure* or *consequence* suggested is not appropriate, not acceptable to you, or will not be successful, simply ask, *"What else?" "What else?" "What else?"* Repeat this question until you both agree. "That won't work for me," "Can you live with that?" and "Tell me what we have agreed to," are additional "magic sentences" you can use following a child's unacceptable suggestion. You may also decide to ask the child to list the pros and cons of the suggestions. This will help the child to further think through the problem and create an effective plan.

With these questions, the parent is *eliciting* from the youngster either a consequence or a procedure—a plan—for helping the child resist inappropriate impulses and for not repeating the same action. Any consequence or procedure should fulfill a few requirements:

- Be related to the original act

- Be reasonable

- Be practical

- Promote self-control

- Have the *young person* take the responsibility

A major reason for the effectiveness of *guided choices* is that children know and feel that they are safe. They understand that the parent's intention is to help—not harm—and that the parent has the youngster's best interests at heart. This is the reason that the approach is still successful even after the questioning approach is repeatedly used and youth, regardless of age, know exactly what the parent is doing.

Guidelines

Talk with your child about victimhood thinking. This topic was discussed in Chapter 2, but the concept is so significant that we will review it here.

Have a short conversation by asking the question, *"Do you want to be a victim of your impulses or would you rather be in charge?"* Having children reflect on this question will bring an immediate response. No one wants to be a victim; people want to be in charge of themselves. When the youngster then responds that he or she prefers to be in control, help the youngster by *eliciting or suggesting some procedure* to rely on when an undesirable impulse arises again. The procedure needs to be practiced before the next such incident. Helping youngsters help themselves is much quicker, less stressful, and more effective than any imposed or coercive approach because, as noted, people don't argue with their own decisions.

When a youngster makes a mistake or does something wrong, *focus on the future,* not on the past. It is counterproductive to harp on past unsuccessful behaviors. For example, if you focus on the past, it might sound like, "You should have been more careful!" However, if you focus on the future, it would sound like, "What can we think of so that it won't happen again?" (Notice the use of the collaborative "we," rather than "you.") *The past cannot be changed.* If you talk about what was done wrong, the person will only resent it (and you) because the act cannot be undone. Focusing on the past will result in criticizing, blaming, complaining, threatening, or punishing. Any of these will result in stress and negative feelings on the part of everyone involved. You promote responsible behavior so much more effectively if you communicate in terms of, "So let's talk about what has been learned and how to do it better next time."

A Driver's License Story

After using the *Raise Responsibility System* in their home, a family had an amazing incident with their 15-year-old son. Here is the story in the mother's own words:

> We live on a very large piece of property and my husband was preparing our son for driving by allowing him to drive the firewood truck from one area to another under guidance and supervision. He would also allow our son to move our vehicles around in the driveway. The expectation was always the same: This was a privilege and only possible when my husband was in the vehicle. One day while we were at work, our son decided to drive the car up and down the driveway on his own. The neighbors reported this to us when we arrived home. We were very disappointed, and my husband grounded our son for two weeks.

That night my son came to me and said, "Mom, I thought we didn't handle things in this way anymore. Being grounded has nothing to do with driving and I won't learn anything from it. I think that instead of being grounded, I shouldn't be allowed to get my learner's permit on my birthday; I should have to wait an extra month. I was not being responsible about driving, and the consequence should be related to that." I told him that this was between him and his dad and that he would have to discuss it with his father.

That night they both agreed that my son's plan was the more acceptable solution. His 16th birthday was five months away. When his birthday arrived, he did not mention his learner's permit. Exactly one month later, he announced that it was time to go to the licensing office.

The best part of this story is that he assumed full responsibility for his behavior. We did not have to suffer through two weeks of grounding, and he never drove the truck unattended again.

A Key Concept

Aside from *eliciting* rather than *imposing* a consequence for continued unacceptable behavior, *guided choices* is also different in that it never announces what will happen ahead of time. This is intentional for a very practical reason.

My experiences in working with young people of all ages in a variety of settings have given me insight into how young people think—as if I didn't know from my own experiences as a youth. People of all ages want security; they want to know where they stand. A prime reason that young people "test" adults is that young people want to know their limits. With this in mind and with the belief that it is only fair to tell people the consequence resulting from an inappropriate behavior, many parents (and schools) inform young people *ahead of time* of the consequences for specific actions. A typical school example is the consequence for coming to a class late. I have heard teens say that nothing happens until the third tardy; therefore, as their thinking goes, it is okay to come to class late two times. When a young person knows the consequence, *the risk is reduced*. Here is my point: In terms of disciplining a young person, *not knowing is far more effective than knowing.* If the consequence is known ahead of time, young people assess its severity and then determine whether or not what they want to do is worth the imposed consequence.

You may want to use an approach I recommend to teachers when a student is acting on an unacceptable level. Just whisper in the youngster's ear, "Don't worry about what will happen; we'll talk about it later." The misbehavior immediately stops because the youngster is then focusing on what will happen later.

You will also discover that when a consequence is *elicited* from a youngster, the consequence chosen is often more severe than the adult would have chosen. In such cases, let the youngster know your thoughts and pursue a procedure or consequence that is not quite so severe but will still assist the youngster from repeating the same offense.

A Reflective Exercise for Older Children

Four questions are particularly useful as a reflective activity to improve decision-making skills. Although you can pose the questions orally, the responses can be in conversation or in writing. If the responses are to be written or typed on a computer, it should be the youngster's decision whether or not to share with the parent. The parent merely requests that the written responses be kept should a future review of the situation prove necessary. The set of four questions from Chapter 2 are:

1. What did I do? *(acknowledgment)*

2. What can I do to prevent it from happening again? *(choice)*

3. What will I do? *(commitment)*

4. What is my plan to help me fulfill my commitment? *(procedure)*

Consistency and Fairness

Consistency is important, but so is fairness. How does a parent resolve a situation where, for example, two siblings are fighting? The usual approach is to *impose* the same consequence on both parties. *But is equality the same as fairness?* What if one sibling continually acts on Level B toward the other? Since one individual may have started the incident and since each person's sensitivity is different, *imposing the same consequence on all parties is the least fair approach.* A more effective and fairer approach is to *elicit a consequence or a procedure from each individual* to redirect impulses that will help each youngster become more responsible.

As was explained earlier, if you think that the consequence or procedure suggested is not appropriate, not acceptable to you, or will not be successful, simply ask, *"What else?" "What else?" "What else?"* Repeat this question until you both agree.

So, the way to resolve this is to be *consistent in your approach,* rather than focusing on the *consequence.*

To prove that this is fair and the most effective approach, just ask your children whether they would rather be treated alike or as individuals. They will readily have a preference to be treated as individuals and have ownership in the decision that will help them. By *being consistent in the procedure of eliciting,* you will be helping each child in the best way possible.

POINTS TO REMEMBER

◆ You can use authority without being punitive.

◆ If a consequence is necessary, rather than impose it, a more effective approach is to *elicit a consequence or a procedure,* thus placing ownership and responsibility on the young person.

◆ Focus on the present and future, not on the past.

◆ Eliciting is the best way to assure both *consistency* and *fairness.*

PART II
The Raise Responsibility System
Summary and Conclusion

*Every time you force a youth to do something
by using your power of authority,
you deny that person a chance to learn
self-discipline and responsibility.*

SUMMARY

The *Raise Responsibility System* has three parts:

(1) *Teaching*—having youngsters learn the **Hierarchy of Social Development**

(2) *Asking*—also known as **checking for understanding**

(3) *Eliciting*—also known as **guided choices**

Teaching

The first part of the system rests on *teaching* four levels of *social (and personal) development*. The levels are displayed in a *hierarchy*, much like the steps of a ladder. An advantage of using a hierarchy is that people have a natural tendency to want to reach the highest level. *Think of the hierarchy as a reference your children can use for making decisions throughout life.*

As children learn the levels, they gain an understanding of how people and societies develop. In the process, they learn to identify behaviors that are responsible and acceptable and those that are not. Contrast this *proactive* approach to the common approach of *reacting* in a negative manner after a child acts irresponsibly. A reactive approach prompts stress and ill will in both parties.

Asking

The second part of the system has to do with *checking for understanding*. This is the basic approach for any learning. First comes the lesson, which is then followed by a "*checking*" to see if what was taught has been learned. This phase is accomplished by *asking a reflective question* to have the youngster identify the chosen level.

Eliciting

The third part of the system is referred to as *guided choices*—or *eliciting*. This action need only be used when a youngster's behavior is continually unacceptable. In these situations, authority is used— but without being punitive.

Rather than doing something *to* the young person, the parent works *with* the youngster. This is accomplished so that irresponsible behavior becomes a learning opportunity rather than a stressful problem for both parent and child. *A procedure is developed* or *a consequence is elicited* to help the youngster control impulses and redirect irresponsible future behaviors.

CONCLUSION

Practitioners of the *Raise Responsibility System* move into a stress-reducing mode, and young people become more responsible because:

- The *youngster* self-evaluates
- The *youngster* acknowledges inappropriate behavior
- The *youngster* takes ownership
- The *youngster* develops a plan
- The *youngster* develops a procedure to implement the plan

Principles Used

The system is so effective because:

1. Positivity is a more constructive teacher than negativity.

2. Choice empowers.

3. Self-evaluation is essential for lasting improvement.

4. People choose their own behaviors.

5. Self-correction is the most effective approach for changing behavior.

6. Acting responsibly is the most satisfying of rewards.

7. Growth is greater when authority is used *without* punishment.

As you implement the *Raise Responsibility System*, you will find the system so simple and effective that you will want to share it with others.

Manipulatives such as rewards for expected behaviors, threats, and punishments are not used because they (a) foster compliance rather than commitment, (b) require an adult presence for monitoring, (c) set up children to be dependent upon external agents, and (d) do not foster long-term motivation for responsibility. These counterproductive approaches are discussed in Part IV of this book. But first we will turn our attention to some additional approaches to promote responsibility, increase effectiveness, and improve relationships.

POINTS TO REMEMBER

◆ Society has changed and requires a different approach to dealing with today's youth.

◆ The *Raise Responsibility System* is a proactive *system*—not merely a list of techniques.

◆ The system is based on promoting responsibility, rather than obedience.

◆ The system has three parts:

    (1) *Teaching*—having youngsters learn the *Hierarchy of Social Development*

    (2) *Asking*—also known as *checking for understanding*

    (3) *Eliciting*—also known as *guided choices*

◆ The system rests on young people's learning the four levels of the hierarchy.

◆ The levels can be used to analyze everyday situations.

◆ As we live, we experience the various levels.

◆ Level D brings the most personal satisfaction.

◆ The young person, rather than the parent, invests the most effort.

————————————————————————

PART III
Additional Assistance

Promoting Responsibility

Increasing Effectiveness
& Improving Relationships

Answers to Questions

INTRODUCTION
Additional Assistance

We can control people, but we cannot change them.
People change themselves.

One of the joys of living is continual learning. Learning to think and communicate in positive ways, offering choices, and asking reflective questions (the topics of Chapters 1, 2, and 3) seem to be rather simple. Teaching levels of social development, asking in order to prompt reflection on the level of choices, and eliciting consequences or procedures (the topics of Chapters 4, 5, and 6) also appear simple to implement. And indeed they are.

Chapter 7 includes a few additional approaches that are particularly effective in promoting responsibility.

Increasing your effectiveness and improving your relationships is the subject of Chapter 8. The *Acorn Principle* will help you in this regard. Teaching a procedure for impulse control and how to work smarter, rather than harder, are just a couple of the additional techniques you will learn in this chapter.

Chapter 9 contains a sampling of answers to questions I have received that relate to the topics of this book. They are from my monthly *free* electronic newsletter (e-zine), *"Promoting Responsibility and Learning."* Each issue has articles dealing with promoting responsibility, increasing effectiveness, improving relationships, promoting learning, disciplining without stress, and parenting. I encourage you to join the growing number of thousands who have subscribed at ***www.MarvinMarshall.com***.

7
Promoting Responsibility

Taking responsibility is the foundation of a civil society.

Asking *reflective questions* and *eliciting a procedure* to manage impulses are two approaches for promoting responsibility. This chapter offers additional suggestions. We start by examining one of the more traditional approaches—relying on *rules*—and then offer a more effective approach.

RULES

As with *imposed* consequences, the use of the term "rules" as a disciplinary tool is often counterproductive. *Rules are used to control—not inspire.* Although essential in games, *rules are counterproductive in relationships.* How? If a rule is broken, a mindset of enforcement is naturally created. The adult's thinking goes something like, "If I don't do something about this, it will occur again. And besides I'll lose my authority." The situation between the adult and child immediately becomes adversarial. The use of the term "rules" prompts the parent to assume the role of a cop—a position of enforcement—rather than a more encouraging stance similar to that of a coach. As a coach, you are more inclined to view a youngster's misbehavior as an *opportunity to promote responsibility* in a positive manner.

Therefore, instead of relying on rules, consider using the term "responsibilities." In contrast to "rules," "responsibilities" empower and elevate. They are stated in positive terms, whereas rules are often stated in negative terms. When communications are in positive terms, there is a natural tendency for you to *help* rather than to *punish.* So, rather than using the term "rules," consider using a term that describes what you *want to encourage.* Notice that the following examples are meant to *teach* and are all expressed in *positive* terms for what is desired, rather than for what is prohibited.

My Responsibilities

Take care of my things.

Be kind to others and to myself.

Accept ownership of my choices.

Respect other people's property.

Plan ahead so that I can be on time.

If you say to a child, "You are always late," the child is not empowered to change. However, by saying to the child, "You have such great habits in many areas, and being on time is something you can improve," you have reminded the youngster of successes upon which to build. You have encouraged the child to *strive* because of the positive picture you have created.

When a child does not follow a rule, the tendency of the parent is to think in negative terms. The reason for this is simple: rules imply "or else." A rule not followed often leads to an accusatory encounter, which results in some type of psychological pain, be it anger or resentment on the part of both parent and child. The rationale is that there must be a punishment for breaking a rule. *Imposing a punishment, by its very nature, is coercive.* It encourages feelings of hostility, which are hardly conducive for positive relationships. As parents, most of us do not operate out of a desire to enforce rules, impose consequences, or dole out punishments. Our desire is to share knowledge, help develop skills, empower with wisdom, and be a role model and mentor—not a police officer. Because rules create an enforcement mentality, the relationship between parent and child can only improve as the reliance on the term "rules" is reduced.

Rules are "left brain hemisphere" oriented. They work with people who are naturally orderly and structured. Not surprisingly, children who "break the rules" often operate spontaneously and process ideas randomly—typical "right brain hemisphere" behavior. Teaching procedures—rather than relying on rules—is significantly more effective with this type of youngster.

The fact that someone *knows* a rule does not ensure that the rule will be *followed.* Just because information has been *taught* does not mean it has been *learned*. The classic example is the trainer who declared that he had taught his dog how to whistle. The trainer doesn't claim that the dog can whistle but does claim that he has taught the dog. Upon discovering that a child hasn't followed what has been taught, effective parents coach and teach. Rather than punishing for that which has not been learned, they re-teach. A child who is having trouble needs to be helped, rather than be hurt or caused to suffer.

Especially with teenagers, relying on rules invites a problem because rules are seen as restrictions. Teenagers are asserting their independence and they view restrictions as controlling. Although it may seem so, rebellion is not their focus; rather, their focus is on finding and asserting their identity. Instead of establishing restrictions, parents can help by communicating expectations or guidelines, which are much more positive. Using self-evaluative questions and entering into dialogue with teenagers is much more effective than *imposing restrictions* and *relying on rules*.

Although the intentions behind rules are noble, they create a desire to search for loopholes. Rules also work against having children *want* to act appropriately. For example, "No hitting" is a rule. In contrast, "In our family, we express our feelings with words," presents *both an expectation and a procedure*. If a child fails to meet this *responsibility of being kind to others* by hitting a younger sibling, the parent assists by helping the young person create a procedure to better control the impulse the next time the urge to hit arises.

PROCEDURES RATHER THAN RULES

Procedures spell out clearly and exactly what should be done. Teaching *procedures* and *expectations* are far more effective than relying on *rules*.

The most common mistake in working with the young is the assumption that they know what adults want them to do *without the adults first showing them how to do it*. The most successful approach is to *assume nothing*. We are not born with the same type of instincts as other species such as turtles that know everything they need to know at birth. Humans cannot survive independently. We need to be taught.

Establishing procedures and then practicing them until they become routine helps young people to know exactly how things should be done. When young people know exactly what is expected of them, they are more likely to behave responsibly. Because there is no having to guess about how something should be done, opportunities for irresponsible behavior are limited. Simply stated, *we live our lives on procedures.* From the time we get out of bed in the morning until we arrive at the same destination at night, we follow procedures. Procedures give structure. It's similar to riding a bicycle or driving a car. We first learned the procedures involved and then the activity becomes so automatic that we engage in it with little conscious thought. The procedures you teach become the habits of your children.

Visualization as a Procedure

To curb an undesirable behavior, have the youngster create a visual image. For example, let's say that the older brother sticks his foot out to trip his younger brother. The parent's conversation goes something like, "Every time you stick your foot out to trip your younger brother, you are a victim of your impulse. Do you really want to go through life being a victim? If you want to be a victor, rather than a victim—if you want to be in charge of yourself—then let's establish a procedure so that when you get that impulse again, you can redirect it. For example, picture your ankle chained to the floor. That image will prompt you to reflect the next time your brother runs past you. It will help you to be in charge and in control, rather than become a victim of your impulse."

Even very young people can learn that, although emotions and thoughts cannot be stopped from erupting, *growth and maturation come according to how people respond to them.* The more an emotion such as anger is responded to with a *procedure,* the less will be both its frequency and intensity. It is very important to understand that you cannot prevent an emotion. Telling someone not to have an emotion is useless. Instead, redirect the thinking, and because attention is now elsewhere, so is the previous emotion.

Procedures to Deal with Impulses

Impulses, emotions, and even behavior reflexes emanate from within ourselves, even though something outside of us might have prompted the stimulation. As with dreams, emanations may "pop up" without any deliberate thinking. Although the bad news is that these eruptions cannot be prevented, the good news is that they can be diminished by our response to them—so they no longer direct our attention and emotions. Learning a *procedure* is the most effective approach to dealing with destructive thoughts, negative emotions, and inappropriate behaviors. Here is a simple approach to use for yourself as well as to teach youngsters, employing traffic signal imagery to redirect attention and resulting emotions.

Let's start with a situation that may be familiar to you. Assume that you are in your car stuck in a traffic jam and that you will be late for an important appointment. You feel yourself getting angry and your self-talk sounds something like, "This traffic is making me so angry!" Of course, the traffic doesn't care! *You* are allowing *yourself* to become angry—to become emotionally hijacked. Here is a procedure to redirect your thought process and prevent stress.

Reflect, then react.

First, stop (red in the signal), and then breathe as though you were gasping for a breath. Take a *deep gasp* a second time and notice that your jaw drops open and your tongue drops to the bottom of your mouth. It is impossible to gasp with a closed mouth. This simple procedure of taking a gasp of air immediately relaxes the jaw as well as the tension in the nearby nerves that otherwise would send the stress throughout the body. Now, in the moment that it takes to gasp and release the tension, your mind has the opportunity to redirect thinking so you can *consider options* (yellow in the signal). You may decide to turn on your car radio, play a CD, or think of plans for the coming weekend. Having considered a few options, *choose one* (green in the signal). This redirecting your thinking will immediately relieve the negative emotion. *The only sure way to relieve or change an emotion is to redirect your thoughts.*

This simple three-step strategy is easy to teach to children. Make or buy a small drawing of a traffic signal and fill in the colors of the signal. With older children, just a mental image of a traffic signal will do.

This procedure needs to be continually practiced until it becomes habitual. The next time the youngster allows emotions to direct behavior, your first action should be to hold up a picture of the traffic signal. (A few of them can be scattered around in various places.) *Trying to reason or imposing consequences means nothing to a person in a highly emotional state.* Using a procedure is more successful than threatening or punishing—and is less stressful on both parties. If you have a teenager, you may have witnessed something like the following: Our daughter was arguing with her mother, my wife. The phone rang; it was one of our daughter's friends. Our daughter's tone of voice and voice volume immediately changed; her voice became suddenly friendly, even sweet. As soon as the conversation with her friend ended, our daughter's previous emotion reappeared—proving that *by redirecting attention even teenagers can control their tempers.*

Sometimes the youngster's emotion is prompted by something you have no idea about, but the emotion is directed at you. Just ask, *"Are you angry at me or the situation?"* This reflective question prompts the young person to stop and evaluate, which so often leads to the child's sharing the frustration with the parent.

UNDERSTANDING BOYS

Whereas good relationships are important to girls, success is more important to boys.

Hopefully, we are past the "politically correct" theory (an oxymoron in a democratic society) that the differences between males and females are due to socialization—that aside from reproductive organs, there is no difference between the sexes neurologically, psychologically, or emotionally.

A boy measures everything he does or says by a single yardstick: "Does this make me look weak?" If it does, he isn't going to do it. That's part of the reason that video games have such a powerful hold on boys. The action is constant; boys can calibrate just how hard the challenges will be; and when they lose, the defeat is somewhat private in that they are not embarrassed. With this in mind, it's important to remember that while *competition improves performance, it does not improve learning.* Some youth will practice for hours spurred on by the competitive spirit in music competition, athletics, or speech contests. Competition motivates and can be fun, as witnessed by the hours that young people invest in such activities. However, competition can be devastating—*especially for the boy who never finds himself in the winner's circle.* Rather than compete, that youngster loses interest and stops trying.

Boys would rather drop out by giving up or by misbehaving than show that they can't perform. Weakness does not motivate them to want to participate. It takes a masterful parent to encourage them to persevere. You should be aware that more and more young boys become "at-risk" as early as kindergarten because of the feeling associated with weakness in academic skills. Lack of success impinges on their self-talk and self-esteem. I repeat a recurrent theme in my presentations: *"People do good when they feel good, not when they feel bad."* You may want to investigate whether the school your young boy attends is replacing important play and creative time with the counterproductive emphasis on academic achievement in the lower primary grades.

OTHER SUGGESTIONS

The media plays a significant role in the lives of youth. Young people have rights, know them, and articulate them to their parents.

However, rights need not be at the expense of responsibility. This is especially important during the adolescent years when parents and youth can be under great stress. By these years, much of what parents want can be worked out successfully—but not through coercion. Parents can no longer physically control youngsters, just as they can no longer control their children's exposure to outside influences or what their children do when not in their presence. When young people understand the difference between internal and external motivation, they find it much easier to make responsible choices.

Start Young

Fostering responsibility should start at a very young age. For example, a young child sits in the highchair having milk. When finished, the infant throws the bottle away. The youngster hears the "thump" sound and likes it. When the mother picks up the bottle, the infant is getting a message that, to a certain extent, the mother can be controlled. The mother decides that she is not going to let her child behave this way. The mother does not threaten or punish; she simply makes sure her hand is ready when the baby finishes the milk. She then removes the bottle and cleans his face while talking to him. The mother begins to teach the child responsible behavior at a very young age.

Very young people cannot be left to their own devices. It is a parent's responsibility to protect the child. For example, if a child runs into the street, a parent can pick up the child and put the youngster on the sidewalk. The parent can talk to the child about the dangers of cars but needs not make the child feel blameworthy for the innocent act. Rather than focusing on what the child did wrong, a wiser approach is to have the youngster develop a procedure to prevent a reoccurrence.

Exhibit Personal Responsibility

We act and communicate from the beliefs we hold, even though these beliefs are often not clear to us. For example, the parent praises the youngster by saying, "I am so proud of you." The implicit message the parent is sending is that if the child really loved the parent, the child would always do things that make the parent proud. To a certain extent, the parent is saying that the youngster is responsible for the parent's feelings. The message being sent is, "If you really loved me you would make me happy." The same message is implied when the parent makes comments like, "You're making me angry," "You're making me upset," or "You're making me sick." When a parent gets upset, stimulated by a child's action, the thinking process often appears to be, "I am upset, and it is my child's fault." In these cases, the parent is not taking personal responsibility for his or her own response. The parent should be thinking, "I'm upset; how can I best handle the situation?" Instead, the parent is putting the responsibility for his or her feelings on the youngster.

Similarly, it is easy to believe that if other people are responsible for our feelings, then we are responsible for other people's feelings. For instance, the parent feels the caretaker role and accepts responsibility for making the child happy and puts his or her own desires aside. This approach is not good for the parent or for the growing child. When the child continually asks the parent to do something, and the parent does what the child requests, the parent sooner or later may feel some resentment and even anger. Notice the implicit learning: It teaches that the child does not need to value the parent's desires or the parent's time—that the child comes first.

The child not only learns to be manipulative *but also becomes more demanding of the parent's time.* It would be better for the parent to sometimes say, "I'll do that with you later," or "I need some time alone. You need to play by yourself now." Children learn that they can indeed make themselves happy. Of course, any parent will often put his or her child first—but not to the point of dependency, and less and less as the child grows more able to take responsibility.

The approach of demonstrating personal responsibility is one of the hardest to implement, but the benefit is most worthwhile because the parent is role-modeling responsible behavior. Needless to say, at first a child will not like it. But after a while, the youngster realizes more satisfaction by taking personal responsibility than by relying on someone else for his or her happiness. When the parent says to the child, "I have to take care of you because you can't do it for yourself," and the child goes along with it, the child's self-esteem is compromised. However, when the parent communicates, "I am here for you if you need me, but I have faith that you can make yourself happy," the child learns to behave in a more autonomous, responsible way.

Challenge the Youngster

A friend was visiting us with his wife and four-year-old and six-month-old sons. As they were about to leave, the four-year-old jumped onto the driver's seat of the van. The mother mentioned that young Adam was becoming an ever-increasing challenge and that trying to get him out of the driver's seat would be a real chore. I suggested to her that every time she tried to make him do something or stop doing something, he would resist and that her most successful approach would be one that did not involve coercion. I recommended that every time she tells him to do something, he would interpret it as an attempt to control him and that she would be creating a challenge for herself. Sharing (rather than telling), asking a reflective question, and creating a challenge for him would be more effective options.

To demonstrate this third option, I leaned toward Adam and said, "My wife and I have just made a bet. She said it would take you two minutes to get into the backseat and buckle your seat belt. I told her that I bet you could do it in one minute." Little Adam jumped out of the driver's seat and almost knocked my wife over as he ran around the van, climbed into his seat, and buckled his seat belt. I told him how surprised and amazed I was that he could do it—and even in less time than I thought he could. Young people love challenges. The youngster knew where to sit. Having him demonstrate responsible behavior merely took some creativity, namely, "What could I say or do to prompt him in a way that he would interpret as a challenge rather than an attempt to control him?"

Put the Person in Charge

A mother of a young boy shared her frustration with me. One of her sons was constantly getting up from the table during dinner, thereby disrupting the environment she wanted to maintain during mealtime. I suggested that she think of the *exact opposite* behavior to what her son was doing. I then suggested that she put her son in charge of that responsibility. The conversation would go something like this: "Jay, I need your help. I want you to be in charge of having all members of the family remain seated during dinner. Can you handle this?" The mother later told me that the procedure worked like a charm. Her son regularly stayed at the dinner table until the meal was over.

Assuming that the youngster is doing the opposite of what you want, ask for help by putting the person in charge. People like to be in charge. The person will then perform the appropriate behavior because incongruity (doing the opposite of what the person is in charge of) is very difficult for young people. This approach to changing behavior immediately is foolproof. If it doesn't work, reflect: Did you think of the exact opposite? Did you use the exact wording of putting the person in charge and phrasing the responsibility in positive terms?

Knowing the Cause

People know when they act irresponsibly. But their knowing does not stop that type of behavior. *Knowing the cause for behavior may be interesting but has nothing to do with changing that behavior.* Until responsibility is accepted, the person will not act differently—even when the person knows the reason. Therefore, rarely ask a person *why* the behavior occurred. "Why?" implies that knowing the reason for the behavior would make a difference in the future, but it does not. A more effective approach would be to ask, "What are we going to do about it?"

Empower with Responsibility

When young people know that others are counting on them, and especially when the youngster has an attachment to the adult, there is a great incentive to carry through with the request. Young people don't want to let down others they care about. A person wants to think of oneself as someone who can be counted on. Having young people be responsible for something, such as a family task, can have a significant effect on developing responsibility.

Use Creative Phrasing

Use creative phrasing with a youngster who has done something that shouldn't have been done, has misbehaved, or has had to suffer the results of a bad choice. "I know you didn't mean for that to happen. What went wrong?" This phrasing sends the message that you think highly of the person regardless of the negative situation and that you know the person didn't want to end up with the bad results. It demonstrates empathy and opens the gate for the young person to think back over the whole issue without getting defensive.

Have the Youngster Feel Important

The great American humorist Will Rogers said, "As long as you live, you'll never find a method so effective in getting through to another person as having that person feel important." He was right. When you make people feel important, you get their cooperation. Rogers was not talking about insincere flattery. He was referring to getting in the habit of recognizing how important people are. This should obviously apply to your children.

> Cavett Robert, the founder of the National Speakers Association, looked out his window one morning and saw a skinny 12-year-old boy going door-to-door selling books. The boy was headed for his house. Robert turned to his wife and said, "Just watch me teach this kid a lesson about selling. After all these years of writing books about communication and lecturing all over the country, I might as well share some of my wisdom with him. I don't want to hurt his feelings, but I'll get rid of him before he knows what's happened. I've used this technique for years, and it works every time. Then I'll go back and teach him how to deal with people like me."
>
> Mrs. Robert watched as the young boy knocked on the door. Mr. Robert opened the door and quickly explained that he was a very busy man. He had no interest in buying any books. "But," he said, "I'll give you one minute, and then I have to leave; I have a plane to catch."
>
> The young salesman was not daunted by Robert's brush-off. He simply stared at the tall, gray-haired, distinguished-looking man, a man who he knew was fairly well known and quite wealthy. The boy said, "Sir, could you be the famous Cavett Robert?" To which Mr. Robert replied, "Come on in, son."
>
> Mr. Robert bought several books from the youngster— books that he might never read. The boy had mastered the principle of making the other person feel important, and it worked. It's an approach that even the rich and famous or the big and strong can rarely resist.

All people, and especially young ones, wear little invisible signs around their necks that say, "Help Me Feel Important!" The truly effective parents do exactly that. They read the signs and act on them.

POINTS TO REMEMBER

◆ Rules are meant to control, not inspire.

◆ Rules are necessary in games but create adversarial relations between people because of the enforcement characteristic inherent with them.

◆ Referring to procedures and expectations is more effective than relying on rules.

◆ The procedures you teach become the routines and habits of your children.

◆ Teach a procedure to deal with impulses.

◆ Putting the person in charge will encourage doing the right thing.

8

Increasing Effectiveness & Improving Relationships

Discover your child's nature,
and then nurture that nature.
—Jim Cathcart

Any positive relationship is based on trust. It assumes that both parties will be safe, will not be harmed. Trust also carries with it an implicit message that you have each other's best interest in mind. That is why we can accept criticism and even anger from those we trust. We know deep down that the other person really means to help us. Trust is an interesting quality because, once it is lost, it is hard to recapture. Many a relationship gasped its last breath with the words, "I just do not trust you anymore." To have optimum relationships, all parties must feel a sense of trust and safety. The feeling must be that harm will not be forthcoming—physically, emotionally, or psychologically.

THE ACORN PRINCIPLE

Jim Cathcart in his book *The Acorn Principle* brings us a very important message regarding how parents help form the path for their children. An acorn is capable of becoming a mighty oak, but it will never become a giant redwood.

> Some people look at that possibility in their child—the acorn that they are trying to grow—and say, *Acorn, I believe you have potential. I believe you could be a giant redwood. I'll tell you what I am going to do for you, Acorn. I'm going to work with you. I'm going to be your mentor. I'm going to teach you to be a giant redwood. Here is a recorded message. It's called "The*

Power of Redwood Thinking." Listen to this recording, and it will change your life. And here's a book that tells about great redwoods. Listen to your own thoughts as you read it. Think about what you could do to be more like the redwoods you read about. Notice their patterns and what will happen is that you'll be more of a redwood.

Question: What would this acorn be when it grows up? Answer: A really insecure oak. It grew with the message that it was not supposed to be an oak; it should have been a redwood. Can it be a redwood? Never! The point is that if you plant an acorn, it can only grow to be an oak because that is its genetic makeup. But it could really do well if the expectation and mentoring you gave it were for an oak. People's greatest, fastest, and easiest growth always comes along the line of their natural abilities. Every person has them in some form of talent, be it in the use of language(s), numbers, organizing, visual arts, music or rhythm, athletics, body maneuverability, skill in working with others, and/or understanding themselves—to name a few. And a great way to foster a youngster's natural abilities is for parents to communicate in positive terms, by allowing the youngster to choose activities that build on strengths, and by prompting reflection.

LIMIT LECTURING

To ensure that children will make responsible decisions, parents begin to lecture. If you reflect on this, you will soon realize that lecturing and telling your children what to do implies that you do not have faith in their decision-making abilities. This can result in their becoming defensive. A person who is defensive does not listen. In addition, these young people can lose faith in their own confidence to make decisions. If young people do not have faith in themselves, then the parents' faith in them decreases even more, and the lecturing begins again.

Even well-intentioned lectures convey the subtle, negative message that what the youngster has done is wrong or not good enough. This often results in defensiveness and resistance, especially with adolescents. Trying to persuade adolescents by using reason often has little effect; they know they are right! In addition, the youngster sees this as, "My parents are trying to control me again!" An adage when dealing with young people is to say no more than 13 words at a time, and with a teenager, make it 12.

Young people are sensitive about being told what to do; yet parental help is perfectly appropriate. Consider using reflective questions, such as, "What do you think about... ?" "Have you thought of... ?" "Would you consider... ?"

LISTEN TO LEARN

Epictetus is credited with the statement: "Man has one tongue but two ears that we may hear from others twice as much as we speak."

Listening to learn and valuing young people's feelings and ideas is what promotes the ability of parents to effectively communicate with and influence children. Listen to *learn* means not inserting your opinion and not judging what the youngster says *while the youngster is speaking.* Parents have a natural tendency to approve or disapprove of young people's statements. Parents' first reaction is to evaluate from their own point of view and then approve or disapprove of what the youngster says. This is listening autobiographically. While the tendency to make evaluations is common in almost all conversations, it is much more intense when feelings are involved. An easy strategy for replacing this tendency of listening autobiographically is to cultivate the habit of *listening to learn.*

Listening is a skill that can be improved. It starts by the procedure of taking the position of a good listener. It's getting ready to hear what is about to be said. It is refraining from the all-too-common practice of hearing a few words and then jumping in with a response. You may have experienced the feeling that arose when someone finished your sentence before you had finished it yourself. The feeling is not a positive one! When a parent interrupts a young person who is attempting to communicate, it prompts a negative emotion. *No one—including a young person—enjoys being interrupted when trying to make a point.*

Listening in anticipation of what a child will say is another habit to break. *Listening in anticipation encourages interruptions.* A child wants to be acknowledged and does not wish to feel that you know what is about to be said. Interrupting is an indication that you don't care about hearing the other person's viewpoint as much as your own. Because humor can dissipate a negative emotion, consider teaching the following phrase to your teenager as a prompt to remind you when you impulsively interrupt: *"Pardon me for speaking while you're interrupting."*

A parent who listens well acknowledges the youngster's feelings and opinions. In addition, listening well can be a model for adolescents, who themselves often have trouble practicing this skill. *"Zipping the lip"* is extremely difficult for a parent, but it is the surest way to improve communications and understanding. *No great insight ever enters the mind through an open mouth.* It is important to let young people know that you are willing to listen, even though it may not result in agreement. A simple "Talk to me about it" is an effective start toward dialogue. Just use the most effective sales principle: *Inquiry precedes advocacy.* In other words, listen before you talk.

Talking is sharing and communicating, but listening is caring. Listening is at the heart of every positive relationship. It has the opposite effect of *indifference, a relationship killer.* As with anyone you care about, listening communicates that the other person is important and that you have respect for the person. When you are attentive to another person, you are saying, "I am listening to you— and only you—right now. You are getting all of me. No distractions. No mind wandering. You're getting all of my attention because you are important to me."

When you feel a temptation to interrupt, redirect that impulse by thinking of the following question: *"Will I be more effective if I listen first?"* Another consideration is to follow former President Harry S Truman's approach: "I have found the best way to give advice to your children is to find out what they want, and then advise them to do it." I personally find it quite easy to totally focus on what the person is saying while taking a few deep breaths. Don't think about what you're going to say before the other person is finished. It's like tennis. When you're playing, you should watch the ball. It doesn't work if you're thinking about your next play. You've got to watch the ball as it's coming toward you.

Checking for understanding is by far the most important thing you can do in listening. In fact, *without* this step you can never be sure that you and the other person actually communicated.

There is a story told about General Alexander Haig, the former commander-in-chief, United States European Command, who spent five years with the North Atlantic Treaty Organization (NATO). One time, at an international party, an Englishman asked him, "General Haig, are you married?" Haig said, "Yes, I am."

The Englishman asked, "Do you have any children." He answered, "No, I don't have any children. My wife can't get pregnant." The Englishman said, "Oh I see, your wife is inconceivable."

A German fellow said, "No, no. You don't understand. What General Haig meant was his wife is impregnable."

But a Frenchman said, "No. What General Haig really meant was his wife was unbearable."

Occasionally paraphrasing in your own words what the other person is saying is a wonderful technique to check for understanding. And whether you understand or misunderstand, both parties win. If you get the person's message right, the person will feel good about the communication and will affirm it with you. If you get the message wrong, the person will clarify.

Your listening attitude is more important than anything you say in response to someone. Your attitude of respect and understanding is more important than your ability to formulate brilliant responses, as the following slightly abridged thought by Ralph Roughton, M.D., illustrates:

When I ask you to listen to me, and you start giving me advice, you have not done what I asked.

When I ask you to listen to me, and you begin to tell me why I shouldn't feel that way, you are trampling on my feelings.

When I ask you to listen to me, and you feel you have to do something to solve my problem, you have failed me—strange as that may seem.

Listen! All I asked was that you listen—not talk or do—just hear me.

When you do something for me that I can and need to do for myself, you contribute to my fear and inadequacy.

So please listen and just hear me. And if you want to talk, wait a minute, and then I'll listen to you.

The Talking Stick: Listening to Solve Problems

One of the most successful approaches to solving disputes comes from the Native American aphorism: "Before we can truly understand another person, we must walk a mile in that person's moccasins." *Before we can walk in another person's moccasins, we must first take off our own.* This means to perceive as with the other person's eyes, ears, mind, and spirit.

One of the deepest desires of humans is to be understood. But how do you do it? The *talking stick* is one approach. One reason for its success is that it uses something tangible. The "stick" can be a spoon, a stuffed animal, or any object that serves as something that can be held and passed from one person to another.

When meeting to resolve an issue, the *talking stick* is present. Only the person holding the stick is permitted to speak until that person is satisfied that everyone understands. *To be understood does not mean to agree.* The procedure is that others are not permitted to make their own points, argue, agree, or disagree. They may need to restate the point to make sure the person feels understood, or the person may just simply feel that all understand.

As soon as the person holding the stick feels understood, the stick is passed to another person. As that person shares, all listen. The others may be required to restate and empathize until that person is understood. Using this approach, all parties are responsible for 100 percent of the communications—both speaking and listening. Once each of the parties feels understood, an amazing thing happens. The focus naturally shifts to problem solving. Negative energy decreases, ill feelings evaporate, mutual respect grows, and people become creative.

An underlying reason for the success of this approach is that the goal is to clarify, rather than to influence. As you may experience in many situations, *when the objective is to clarify, the result often leads to influence.*

FAMILY MEETINGS

Family meetings are a wonderful approach for improving relationships and also for solving problems in a constructive manner. The meeting should involve all members of the family and should occur on a regular basis, such as once each week at a predetermined agreed-upon time.

Successful meetings start with *procedures* or *guidelines* created by the participants. Again, shy away from the term "rules," which, as noted, creates an enforcement mentality. A key to success is to focus on solutions, rather than on problems. Deal in the present. The past cannot be changed. When the past is re-lived, it becomes the present and builds frustration. The following question should continually be the focus: *"What can we do about it?"*

Guidelines for conducting the meeting may include:

- Sitting so that everyone can have eye contact with everyone else

- Talking about what you—not what others—will do

- Speaking in a conversational tone and volume

- Aiming for clarification and understanding

- Helping, not hurting, each other

- Refraining from accusations

- Focusing on solutions

If any of the guidelines are not followed, a simple solution is to have a procedure to handle the situation. This can be as simple as someone's asking, *"Is this following the guidelines?"* Avoid accusatory phrases, such as, *"Are you following the guidelines?"* Comments like this will prompt a defensive reaction. Sometimes, an underlying problem is beneath the surface and requires patience to uncover. Members need to feel that they will not be emotionally harmed, especially when sharing something that bothers them. *Both trust and noncoercion are essential.* To reinforce how important this is, think of any friend you have. Chances are that if the person attempted to coerce you or if you did not trust that person, the friendship would not last very long.

Determine a location for the agenda sheet. Anyone can add to it before or at the beginning of the meeting. Here are a few starter questions to consider using:

1. "What did you learn this week that's valuable or useful?"

2. "Do you have an issue or concern that should be shared?"

3. "What did you feel good about or proud of last week?" (for younger children)

Conducting a family meeting is a skill, and as you know by now, as with any skill it requires patience and practice. The goal should be to share problems and feelings in order to improve family relationships and for each person to feel good about the family community. As long as the meetings are moving in these directions, you will find them well worth the time and effort.

ADDITIONAL SUGGESTIONS

Check Assumptions

Some of the decisions we make are based on inaccurate assumptions. We may know exactly what we are thinking and what we mean, but the child may have a completely different perspective.

> A father is walking through the forest with his three-year-old daughter. As they are walking, he repeatedly tells her to stay on the path. The little girl is walking all around. She looks at a tree, then a bush, and meanders here and there. The father continually says, "Stay on the path. I told you to stay on the path." Eventually, he gets so angry with her that he pulls her over, shakes her a bit, and shouts, "I told you to stay on the path!" The little girl looks up at him with tears in her eyes and says, "Daddy, what's a path?"

> The youngster says to his mother, "I'm hungry. Can I have a snack?" His mother says, "Sure. Help yourself." The boy takes two cookies from the jar in the kitchen cupboard. He then hears his mom say, "You can have an apple or an orange." The youngster thinks, "Are we both speaking the same language?" The youngster assumes two cookies would be a good snack. His mother's definition is quite different.

As has been emphasized throughout this book, one technique to reduce parental stress is to check for understanding.

Focus on the Important

Choose your battles. While clashes may be unavoidable, it is not necessary to get pulled into every skirmish. An effective strategy here is to ponder the answer to the question, *"Will this matter a week from now?"*

Youngsters explore and try out different roles. These can be irritating and bewildering to a parent. As painful as it may be to watch, it is one way that young people learn to function on their own. As a rule of thumb, *only make a fuss about those issues that are harmful to the youngster or others—or are irreversible.* Wearing baggy pants or an "outrageous" hairdo at 13 may not be very serious; getting a large tattoo on your arm with controversial language is serious. Situations that involve safety or that are illegal or immoral are non-negotiable.

Ask for Assistance

In past generations, the parents were the center of the household and children were expected to assist in the running of that household. Very often in today's family, the parental focus is on *giving to* children, rather than on the children's doing the giving. You can increase your effectiveness and assist in the maturing of your children if you give them the opportunity to lend assistance. A simple way to do this is for the parent to express a need, giving the child an opportunity to help parents. *Children grow by giving.* Some examples are, "I need you to help me put the groceries away," "I need your help with dinner," "I need quiet time. Please find an activity for the next 30 minutes until I feel better." Machiavelli made the point: *People are by nature as much bound by the benefits they confer as by those they receive.* A request for assistance is easy to hear. This approach is proactive and is more effective than a reactive approach that criticizes, blames, or complains, such as, "You should have helped me with the groceries."

Recognize Implicit Messages

Parents often deliver *explicit* messages unaware of sending *implicit* ones. "Explicit" refers to the actual words you state. "Implicit" refers to what the receiver of the message is learning by inference. For example, tickets for a movie theater are more expensive for a 13-year-old than for a 12-year-old. In order to save money, the parent tells the 13-year-old daughter to state her age as 12. The explicit message is that saving money is desirable; however, the *implicit* message is that being dishonest is acceptable.

The teenager tells the parent, "I may be home late tonight." The parent asks, "Will there be alcohol or drugs where you are going?"

The response is, "I don't know." The parent responds by saying, "You're not going!" The explicit message to the offspring is very clear; yet, so is the *implicit message: "I don't trust you."*

An 18-year-old calls her parent and says she drank a little too much at the party she is at and that she wants to be picked up. This is a very responsible thing to do. However, the parent becomes angry with the daughter. On the drive home, the parent relentlessly chastises her daughter, who concludes, "I'm not going to tell my parent next time." If parents get angry and forbid young people to do certain things, they can put their heads in the sand believing their prohibition is going to be effective. However, in more cases than we would like, young people will do what they want anyway; they just won't talk about it to their parents. In such situations, the parents *have lost the opportunity to influence their children*—to tell them how they see the situation, to share what they did when younger, and to share their parental feelings about the situation.

Parents always need to be aware of implicit messages. When parents become upset and yell at children, the implicit message taught is that when upset, yelling is acceptable. The same goes for hitting. The parents, usually without realizing it, are teaching the youngster to deal with upsetting situations by losing control and even striking out.

Maintain Standards

An admirer visited Samuel Taylor Coleridge, the British poet. During the conversation, the subject came around to children. The visitor stated that he believed children should be given free rein to think and act and learn at an early age and to make their own decisions, arguing that this is the only way they can grow into their full potential. Coleridge invited the visitor outside to see his flower garden. The visitor took one look and exclaimed that it was nothing but a yard full of weeds. Coleridge retorted that the garden used to be filled with roses, but this year he thought that he would let the garden grow as it willed without tending to it, and that this mess was the result.

At times children—and especially adolescents—will not like what is required of them and will act as if they do not like their parents. Remarks such as, "You don't understand," or "I'm the *only* one who has to," or "I'll die if you don't let me," are attempts to have the parent relent and say "Yes" when the parent knows it is really best not to allow what the youth desires. In these situations, the parent should focus on what is best for the youngster *in the long run*. However, in the process, the child needs to understand the reasons for the decision. A simple technique to employ when a "No" needs to be given is to place the challenge on the youngster by simply saying, *"Convince me."* The challenge encourages reflection and responsible thinking. This is especially important with teenagers who want to feel right even when they are wrong.

Another simple but underused technique is for the *parent* to first reflect on the reason for the parental decision. Then share the reason with the child. This can be very significant. The youngster has a reason for what he or she wants, for what is desired, and so, too, should the parent have a reason.

Just as our democratic system of government needs to be learned by each generation, so do the morals, values, and ethics upon which democracy rests. As parents, it is our job to teach these principles. The young boy in the park, for example, goes up to a smaller boy and pushes him down, hurting the smaller boy. The mother runs to the pusher, her son, and asks, "What made you feel so bad to do a thing like that?" Even if the boy could articulate the reason, it is no excuse for his bullying the smaller boy. Rather than feelings or excuses, the *behavior* should be addressed. *Developing a sense of right and wrong takes precedence over feelings and impulses.* Although it is perfectly acceptable for the mother to inquire, pushing a smaller child is still not acceptable. The opportunity was lost for teaching acceptable behavior.

Let the Youngster Lead

If a youngster is critical of the way a parent does things, a good strategy is to let the youngster plan an activity. Parents can assist by providing a few guidelines and a budget.

A forgetful or unreliable child can also lead by being in charge of a message center, such as a "Things to Remember" board (on or near the refrigerator). Things that are important, such as appointments and activities, are on the board and read each day. The youngster can post messages on the board. The strategy also ensures that the youngster, being in charge of the board, will not "forget" what is on it.

Working Smarter

Do not do things for young people that they can do for themselves. When you do, the youngster is deprived of an opportunity to become more responsible. Performing tasks promotes responsibility. Accept the fact that growth comes through struggle. Babying children keeps them dependent and hinders their development. Focus on treating children as if they are who, how, and what you would like them to be. *Treating people as if they are responsible increases their chances of becoming so.*

Once a task has been performed, the objective should be to focus on progress—rather than on perfection. If the activity does not meet parental expectations, something positive can still be found to comment on. This is far more effective than comments that foster guilt or a sense of failure. A positive approach prompts an incentive for the task—in contrast to criticizing, which provides a disincentive.

Choose a specific time of day for required activities. When tasks are structured and organized, they are easier to accomplish. When establishing routines, consider the timing, such as whether or not the child is tired or hungry. There may be causes for being cranky or uncooperative. Similarly, if you are interrupting a child's favorite activity or television program, don't expect the youngster to be very cooperative. With an adolescent, the "state of mind" needs to be considered. A typical example is a parent's demand on a youngster's time. Let's say that the son has not taken out the trash or completed some other chore, and he is watching television. The parent reminds him. The timing is met with a negative reaction. A more successful approach would be to ask later or wait until he is upright, preferably in motion. Once on his feet and moving, the young man will be in a state of mind much more receptive to taking out the trash. In addition, the implicit message will not be that what the parent wants is more important than what the youngster wants. A key phrase to remember is, *"Under duress, they do less."*

Offering help to start an activity is a good technique. Younger children prefer starting tasks with others rather than in isolation. After the youngster is involved, then withdraw, saying something like, "I'm sure you have the skills to do the rest without my help."

Any task should be age appropriate. "Have you picked up your clothes?" is more manageable and not so discouraging as, "Clean your room." In addition, once the clothes are picked up, cleaning the rest of the room may naturally follow.

As noted earlier in the book, *there isn't any empowerment more effective than self-empowerment.* Because being positive is so enabling, it is best to displace thoughts and communications that are destructive. Continually ask yourself how what you want to communicate can be put in a positive way. For example, saying, "You are bad tempered," has the same meaning as, "You need to work on controlling your temper." However, the first *labels* the person, whereas the second *enables* the person. People change more by building on their strengths and aptitudes than by working on their weaknesses. This does not mean that an area of weakness should not be worked on, but it does mean that a parent's emphasis should be on what the child *can* do, rather than on what the child cannot do. The simple belief that something can be done is the spark that ignites the brain to act.

If a child is acting irresponsibly, acknowledge the action, but do not call the child irresponsible. Label the behavior, rather than the person. "Do you consider that the responsible thing to do?" and "That was not worthy of you," are better choices than, "You are irresponsible."

Refrain from arguing. It only fuels hostility and diminishes healthy communications. Arguments *rarely* focus on solutions, and reasoning with someone who is upset is futile. One approach is simply to hold up your hand, palm out, making the "stop" sign, or signal "time out" with hands overhead like a referee. Then determine a later time to resolve the issue.

Avoid attempting to talk young people out of their feelings. Young people have the right to feel hurt, upset, and disappointed. Their reactions should be acknowledged without being condoned. However, negative feelings should not be allowed to infect other members of the family. If the person chooses to anger, let it be done in isolation.

Recognize Styles

The Swiss psychiatrist Carl Jung was the first to categorize behavioral styles. No style is good or bad, right or wrong. Neither is one style better or worse than another; they are just different. Jung articulated a theory of personality behavior styles that he believed are genetically determined. Styles can be discerned by watching young children. You will discover how they process experiences in different ways. Jung postulated that every individual develops a primacy in one of four major behavioral functions: intuiting, thinking, feeling, and sensing.

Over the years a number of personality inventories have been developed using Jung's "forced-choice" approach. If you have ever taken such an inventory, you might have had difficulty making choices between two opposites. For example, would you classify yourself as an introvert or an extrovert? Your choice may be more representative of one but not to the complete exclusion of the other. Therefore, any inventory that uses a forced-choice approach is an artificial attempt to categorize and describe. If we keep this in mind and do not pigeonhole people by the results of such an inventory, the descriptions can be useful.

From the many instruments now available using this forced-choice approach, four behavioral styles seem to emerge. To help understand this approach and in understanding a child, visualize a directional scale with a thinker in the north, a feeler in the south, a doer in the west, and a relater in the east.

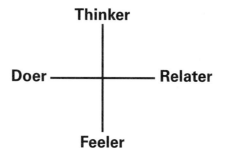

A thinker (north) analyzes and can be described as someone who processes information using a great deal of thought. A feeler (south) can be described as being more directed through emotions than through cognition. A doer (west) is orientated toward results, while a relater (east) is into relationships. Since directions are not limited to north, south, east, and west, think in terms of general areas or neighborhoods, such as the north and west, south and east, etc. My styles are predominantly in the thinker and doer areas. I am cognitive (thinker) and project-oriented (doer). My wife is a writer (thinker) and enjoys social interactions (relater). However, our daughter is guided by her feelings (feeler) and has a great desire to be with people (relater). Knowing our daughter's styles allows my wife and me to be much more understanding of her and her decisions. A parent who is aware of styles has a decided advantage in relating to the child. The same holds true for a husband and wife. Just knowing that my wife wants time to relate prompts me to redirect my impulse of "getting on with a task." I deliberately take time to listen. Being aware of styles enhances communications. When you observe a youth's style and start relating with this understanding, you will experience less stress and more joy in your parenting.

Since this book is a manual for raising responsible children while reducing stress, the next chapter focuses on suggestions not previously addressed.

POINTS TO REMEMBER

◆ Your child is born with certain genetic dispositions. Nurture your child's nature.

◆ When you talk, you repeat what you already know; when you listen, you often learn.

◆ A person who is defensive does not listen.

◆ Listening is the surest way to increase your effectiveness.

◆ Family meetings are a very successful approach for solving problems.

◆ Ask your child for help. This is a simple but highly effective approach.

◆ Recognize implicit communications—those not stated but that still convey a message.

◆ Understand your child's styles.

9
Answers to Questions

A guaranteed way to help children become miserable
is to satisfy all of their wishes.

In order to categorize frequently asked questions and responses in a convenient manner, this chapter is divided into three sections. The first applies primarily to children of all ages. The second section deals with young children—preschoolers and those of elementary ages. The third section deals with older youth.

GENERAL

We have the freedom to choose how we act, what we say, how we respond to situations, how we treat other people, and how we deal with an impulse. We also choose our self-talk. Each choice, no matter how small, is always accompanied by a cost, a consequence, or a result. Economists refer to "opportunity costs." If, for example, you watch a television program, it was at the "cost" of *not* doing something else. If you get angry and kick the machine you are working on, the cost or consequence can be a broken toe. If you create a relationship with a server at a restaurant by asking the server's name, the result may be better service.

Self-disciplined people make a point to think before they act or speak. They think about where each particular choice will lead—to something positive or negative. They think ahead to see if they are going to be satisfied with the consequence that a particular choice will bring. If they are satisfied, they go ahead in that direction. If not, they think again and choose to act or speak differently—in a way that will bring a consequence that they can more happily accept. So, how do you help a child become more self-disciplined? The key is to hone the skill of *asking reflective questions*—questions that prompt the child to think. It's *not* necessary for the youngster to tell the parent what the thoughts are. *It's enough just to pose the questions.* If you ask a question in a calm way, the youngster will think about it—even if the child will not admit a mistake or share thoughts with you. In fact, it's even a good idea to say, "You don't need to tell *me* what you're thinking. That's not so important. What is important is that you *be honest with yourself.*"

Questions Regarding Consequences

A parent might be frustrated and angrily blurt out:

> "WHY did you do that?"

> "WHAT on earth were you thinking of to say that?"

> "HOW could you do such a thing?"

These kinds of questions immediately put a child on the spot and lead to defensiveness and confrontation. They encourage a child to make up excuses, become sullen or defiant, or blame his actions on circumstances or someone else. They will *not* prompt reflection or responsibility.

If you feel it necessary to have a suitable consequence for misbehavior or if you want to set up a procedure in the event that the same irresponsible choice occurs again, be sure that what is chosen *comes from the youngster.* For example, if you feel that your child's suggestion is not appropriate, say *"What else?"* until you both agree. If the youngster has no ideas, offer a choice of several suggestions. Or, your child might say something like, "If I do it again, I'll have to miss my favorite TV show." You could say, "Does that have anything to do with this particular situation?" The response then might be, "I'll apologize," or if that is not satisfactory to you, you might respond with, *"And what else?"* Then, if done again, it's very clear what should occur. You would say, "What was it you said should happen if you did that again?" You will find that the youngster will sheepishly tell you what has been set up and then carry through with that consequence. *Your child takes responsibility for the actions—which is the goal.*

Picking on a Sibling

Let's say that the older brother is picking on his younger brother. Raise expectations and empower by saying, "You're stronger and bigger than your brother. I would think that you would want to protect him?"

Sibling Squabbles

Positive sibling relationships can be a source of strength for life, whereas unresolved early conflicts can create wounds that never quite heal. Parents need not intervene in every quarrel. However, parents should obviously intervene whenever an argument turns violent or threatens to do so. When an older child is hitting his baby sister, the parent intervenes immediately and makes it clear that hurting others is not acceptable. The same is true for verbal abuse between siblings that leaves one or both angry or with negative feelings about the other. Establish guidelines, such as treating the word "hate" as a forbidden one and not allowing "shut up" between siblings. A "no hitting, no hurting" expectation can be established so the youngsters will know that they are to work out their problems peacefully. *Solving circles*, described in Chapter 2, is a very effective approach in such situations.

Most children hate fighting—even when they are winning. They do it because they do not have the tools for dealing with their frustrations. Fighters should be separated to cool off. An effective technique is to have them sit down together until each gives the other permission to get up. *This technique diminishes anger more speedily than if the children are separated completely.* Youngsters often realize the situation they are in (not able to get up until permission is given by the other person) and actually start laughing. Humor is a great problem solver.

Another approach is for a parent to listen to both parties while the youngsters come up with a solution. Still another is to have each sibling write down his or her side of the story. When the parent looks at the two stories, each will be different. The charge is then given for the siblings to present an ending to the stories that both can live with. A variation is to have them write their individual stories and then read each other's. Then have them create a plan they both agree on, even an impractical one. Anger dissipates even more as they come up with zany endings.

Understanding Differences

One of the most important teachings a parent can give is that *being different is not being wrong.* Understanding differences is crucial in our diverse society. Understanding differences includes how males and females operate. Generally, girls will sit and discuss feelings rather easily. Boys usually will not. In order to get boys to express feelings, *engage them in some activity*, such as throwing a baseball, playing basketball, or taking a walk. Boys have a strong desire to feel competent. That's how they achieve self-esteem and self-respect. Telling a boy what to do interferes with his desire for competency, which is why boys so often react negatively even when they know a parent is correct.

Understanding the differences between parents is also helpful. Whereas a mother has a desire to protect a boy and prevent him from doing something because he may get hurt, a father may say, "Let him do it. That is how he will learn." A father is more likely to think that as long as an activity is *not life threatening, unhealthy,* or *morally wrong,* it should be allowed. For example, a father is more willing to allow boys to engage in rough-and-tumble play. This "boy-play" is natural, as can be seen by how boys physically greet each other. It is different from what we normally think of as negatively aggressive behavior, such as bullying. In the case of bullying, however, the sooner the parent intervenes when a youngster bullies, the better. Bullies tend to grow into, not out of, such behavior.

Giving Allowances

A prime purpose for giving an allowance is to engage youngsters in making decisions regarding savings, spending, and charity. This is totally different from family obligations. The allowance should not be turned into a reward that is contingent on pleasing the parent. If a parent is not satisfied with behavior or how chores are done, these should be dealt with separately. In such cases, eliciting a procedure or consequence from the young person, rather than your imposing a consequence, is the path to success.

Homework

The most obvious reason for homework is to practice and improve skills or to gain further knowledge or understanding. Practice is essential for skill mastery and reinforces what has been learned in the classroom. Gaining knowledge and understanding is not limited to class time. Homework also teaches other lessons: responsibility, self-discipline, perseverance, and time management. Homework provides practice in how to begin a task, complete it, and be responsible for the outcome. When homework is difficult and the young person begins to struggle, parents want to help, and they should—up to a point. When the helping has reached the point where the youngster knows how to do the assignment, then the parent should back away; otherwise, the rescuing and over-involvement result in a gradual dependence on others.

Homework should be something done on a regular basis. A regular time is most effective because it establishes a routine. An encouraging comment, such as, "What do you expect to learn or reinforce from this assignment?" is better than one that is negative or nagging, such as, "Have you finished your assignment?" Negative comments only encourage doing the assignment in order to get away from the negativity of nagging. This often results in the youngster's doing the assignment but then forgetting to take it to school. Again, the motivation in such cases is not the assignment, but rather getting away from the nagging.

According to the recommendation by most experts, homework should be limited to 30 minutes in the elementary grades. For example, Harris Cooper, a Duke University psychology professor, has reviewed more than 120 studies on homework. He suggests a moderate amount in the early years but for older students the amount of homework done usually translates into higher achievement scores.

Establishing a procedure helps youngsters complete homework assignments. Some questions you can ask to assist in setting up this kind of a routine are:

"What time will you do your homework?"

"Where will you do it?"

"What materials will you need?"

"Will you be watching TV while doing your work?"

"How will you know that you have done quality work?"

Attention Deficit

Attention deficit disorder (ADD) and attention deficit hyperactivity disorder (ADHD) are often used interchangeably because they both have to do with attention. However, they are both mislabeled. People who have either of these characteristics can have laser-like attention when they are involved in something that interests them. What they lack is good impulse control. Chapter 7 discusses this topic along with a suggested procedure.

These people need to develop procedures because procedures give structure. Cindy wrote me:

> I was an ADD kid. It wasn't that I couldn't control myself but that I had a hard time remembering what I was supposed to be doing. My parents organized my life around *structure.* Everything was done a certain way, every time. That way it became habitual vs. something I had to consciously think about. Cleaning my room was done by starting on the right-hand side of the door and then going around my room, spot by spot. Stuff that was in the wrong spot went in the center till I got to the part of the room it belonged in. Anything remaining in the center of my room when I was done either got thrown out or brought to the part of the house in which it belonged. When it came to homework, my dad sat by my side. Every time I looked up, he told me to look back down. It took a strong commitment by my parents and my teachers, but it was worth it. I ended up with some real life-strategies that I still use today. I think that any child, ADD or not, needs structure and they need to know that there is "a way" to do certain things.

Sexual Harassment

My advice was asked regarding the following dilemma:

> My son is in trouble AGAIN! Yesterday I got a phone call from his PE teacher about something he did in class (a mixed boy/girl PE class). The teacher said that my son was bordering on sexual harassment. During a volleyball game he cracked a crude joke by commenting on a play made by one of the girls in the class. When I asked my son why he did this, he said, "It was a funny thing to say." I don't know what I should say to him or do about this.

I responded that the son most likely realized that his being funny in the situation would be a problem. He had poor impulse control or believed that the satisfaction from his humor was worth more than any consequence. So don't *say* anything to him. Instead, use the recommended approach. *Ask* him by eliciting responses to two questions: (1) What will he do to amend this situation? (2) What should occur if he pulls a similar poor choice again? After eliciting responses, have him write them down. Give him a choice as to whether he wants to keep the paper or have you keep it. Let him know that keeping the paper has nothing to do with trust. It is simply to remind him what he has chosen to do if he makes the same unacceptable choice again. The way the human brain works, committing the consequence to writing is the only sure way of total recall. Acknowledge that he is socially adept to know when he says or does something that is inappropriate. Let him know that you appreciate his sense of humor but if he is going to be successful in future relationships, he needs to learn when humor is appropriate and when it is not.

In another example related to sexual harassment, a close friend asked for assistance, as described in her communication below:

> A parent near and dear to me has a seven-year-old boy who frequently touches/grabs his four-year-old sister in her "private" area. My understanding is that he has been reprimanded, yelled at, had his hand pulled away, as well as talked to calmly about personal boundaries, and still continues to do it. My worst fear of course is that this behavior amounts to early sexual abuse and could cause lifelong damage to the girl as well as establish habits and a mindset for the boy that will continue into a life of abusing girls!

I suggested for the mother to teach the four levels of social development described in Chapter 4. The mother then has the youngster identify the unacceptable level of the behavior in question. The suggestions in the preceding situation should also be followed: "What should occur if he pulls a similar poor choice again?"

The mother realizes that her attempts to *control* his behavior have been unsuccessful. Have her move to the more successful approach of how her son can influence himself to change his own behavior—since he is the only one who can do it. The mother should also have the youngster reflect that he is a victim of his impulses when he continues this behavior. Remind her to ask, "Do you really want to go through life being a victim or are you old enough to control yourself and be in charge? If you want to be a victor, let's figure out what you can do when you get the impulse again." Be sure to follow up on the procedure or consequence that has been previously agreed upon. If unsuccessful, elicit a new procedure/consequence. It may take this process a few times before the behavior is completely stopped.

THE YOUNG

With infants, the world revolves around themselves. Their desires and needs are all they sense. At about eight months, they become aware of separation. Soon after, they learn that parents have relationships with each other—and that children are not the center of the universe.

A parent related the following to me:

> One night I was very tired, and our daughter was cranky. She wouldn't go to sleep; she was crying and wouldn't even lie down. She was hysterical. I started out just talking to her, to no avail. Her crying kept going on and on, and my hostility level started rising. "Yes, you're going to bed right now; no, you are not going to play!" My tone got louder, and then I just spanked her and said, "You will go to bed, now! I've had enough of this!" That didn't do it. She was still crying. I was desperate, wondering, "What do I do now?" So I went back to her and sat down on the bed and held her a bit. But I didn't take her out of the bed. I said, "Daddy and I don't get much time together, and I spend most of the day with you. I would like to spend a little time with Daddy. We need to relax at night and talk to each other. Sometimes we like to go to bed early, too. But we can't go to bed if you're crying." My daughter said, "Okay, Mommy." That was it. I couldn't believe it! While she didn't instantly go to sleep, there was no more crying.

Role-Modeling

The parent is the first teacher—and the most influential. In fact, you cannot help but teach because you are always modeling.

> Every morning a father drove his three-year-old daughter to preschool. One day, the father was away at a conference

and the mother drove the girl. The youngster, sitting next to her mother, could hardly see over the dashboard and asked, "Mommy, where are all of the bastards today?"

The mother replied, "I don't know, honey. I guess they're only out when your father drives."

Nonverbal Communications

When children are too young to understand concepts such as *internal motivation,* appropriate behavior can still be taught without using rewards or coercion. For example, when a child does something that is not appropriate, lightly touch the child's wrist and shake your head *no.* Persevere. You may have to do this a number of times before understanding sets in.

> When Dad is carrying little Tyler in the supermarket, Tyler starts to kick Dad in the stomach, laughing with each kick. Dad immediately puts Tyler down, steps back, and rubs his tummy where it hurts, and continues walking.

> Another young child, Jenny, stalls and pokes around before getting into the car when the mother is in a hurry. The mother puts her hand on Jenny's rear and gently guides the child onto the front seat. When the child starts to cry, the mother hugs the child. If crying continues, the child is hugged harder. The crying will stop unless the child is in physical pain before the mother starts hugging. When the child is old enough to understand, the parent should say, "Show me what is the right thing to do."

Going to Sleep

Have the youngster talk about what was enjoyed during the day. By reflecting on something good, the child will go to sleep in a pleasant mood. In addition, have the youngster talk while lying down because more effort will be exerted than if the youngster were sitting or standing up. After the child finishes, speak or read in a soft volume. Exerting effort by talking and then relaxing by listening prompts sleepiness.

Cleaning Up

To have your three-year-old pick up toys, make a game out of the activity. Play some music and dance. You pick up one item and say,

"Where does this go?" Or say something like, "You pick up a little thing and I'll pick up a big thing." Then switch. You find something small and the child finds something big. Or make a parade, and pick up something and march over to the shelf where the item goes. Or just pick up all the red things. Then ask the child to find a new color to put away. Or you can say, "How many can we pick up before the music goes off?"

Actually, almost any goofy thing you can think of will usually motivate a three-year-old. Then when the room is clean, survey the success by asking the child a reflective question. "Wow! Look at this beautiful room! How does it feel to have such a clean room?" Or, "How does it feel to get a job all done?"

Getting Dressed

Getting a youngster to dress is a challenge for many parents, as this communication to me describes:

> I'm having a problem dressing my five-year-old son. He often takes a very long time to get dressed in the morning. We give him 20 minutes, which we know is ample because when he's motivated he can do it in 3 minutes flat. Yet 20 minutes later he's still only half dressed, having been distracted by toys, books, a dripping faucet, an ant on the floor, or just about anything. This behavior is making my husband late for work every morning. We've tried taking the offending toy or book away from him, but we can't take away the world.
>
> When I talk with him about coming up with possible solutions, all he says is "I don't know" or suggests unreasonable solutions like having me come in every minute to remind him. (I'm doing that already and it's not helping!) He's even suggested that I yell at him. He did suggest letting him eat breakfast first before getting dressed, but it didn't help. He'd eat and then waste time afterward. I've pointed out that his behavior is Level B, and by doing so he's asking to be bossed. His response is that he wants to be bossed. So now what? How do I get someone to *want* to move beyond Level B?

My response to the parent follows:

> As you indicated, continued operation on Level B indicates the need for using authority. Since you have already explained this to your son, emphasize that his not getting dressed indicates that he's not acting in a mature way and that you'll have to direct him until he can raise himself up to a higher level. Let him know that you know that he is capable of doing this himself. However, as a mother you must be consistent in how you deal with him. Unless he takes responsibility for acting his age, you will have to teach him how to dress as if he were a three- or four-year-old. This means that you will lead him around through all the steps just as you would a much smaller child. But you will also have to treat him in other ways such as using a high chair and having him play in a crib as younger children do. Give him a day to think about how he wants to be treated and then follow up on his decision. (Psychologists refer to this approach as paradoxical in that the choice offered is not the one the client—think youngster here—would choose.)

Problem at Mealtime

Having children eat as adults do is oftentimes frustrating.

A request was posed to me:

> My four-year-old granddaughter creates hell at lunch and dinner. Your suggestions would be appreciated.

I responded:

> Mealtime should be a pleasant experience, but with preschoolers it is often the opposite. Here are my recommendations:
>
> - Allow no eating between meals.
>
> - Serve small portions.
>
> - Set a kitchen timer for 10 minutes. While you are there with her, do not prompt her to eat in any way. The timer will do that for you. If she finishes eating before the 10 minutes are up, acknowledge her for doing so. If she does not, lead her away from

the table and let her know that she may eat at the next meal. She will not starve and will be ready to eat next time.

- Repeat the procedure if necessary.

Be Creative

Every morning when it was time to go to school, Jared would rush out the door leaving the room a mess with clothes all over the floor. His mother was stuck either yelling for him to come back and pick up his clothes (and feeling guilty about making him late for school) or fuming and getting on him when he came home from school (and feeling awful because it seemed useless to be so upset).

One day, the mother actually helped Jared hurry off to school on time with a warm smile and a happy wave. She then went into the room, took a pair of pants off the floor, and hung them from the ceiling light fixture. She walked out and shut the door behind her. When the boy came home, his mother met him pleasantly. When he eventually went to his room, he hollered, "Hey! What are my pants doing hanging from the light?"

The mother blithely replied, "They were on the floor. I hung them on the light." The stunned Jared said, "Well, what's that supposed to mean?" His mother replied, "It doesn't mean anything."

A week later the boy was still repeating to his friends, "You won't believe my mother. She hung my pants on the light!" Even later, when the mother stuck her head in the door to be sure the boy knew what time it was, the boy piped up, "Don't worry, I'll hang them up." Needless to say, his mother grinned and thought, "What a great kid!"

Siblings Wanting Immediate Attention

Youngsters are impetuous. They want to know an answer immediately. One child wants one thing and another child wants something else. They try to back you into a corner. Give them your stock answer: "If you need to know right now, the answer is, 'Not yet!' But if I can think about it for a while, I might consider saying, 'Yes.'" Their usual response will sound something like, "Take all the time you want."

Reducing Noise Levels

As usual, being proactive by teaching a procedure is often the most effective approach, as indicated by the following:

> With my five-year-old, I do what Dr. Marshall suggested. I speak very softly and say, "If you can hear me, touch your nose. If you can hear me, touch your ears," and so on. After a minute it catches on.

Here is a technique you can use to communicate acceptable loudness levels:

> Level 0 – *Silence:* Raise your thumb and an index finger to form a zero.
>
> Level 1 – *Whispering:* Raise an index finger.
>
> Level 2 – *Speaking*, as in the volume used in conversation. Raise two fingers.
>
> Level 3 – *Playing*, as in the volume used outside in a game. (no visual necessary)

Weaning Off Rewards

So many parents and teachers believe that it is necessary to give young people a reward for doing the right thing that it is a challenging endeavor to stop the practice.

I was asked:

> How do I wean my five-year-old son from expecting rewards? He'll make his bed, straighten all his shoes, and hang up his clothes, all without being asked, and then he comes running up to me with a smiling face and says, "NOW can I have something?" Oh, boy! Have I turned his taking responsibility into a reward? Do I then say "no" and crush his attempt to do the right thing?

My response to the parent:

> Explain to him that there are things that a family does to make life smoother and more organized. When he has finished a chore, help him realize that he is a member of the family team and he has contributed to the well-being of the family. "Isn't it great that you made your own bed!" "How do you feel now that you did it yourself?" "Don't you

feel proud when you have helped the family by doing your own tasks so Mother doesn't have to do it for you?"

Here is a cute story about rewards in a classroom:

> I teach first grade, and sometimes just getting the kids to remember their folders and to sharpen pencils is a chore. I usually start out the year reminding them, nagging them, and finally giving up. THEY don't care if they have a folder or a pencil. I'm the only one who seems bothered. So I put a sticker chart in their folders and offer stickers and trips to the treasure box if they come prepared. I KNOW it's not helping, and it bothers me every day as I waste time on this activity, but at least they have pencils when we start to work.
>
> One day recently I was monitoring the kids' work. I commented to one boy about his pencil; it was really short and dull. He said it was all he had, but in his pencil holder on his desk there were three long, sharp pencils just sitting there. I asked him about those. He said, "But those are my sharp pencils! I don't use those. Those are just for getting stickers." It took me all year to realize that this kid had used the same sharp pencils EVERY DAY to get a sticker, but never once used them to write with. So much for external motivation transferring to internal motivation!

OLDER YOUTH

Focus on the objective of parenthood, which is to have your youngsters become independent so that by the time they are about 13 or 14 years old, you should be through *telling* them what to do. Of course they still need guidance, but it should be accomplished by persuasion—not coercion. Teenagers want to cut the umbilical cord, but at the same time they still want security. This is a challenge for both the teenager and the parent. Implementing the three practices is a very effective way to avoid the trap that teenagers (oftentimes unknowingly) create for the parent—who is also torn between giving wings and having the adolescent stay in the nest. The beauty of practicing the three principles is that you don't need to choose punishments or rewards; you don't need to alienate; you simply ask questions to elicit reflection. As one parent told me, *"First, I spent*

most of the time training myself—cleaning out the old questions that were
accusatory and judgmental and I replaced them with questions that elicit
thoughtful, honest responses."

Teenager and Dinner Cleanup

Having adolescents clean up after themselves is a real challenge
for many adults.

Here is a question I received:

> Last night I requested my 14-year-old daughter to assist
> me with work in the kitchen unloading the dishwasher
> and loading it again with dirty dishes. She said she would
> do it but had her own timetable as to when she was going
> to do it. She said in five minutes and continued to watch
> television. By then I had already requested her help four
> or five times. Suddenly, out of sheer fatigue and irritation
> (I am diabetic and sometimes I express myself this way
> out of exhaustion!), I yelled at her that I needed it to be
> done "right now." She yelled back at me!
>
> Upon reflecting, I thought maybe I could have han-
> dled it more calmly. But I am unable to impress upon
> both my daughter and husband that I need help in the
> household chores because I am unable to cope with the
> stress. I do explain this need to them very calmly and they
> listen to me, but when it actually comes to action, we all
> lose it. I would appreciate any insight you can shed on my
> situation and advice you can give me on handling this.

My response follows:

> First, a word needs to be said about "losing it" (becoming
> emotionally hijacked). Review the traffic signal example
> in Chapter 7. Practice the impulse management technique
> visualizing a traffic light with the red on top *(stop and take*
> *a deep gasp),* yellow in the middle *(think of your options),* and
> green at the bottom *(go with your choice).* Practice it a few
> times a day. Then when a situation arises when you may
> become emotionally hijacked, the neural connections to
> stop it from happening will already have been partially
> established. The more you practice this, the easier it will
> be for you to prevent yourself from "losing it."

Ask your daughter what she suggests. Be willing to listen to her ideas. If you can live with her suggestions, give them a try. Remember that the key to changing someone else's behavior very often starts with a change in our own. Assuming that you shop for dinner, prepare the meal, serve the meal, and clean up after the meal, other members can share some of what you are doing. The following may be very difficult for you, but offer it anyway. Let others know that you will continue to shop, prepare, and serve, but you will only clean your own dishes. Have a family discussion explaining the procedure you have established. Of course, another approach is to *elicit* which part of the meal others prefer to participate in—aside from the eating.

Resolving Conflicts between Two Teenagers
Conflicts between teenagers are inevitable.

I received the following:

> I have two sons, ages 13 and 15. They fight all the time. It's not just a punch here and a shove there; it escalates to a down-and-out brawl! My older son tells me that I favor the younger. I try to be fair, but my older son likes to "pick, pick, pick" at the younger one. My younger son has a quick-fire temper; he just can't ignore the "picking." He retaliates. When they each tell me how a fight started, they both have a different story. Whom do I believe? How can I stop the fighting, and how can I make them respect me again? The stress of these daily fights is affecting my health. It can't be good for them either.

I suggested that the next time a fight occurs, have each of them write down his version of how the fight started and also a solution to prevent it from occurring again. *The guidelines are that each brother can only say what he himself will do or refrain from doing in the future.* After you read their little assignment, have the brothers read each other's paper out loud to each other—with no interruptions allowed. This will help each to understand the viewpoint and feelings of the other. The brothers are not "released" until they come to agreement on how to prevent a future incident. Then elicit from them a procedure or consequence if they do not live up to what *they* have decided.

Regarding respect for you, inform the boys that they diminish respect for themselves when they do not respect your desires. Then, absolutely do not tell them what to do or not do. Simply ask, "What would a responsible person do in this situation? What will you choose to do next time?"

Curfew

Although some parents feel no need to set a time when young people should be home, others believe it is a necessity. The following letter I received may be of assistance:

> Your approach has helped me to be more of a human being with my children. I also appreciate what it has done for my personal life. My savvy teens catch on quickly. It really has helped us deflate some escalating situations. I've become a better mom, guiding my daughter to make better choices. For example, when she started dating, she wanted to know what the rules were. (All of her friends' parents mandated a bunch of rules for dating.) I asked her what kind of rules she thought teenagers needed. I kept asking, "What else?" until she had named those that were important to us. I asked her to tell me what problems she might encounter and how she thought she might solve them.
>
> Finally, she asked me, "Mom, what's my curfew?" I asked her what she thought was a reasonable time. Glory be, she gave me a time that was an hour EARLIER than I would have set! The best part was that she set the curfew. As time went by, and she showed respect for the curfew by honoring it, I've increased the curfew by 30 minutes until we are now at the time I would have set. She's only been more than 10 minutes late two times, and both times she called 10 minutes earlier to tell me.
>
> I've noticed that she comes to me more frequently for guidance since I've started asking her reflective questions. She doesn't seem to mind when I ask who, what, where, when, etc., about things she wants to do.

Getting to Bed

For optimum growth, young bodies need good nutrition, exercise, and sufficient sleep. Sometimes this last requirement becomes the most challenging.

This new way of thinking has made bedtime more peaceful at our house. Of my three kids, I have two still at home. One is 16 and he was born an adult. You know the type. We've never had to encourage him to be responsible; he just came that way. He basically does a good job of looking after everything he needs to look after without reminders from adults and he makes our life easy in that respect. Now, my youngest son, aged 13, on the other hand, is just the opposite. He provides me with plenty of opportunities to use the system.

In our house, we've always had a set bedtime that was decided by an adult until each child was of seventh-grade age. About that age, it just seemed that they started to want more independence and also seemed old enough to handle choosing their own bedtime. Both my older kids slipped into this routine easily. They occasionally stayed up too late, but through experience they seemed to come to the conclusion that they felt better if they went to bed at a reasonable hour, so bedtime was never really an issue with them. My youngest son, however, doesn't seem to learn as quickly from experience as the other two. Being inconvenienced by his own lack of responsibility and self-discipline doesn't seem to bother him in the least. For instance, frequently he's down to almost no clothes to wear because he leaves them all over town, and I don't know how many times he's been locked out of the house after school, dying to use the bathroom and starving to death simply because he rarely bothers or remembers to return the key to the outdoor hiding spot after he uses it. Just a few weeks ago, at the end of school, he had to withdraw very nearly his whole life savings to pay for a social studies textbook that he carelessly lost—just one of several textbooks that somehow were misplaced during the year. As is his style, he was quite happy to turn over the money, not really upset in the least. His general philosophy of life seems to be "easy come, easy go." He will never have an ulcer. (Just as an aside, wouldn't you know it, as he went into the school office to pay his considerable debt, he met his English teacher who remarked that a social studies book had been left in her classroom and since she didn't know whom it belonged to, he might check it out. Of course, it was his. In the end he never had to part with his $65 after all. Darn it! There goes another great learning opportunity. This kind of luck happens to him all the time.)

He never seemed to figure out that if you go to bed late at night, early morning risings for practices and school aren't pleasant (not for him and certainly not for me). So, as we switched over to daylight saving time and the evenings got lighter, he became increasingly more tired and ornery (not to mention how ornery I was getting).

My automatic "re-action" (an action that I was simply acting out over and over again) was to badger him to go to bed by trying to convince him of his need for sleep. The more I suggested and nagged and reminded him to go to bed, the more insistent he became that he WASN'T tired and so didn't need to go to bed. After awhile, I started to wake up to the fact that we had quite an ineffective pattern going. So I took time to think about it a bit. Hmmm, what would Marv do? Well, I was sure he would ask me:

"Are you employing the three practices of positivity, choice, and reflection?"

"Not at all," I would have to reply!

1. Going to bed was becoming a very negative evening ritual between the two of us. I was annoyed and frustrated and he was uncooperative and somewhat defiant.

2. He felt that since he was supposed to be able to choose his own bedtime, I shouldn't be trying to take away his choice in the matter. (He was right. I was trying to take away his choice in the matter because as far as I

was concerned, he wasn't making the right choice; so I had better make the choice for him.) The less choice he felt he had, and the more he felt I was trying to impose a bedtime (which I was), the more resistant and uncooperative he became. A downward spiral!

3. Instead of asking him questions that would lead him to reflect, I was telling him what I thought he should do. This felt like coercion to him (and of course that's what it was). Although my intentions were good—I only wanted to help him feel well rested in the morning—my method was ineffective.

In addition to not employing the three practices at all, I realized that I was not being proactive. Instead, I was always waiting till late at night to deal with the situation by reacting to the fact that he hadn't gone to bed when I thought he should have. So, from there it was pretty obvious what to do.

I began being proactive by dealing with the issue before it became a REAL issue, trying to get rid of negativity surrounding bedtime, ensuring that my son felt that he had a real choice in terms of when he went to bed, and asking questions that would make him think about the positive benefits of being well rested.

Things have greatly improved, and it was really very simple. Early each evening, before either my son or I were tired and while bedtime seemed still a long way off with plenty of free time yet to come, I simply started asking him a nonchalant question or two such as, "Don't you have a basketball practice tomorrow morning?" "What time do you have to get up?" and then a few minutes later, "What time do you think you'll have to go to bed tonight in order to feel well rested tomorrow?" Not every time, but most often, he would come up with the same bedtime that I was thinking to myself would be a good choice. And not every time, but most often, he would get himself into bed by that time without waiting for me to tell him to do so.

The three practices really do work. The challenge is to remember to use them!

Stealing/Borrowing

Some parents have more challenging problems with adolescents than other parents. It is critical to understand that *you are not responsible for your children's behavior. Their behavior is theirs, not yours, and they are responsible for their own behavior.* Yes, you influence them by your modeling and your relationships with them—along with many other factors. However, there are many influences over young people for which *you* have no control.

I received the following request for assistance:

> This is an embarrassing situation for me. I have a strange problem with my son that I have never heard about before. He is 15 years old and has been stealing my clothes or his sister's clothing and cutting them up into little pieces with scissors or cutting our underwear into a thong. We have had him seeing a psychiatric therapist for over a year, with no resolution to this problem. He seems to do this without any warning or reason. I can't link it to anger at us, although he may just not be expressing his anger. It seems like an act of anger. He doesn't talk or express his emotions much at all.
>
> I have required him to earn the money to buy us new clothing to replace the items he destroyed, but that has not stopped him from doing it again. Is there anything you can suggest?

I responded that situations out of the ordinary are occurring all too often with today's youth. Start by completely stopping all forms of coercion. Have a conversation with your son letting him know that when he feels pressure from you, he is to let you know—so that you will be aware of it. But keep your standards. When he does something that is not acceptable, simply say in a calm voice and relaxed body, "That is not acceptable. What do you suggest we do about it?" Notice that rather than imposing a consequence you are *eliciting* one. Also, focus on a procedure he can use when he gets the urge again. If he says, "I don't know." Reply with, "What would an extraordinary person think of?" If you are still not successful, encourage him to share with one of his friends or counselor what he has done and suggest that they might help him come up with a procedure that may assist him.

He won't want to take you up on this, but you have reinforced the idea that only by establishing and practicing a procedure will he be able to redirect his impulses.

POINTS TO REMEMBER

◆ An understanding of gender differences assists in solving problems.

◆ Sibling squabbles are best solved by the participants themselves, rather than by parents.

◆ Giving allowances aimed at managing finances should not be confused with chores.

◆ Parents are always teaching simply by the fact that they are modeling for children.

◆ Getting a youngster to go to sleep, clean up, get dressed, eat at mealtime, reduce noise levels, and other challenges are solved without stress when parents aim at establishing procedures and eliciting consequences, rather than forcing and controlling.

◆ No one can change another person. People are the way they are, and if you want to change someone else, the change always starts with yourself—what you will do differently.

PART III
Additional Assistance
Summary and Conclusion

We are always influencing children by what we say and do.
We are always modeling for them.

SUMMARY

Sharing the hierarchy's levels of development with a focus on the difference between external and internal motivation (the difference between Levels C and D) is a simple way to promote responsible behavior. The reason is that young people learn the difference between doing something to please others (external motivation) and doing something because it is the right thing to do (internal motivation).

Chapter 7 offers additional suggestions and examples that foster both social and personal responsibility. The suggestions in Chapter 8 dealing with increasing effectiveness and improving relationships help promote your desired behaviors in others. Chapter 9 deals with questions in three sections. The first section applies to children of all ages. The second section deals with young children—preschoolers and those of elementary ages. The third deals with older youth.

CONCLUSION

The nature of childhood has dramatically changed in the last few generations. Young people spend time in front of the television, a passive activity that robs them of playtime and imagination. Hours are spent in front of computers. These types of activities—relying on technology—are often lone activities in that people generally engage in them by themselves. Learning about personal relationship skills and developing social intelligences are largely ignored. In contrast to former generations, young people today are more independent, more anxious, more impulsive, more disruptive, and more disobedient. To many parents, youth today seem like a real pain.

Although the young today are different, they aren't worse.

Current generations are not like any other in history. "New features" such as multi-tasking (really multi-switching); technology-savvy skills; and "social networking" without in-person, face-to-face communications are not what former generations experienced. Young people today believe that their role is just as important as anyone else's role—that they are equal to anyone. And they have the presumption that things should be explained or justified to them. Especially with teenagers, if they feel that they *have* to do something, they don't want to do it. Recent generations are more apt to cut and run if there is no challenge or satisfaction from an activity.

We cannot make our children experience what we have experienced in our own younger years. However, we still need to promote those basic values we cherish—such as responsibility, integrity, and perseverance—in ways that they understand and that fit with their nature, their environments, and their experiences.

It should be apparent that as much as we may desire it, society will never revert to the past. It should also be clear that traditional approaches of coercion, force, and domination are ineffective with many young people today.

The next section, Part IV, describes traditional approaches. The chapters explain how rewarding, imposing punishments, and telling youngsters what to do are less effective than approaches shared in earlier chapters.

PART IV
Parenting Pitfalls

Rewarding
Expected Behavior

Imposing Punishments

Telling

INTRODUCTION
Parenting Pitfalls

If discipline is stressful or unsuccessful,
external approaches may be the problem.

Traditional approaches use *external* motivators in attempts to change behavior. They aim to obtain obedience and compliance. These approaches focus on telling young people what to do, rewarding them if they do as expected, and threatening or punishing them if they don't. From the young person's point of view, rewards and punishments are often perceived as being unfair—a valid feeling. It is almost impossible to give rewards and use punishments in a consistent, fair, and just manner. What is fair to one is often perceived as being unfair to another. An additional shortcoming of aiming at obedience becomes apparent as young people grow and spend less time under the direct supervision of parents; they increasingly will do what *they want* to do.

The following testimony illustrates this point:

> Our son started having difficulties in school in the intermediate years (grades 4 and up). He had attention and impulse control problems. We wanted to find solutions and so we worked very hard to support the school. Thinking we would see big changes, we did as the teachers and principal suggested. We prided ourselves on being consistent and always following through. Although I'm no longer proud of it, I have to tell you that as incidences at school occurred, we imposed consequences, threatened the withdrawal of activities, punished, and bribed.
>
> However, things didn't improve. Even more distressing, the wonderfully close relationship we had with our son was being destroyed. The more we used these

tactics, the more he withdrew from us. Our happy, loving, and easy-going child was becoming increasingly
angry and frustrated; he no longer viewed us as being
on his team.

Once we started using the *Raise Responsibility System,*
the situation improved. When incidences occurred, we
had a positive approach to deal with them. Our relationship with our son healed and we were able to truly
support him in facing and overcoming challenges. The
system gave us back our close, loving relationship with
our son.

As you can see from this experience, the external approach of
coercing children to behave appropriately by using punishments
and rewards requires too high a price. Although the *theory* seems
plausible and effective, in practice external manipulators are
counterproductive by increasing stress and diminishing good
relationships.

The traditional approach based on a belief that *external* motivation—motivation coming from someone or something outside of
oneself—will *cause* a person to correct or change behavior is a myth.
External tactics are various forms of manipulation, pressure, or coercion. They vary from "hard" to "soft." A "soft" approach seeks obedience by bribing children with rewards. A "hard" approach might
look like that of a drill sergeant. When a child acts irresponsibly, the
parent seeks to alter the child's behavior by imposing a consequence
that is often painful or unpleasant—hoping that the discomfort will
prevent the child from repeating the offense. Parents who rely on
punishments and rewards are limiting themselves as well as their
children with these unsophisticated and ineffective approaches.
Manipulation is not long lasting. Coercion, in particular, *never*
prompts a youngster to *want* to do what the adult desires.

A coercive approach is never joyful. It may be temporarily satisfying to the punisher, yet it has little long-lasting effect on the person
being coerced. It is something done *to* another person. This is in
contrast to collaboration—working *with* a person. Nothing that is
imposed has a long life because the person doesn't have any ownership in it. If these external motivational approaches were effective,
irresponsible behaviors would be a mere footnote to parenting,

rather than a leading cause of stress. *The irony of coercion is that the more you use it in an attempt to control others, the less real influence you exert over them.* Clearly, coercion breeds resentment. In addition, if children behave because they are forced to behave, the parent has not really succeeded. True responsibility means behaving appropriately because people *want* to—not because they *have* to.

Here is the paradox: We want to assist young people to be self-disciplined and responsible. Both traits require *internal* motivation. Yet, rewards and punishments are external motivators and *place the responsibility on someone else to instigate a change.*

The following three chapters describe external approaches that—as the stories and experiences in this book share—are not nearly as successful as internal approaches of inducing young people to change themselves. Chapter 10 addresses rewarding young people for expected standards of behavior. Chapter 11 takes a close look at imposing punishments on the young. The book concludes with Chapter 12, the most common of parenting approaches—telling children what to do.

10
Rewarding Expected Behavior

The highest reward is not what young people get,
but rather what they become.

Punishments and rewards are two sides of the same motivational coin. Rewards ask, "What do they want me to do, and *what will I get for doing it*?" Punishments ask, "What do they want me to do, and *what happens to me if I don't*?" In both cases, the attempt is made to manipulate behavior by doing things *to*, rather than *with*, young people. At best, such approaches bring only temporary compliance. Most importantly, the foundations of both are based on consequences. Carrots are no more effective than sticks for helping young people make responsible choices and become moral and ethical adults.

As indicated at the outset, this book is the result of numerous requests for me to write a book especially for parents based upon my previous book, *Discipline without Stress® Punishments or Rewards: How Teachers and Parents Promote Responsibility & Learning*. The book is used in many college courses for those entering the teaching profession. However, many people entering teaching are still taught that it is essential to use external motivational approaches to foster responsible behavior. You decide if using such approaches uplifts and empowers students to behave responsibly.

Half of all people entering teaching leave the profession within five years. As studies have repeatedly shown, a major reason has to do with discipline. My point is that these external motivational approaches are not successful enough with too many of today's young people.

Here is a challenge: Inquire if an approach as in the following story is used in the school your child attends. If so, take the initiative (Level D) to make a significant impact on promoting responsible behavior by sharing the approaches in this book with the school.

The elementary school hired a substitute during the absence of the regular teacher.

Upon returning from lunch, a student asked if the class had earned a star to put on the bulletin board for the quiet way in which the class had returned.

The substitute didn't understand the request and asked about the procedure.

Another student explained that when students enter the classroom quietly, the teacher puts a star on the bulletin board. When a certain number of stars are reached, the class is given an afternoon without any work.

The substitute asked, "But aren't you supposed to walk quietly in the hall so that you don't disturb the other classes? Why should you earn a star for doing what is right?"

Students looked at each other, puzzled. Finally, one student explained, "We always get a reward. Why else should we do it?"

REASONS REWARDS ARE USED TO CHANGE BEHAVIOR

Rewarding young people for expected standards of behavior is counterproductive for promoting responsibility. Yet so many parents and teachers use rewards. Let's explore some of the reasons.

Rewards offer a seductively quick and easy way to create obedience. Asking a child to do something in order to gain a reward is an effective way to manipulate behavior in the short term. For example, promising, "If you sit here quietly for Mommy, in just a little while I'll buy you some ice cream," often produces the desired result. When the child suddenly chooses to behave, rewards can seem very effective. Candy, games, and movies can all be used to manipulate young people toward good behavior. But consider how long the effect lasts. The answer: only until the ice cream is gone, the candy swallowed, the game played, or the movie ended. Attitudes and commitment remain largely untouched.

Another reason rewards are so commonly used is that people believe that stimulus-response psychology is effective in changing human behavior. This approach is based on the theory that human beings can be motivated and trained like animals. Stephen Covey, in his book *The 8th Habit*, refers to this as "the Great Jackass Technique that motivates with a carrot in front (reward) and drives with a stick from behind (fear and punishment)." Humans—unlike animals— have the cognitive ability and power to choose. As Covey points out, you cannot buy someone's heart, mind, or spirit.

Along this same line of reasoning, many people have come to believe that the carrot and the stick are necessary. A teacher told me about a parent whose son was in her seventh-grade class. The father insisted that his son needed a positive note to bring home when he *didn't* make disruptive noises in class. A belief that a stimulus-response approach is necessary to change behavior is not unique to this parent. It is prevalent among many parents, teachers, and educational professionals. School districts—and even some states in the U.S.—have mandated programs that originated with helping special needs students because, as the theory goes, these learning disabled students need something concrete, something tangible, such as stickers, when something good is done. "Catch them doing something good and then reward them for it" has left an untold number of students punished because they also did "something good" but were not given the expected reward. This approach is a variation of the old behavior-modification approach designed to reinforce desired behavior by using rewards. In the process of using external manipulators for motivation, *intrinsic motivation for long-lasting responsible behavior is reduced*—as has been repeatedly proven.

People assume that an external manipulator, such as a reward, *causes* young people to change. But this is not true; people change because of a *decision* to do so. No amount of ringing Dr. Pavlov's bell would stimulate an animal to drink if it were not thirsty. Besides, Pavlov was no fool; he used dogs rather than cats, which, like people, are much more independent.

REWARDS AND COMPENSATION

Rewards are often confused with compensation—the argument being that people will not work unless they receive a reward. Salaries in the job marketplace are contractual agreements of *compensation for service*. They are not bribes to manipulate behavior. When was the last time you looked at your paycheck and thanked your employer for the reward?

Of course, if the compensation were not satisfactory, the person may choose to look elsewhere. As an aside, many studies have shown that "merit pay" is a poor motivator and low on a list of employee priorities. Rewards like these also create more problems than they solve, which is a prime reason they rarely last for any length of time. Merit pay, for example, requires competition between employees. *Collaboration among individuals* is more effective for improved efficiency, relationships, and employee morale than *competition between individuals*—not to be confused with competition between *teams*.

Although reduced compensation for work can affect motivation, the opposite is not true. Increased compensation does not increase motivation. Answering the following question can assess money as a motivating force: *"Would you work harder if you were paid more?"* Similarly, *"Would you work harder if you were paid as a parent?"*

REWARDS AS INCENTIVES

Rewards can serve as great incentives. This is true in all situations—whether it is a salesperson reaching a goal, a pieceworker paid for production, a student working to earn good grades, or someone participating in a contest. However, if the reward for winning a contest is a cruise and you are prone to severe seasickness, chances are that the reward would not be much of an incentive. The point is simple: *In order for a reward to work as an incentive, the person must be interested in the reward.*

In school, the incentive of receiving a good grade may prompt a student to pay attention in class, concentrate more, complete homework assignments, and do whatever else is necessary to receive that reward. But schools have great numbers of students who do *not* believe that receiving a good grade is important. Good grades are not in their "quality world," to use a phrase from psychiatrist William Glasser. Put more simply, a good grade is not an incentive for *them*. This realization helps parents as well as teachers understand the reason some young people do not expend energy to improve their grades. Of course, rather than grades, *learning* should be the incentive. Jerome Bruner made the point in his classic *The Process of Education,* in which he states, "Ideally, interest in the material to be learned is the best stimulus to learning, rather than such external goals as grades or later competitive advantage," and "the goal should be to help students experience success and failure—not as reward or punishment—but as information."

If a good grade or any other reward is not important to the person, it has little value as an incentive. In sum, *rewards—of any kind—are effective incentives only if the person is interested enough to work toward achieving them.* The following story is a vivid example of this, shared with me by a school principal after my presentation at a conference of the National Association of Elementary School Principals:

> The father of a fifth-grader rewarded his son with $5 for each A on the boy's report card. During the first grading period the child received eight A's and $40 from his father.
>
> The second grading period ended in January, and report cards went home at the beginning of February. This time the father was quite upset; his son's grades had dropped to only one A, two B's, and the rest C's.
>
> In a conference with the father, I suggested to call the son into the office to see what the problem was. The boy came in, sat down, and we began to talk. My first question was, "How is it that your grades have slipped so much this grading period?" The boy quickly replied, "I didn't need the money."
>
> I saw the father slump in the chair.

REWARDS AS ACKNOWLEDGMENTS

Rewards can serve as wonderful acknowledgments—ways of congratulating and demonstrating appreciation. "Employee of the Month," "Parent of the Year," and "Oscar-winning actor" are examples of such acknowledgments. They are worthy of celebration. But notice that these are awarded *after* the behavior and not as bribes beforehand, as in, "Do this and you'll get that."

REWARDS CHANGE MOTIVATION

External rewards change motivation, as the following indicates:

> An elderly gentleman spent each afternoon tending his large garden on his corner lot. A group of 10-year-olds began harassing him on their way home from school.

After a few days of hearing their jeers and insults, he decided to act.

The next day as the boys turned the corner and approached his house, he met them. The gentleman told the youths that he lived alone and was enjoying the attention they were giving him. To show his appreciation, he told them that if they continued the following day, he would give them each a dollar. Amazed and excited, the boys showed up right after school the next afternoon. They shouted at the elderly man with epithets and jeers as he was working in his front garden.

True to his word, the man put down his gardening tools, walked over to the youngsters, and pulled out a roll of dollar bills from his pocket. He handed each boy a dollar and encouraged a repeat the next day. He told them that he would give each a quarter for their efforts. He again informed his antagonists that he was enjoying their attention.

They came back the next day and again started to call him rude names and were quite disrespectful. The elderly gentleman put down his gardening tools and walked over to the boys with a roll of quarters and again paid off his hecklers. He then announced that in the future, he would give them a penny for their efforts.

Do you think the boys came back?

The sly gentleman's plan was elegantly simple. *By rewarding the boys, he changed their motivation* from that of harassing him for the fun of it to the motivation of getting a reward. As soon as a meaningful reward was gone, so were the boys.

Research studies consistently show that *when Level D motivation is repeatedly reinforced with Level C–type recognition, there is a greater likelihood that in the future, the internal motivational level will actually drop* to that of Level C. For example, studies show that children rewarded or praised for demonstrating caring and kind behavior will actually exhibit *less* genuine caring and kindness in the future, which of course is *not* what the well-meaning adults intended at all.

REWARDS TO PROMOTE RESPONSIBLE BEHAVIOR

When we give young people rewards for appropriate behavior, we are sending a false message. In the world outside of home and school, no one receives a reward for doing what is appropriate and expected. Rewards are not given for paying bills on time or standing in line in a respectful manner.

Giving rewards to encourage children to behave in ways that are *expected in a civil society* gives the impression to young people that, as they get older, society will continue to reward them for such behavior. This simply is not the case. When was the last time you were given a reward for stopping at a red light?

A major concern that results when people are rewarded for responsible behavior is that *the cost inevitably increases.* Although candy may induce a 5-year-old to behave appropriately, persuading a 15-year-old will cost much more.

The hidden message sent when we reward expected standards of behavior is that being good for its own sake is not reason enough. Giving rewards for good behavior teaches children that if they are good they will receive something in return. This leads young people to eventually realize that being good can be bargained or bartered and, in a very broad sense, has commercial worth. This type of attitude is reflected in remarks such as, "If I'm good, what will I get?" and "What's in it for me?" *Any sense of moral development or social responsibility is lacking in this type of mindset.* Whether a behavior is good or bad, right or wrong, just or unjust, moral or immoral—are values not considered. Winning the prize becomes the incentive, pushing aside important questions such as, "Is this good?" "Is this a responsible thing to do?" and "Is this both good for me and considerate of others?" *Rewarding appropriate behavior implies that such behavior is not inherently worthwhile* and gives the false value: "What I am doing must be good because I am being rewarded for it."

When we give rewards for expected behavior, we create the problem of *entitlement* so common in today's young generation. It gives them a false sense of security—a bubble that will certainly burst when they are on their own in the "real" world.

Finally, and perhaps most importantly, by employing a behavior-modification approach of using rewards that young people value (candy, stickers, etc.), we reinforce *their* values. In the process, we lose opportunities to pass on *our values*. What we really should be doing is fostering those values that promote responsible behavior, bring long-term satisfaction, and promote civic characteristics that can last a lifetime.

SELF-ESTEEM

It was a common belief that external rewards provided an effective way to increase a young person's self-esteem. Yet the self-esteem movement had such disappointing returns that one rarely hears about the topic. The fatal flaw of the movement was the mistaken belief that *external* approaches could increase *internal* self-talk.

Self-esteem is an outgrowth of *self-talk*. Self-acceptance and self-improvement are the key requirements. These are built and attained through success and continual progress. This is especially the case when the person attempts something that is difficult or challenging. For example, when an infant is learning how to walk, it is through much effort and perseverance—through achievement—that brings success, self-satisfaction, and increased self-esteem. It is the result of *effort* and *mastery*, rather than from any external reward.

ADDITIONAL CONSIDERATIONS ABOUT REWARDS

Rewards Can Be Counterproductive

When a parent praises child "A" while child "B" is not praised for the same or similar behavior, this "reward" can become counterproductive. "I really like the way 'A' is helping us," is not doing sibling "B" a service. In fact, the exact opposite can occur. Not only can children see the attempt to manipulate behavior, but "A" is also not endeared to sibling "B." On the contrary, "A" feels resentful. In addition, if the child is the type who is embarrassed by the recognition, then that child feels punished by the parent's comment. Along the same lines, *it is not uncommon for a parent to compliment a child whose behavior has improved only to have the child immediately misbehave again.* Some children simply do not like to be pointed out—or the comment contradicts the self-image of the child, who then attempts to reinforce the usual self-perception by acting out the usual behavioral pattern.

Rewards Can Promote Failure

Rewards open the possibility of failure—failure to obtain the reward and failure to please the parent. In addition, the possibility of failure inherently brings *fear of failure*. When a child is afraid, the emotion is so powerful that thinking and effort are diminished.

Rewards Can Diminish Self-Confidence

Giving rewards on a regular basis can prompt youngsters to think the only things that are important are those for which they are rewarded. The result can be a diminished appreciation and disregard for their natural talents and preferences. Trusting their own decisions is also diminished along with their own perceptions and intuitions. They may begin to question their own choices and preferences.

Rewards Infer an Unpleasant Task

Why would someone take the trouble to set up a reward unless the task would be difficult or unpleasant? Offering rewards works against the satisfaction that comes from the diligence and perseverance of completing such tasks. When helping a child to learn something challenging, it is far better to stay focused on the satisfaction from the task. For example, helping a child learn the importance of keeping one's room orderly and clean would mean helping the child to appreciate the *inherent* rewards: ease of finding wanted items, avoidance of breakage and accidents, and the fact that there is simply a good feeling in an orderly environment. Also, when focused on this approach of satisfaction from the task, you are more inclined to work with the child. You and your child are working in collaboration. Both can contribute ideas to make certain projects easier. When external rewards are used, you are more likely to feel that the child must perform the task alone.

Rewards Redirect Satisfaction

Giving rewards for expected standards of behavior deprives children of the satisfaction that comes with doing what is socially responsible and right. The highest, most meaningful and significant reward is not what a person gets from outside of the self, but rather the satisfaction and joy that he or she experiences within. These feelings are the result of taking the initiative to do the right thing, rather than because something externally is received. Even more important is the consideration of what the young person *becomes*: *inner-directed and responsible* vs. *outer-directed and dependent on others.*

Rewards Affect Character Development

The use of rewards has a damaging effect on character development. Studies at the University of Toronto and Arizona State University show that external rewards for socially responsible behaviors are associated with *less* commitment for helping, caring, and sharing over the long haul.

Rewards Change the Focus of Self-Development

Many of the founding fathers of the United States had a mindset for improvement. Benjamin Franklin, George Washington, Thomas Jefferson, and countless others focused inwardly. They believed that by improving themselves, society itself would gain. In recent years with the litigious nature of our society, victimhood thinking, and a focus on things outside of the individual, the inherent struggle for self-improvement has become diminished. For example, school drives to clean up the environment and provide service to others is an important contribution to society. However, something is lost when the focus becomes "being a good person" *because of this type of activity.* You can see this, for example, when a youngster engages in a service such as cleaning up an area full of trash but is mean or disrespectful to others. Focus on the "outside" too often comes at the expense of improving the "inside."

POINTS TO REMEMBER

◆ Rewards are wonderful *acknowledgments.*

◆ A reward can serve as an effective incentive *only if the person is interested in the reward.*

◆ Rewards should not be confused with a salary, which is compensation for service.

◆ Rewarding young people for acting appropriately is counterproductive to promoting responsibility.

◆ A prime point to remember about the use of rewards is that they change motivation.

◆ Rewards do not help children become more moral or ethical because rewards do not change attitudes or commitments.

◆ Rewards foster competition, rather than cooperation, and are counterproductive to the establishment and maintenance of a friendly and kind home atmosphere.

◆ Although rewards may seem kinder than punishments, they are simply *another external approach* that leads away from the goal of promoting *responsibility*.

11
Imposing Punishments

Punishments are based on the belief
that you have to hurt to teach, to harm to instruct.

While punishment can sometimes succeed in forcing an immediate stop to irresponsible behaviors, viewed as a tool for creating lasting change for young people, punishments are ineffective. This is not an argument against society's use of punishments for *adults convicted of socially harmful behavior*. However, if you believe that a 5-, 10-, or 15-year-old is an adult, then it may seem natural to treat the young person's irresponsible behavior with similar punitive approaches. But if you believe, as I do, that *young people are not yet adults*, and we have a goal of leading them to become responsible members of society, then the use of punishments or *imposed consequences must be seriously questioned*. The focus needs to be kept clear here: We are talking about *young people*—not adults.

Young children are cute and we feel comfortable empowering them; we find it easy and it feels natural to communicate with them in positive ways. But we often treat them differently when the same children become adolescents. *Should we?*

If a youngster doesn't know how to ride a bike, we teach.

If a youngster doesn't know how to mow the lawn, we teach.

If a youngster doesn't know how to demonstrate good manners, we teach.

If an *adolescent* doesn't know how to behave, we teach? Or do we punish?

Few young people are maliciously non-compliant. Too often, instead of using a positive approach to promote responsible behavior, we resort to negative methods. Rather than resorting to punishing, we can create a positive mindset toward discipline that allows us to view inappropriate behaviors as an opportunity to teach—certainly a less stressful and far more effective approach.

If you wanted to teach a young person how to swing a baseball bat, play a musical instrument, or hit a nail with a hammer, it would never occur to you to use punishment as a way to help the youngster be successful. In such situations it seems obvious that you would teach and coach. By adopting the same attitude and choosing to think of children as *merely lacking skills*—rather than as being non-compliant when they make mistakes or misbehave—you will find it easy to respond in positive and constructive ways.

THE MYTH OF PUNISHMENTS

A common myth is that punishments are necessary to change young people's behavior. Prisons are full of *repeat* offenders. Schools have the same students reporting to detentions. As a parent, have you had an experience where a youngster had been punished and still repeated the same behavior? Although numerous reasons can be given for being repeatedly incarcerated, or being assigned detention at school, or being punished more than once for the same offense, the record clearly shows that *punishments do not change behaviors* with too many young people.

Some suggest that punishments are simply "natural consequences" or "logical consequences." However, *any* form of *imposed* punishment deprives the youngster of an opportunity to *take the responsibility for changing the behavior.* If the youngster has no part in the decision-making process to redress inappropriate behavior, a victimhood mentality is automatically established.

Few people would suggest returning to the pre-automobile times when the horse pulling the buggy was urged on by a flick of the whip or when information was pounded into students by the cane. The ineffectiveness of traditional approaches with 21st-century youth is not limited to just physical punishment. Approaches that deprive young people of their dignity are also not only ineffective but are counterproductive. This includes shaming, threatening, yelling, sarcasm, and labeling with derogatory names. Yet, even though today we have found better ways to parent, we often continue to use the horse-and-buggy approach to foster social responsibility when both society and the nature of youth have changed dramatically.

Punishments are based on the idea that *young people must experience pain* in order to grow into responsibility—*that they must be harmed in order to learn.* This premise suggests it is reasonable to expect that people whom we "intentionally hurt" will then *want* to respond in a constructive manner. Human nature doesn't work this way. Can you ever recall a time when you *felt bad,* yet were happily prompted to do something *good* in response? When young people feel negative, they do not have positive, constructive thoughts. The significant point is emphasized: People do "good" when they feel good, not when they feel bad.

Parents may *force compliance* by imposing punishments, but this shortsighted approach will never *create commitment* in the long term. Punishments work against the very thing we are attempting to accomplish—to teach young people to be self-disciplined so that they will *want* to act in positive and socially appropriate ways.

One reason we keep thinking punishments work is that sometimes an irresponsible behavior stops as a result of a parent's punitive actions. This can be the case with very young children if the behavior is caught early before it becomes a habit *and* if the punishment itself is a novel experience. In such cases, though, we must consider whether or not the youngster understands exactly which action is being punished. The other scenario where punishments are "successful" is when the threat of punishment, or the punishment itself, is so terrifying to the youngster that the motivation is based in fear—fear of the punishment and often fear of the *punisher.* As you can imagine, this is not the optimum scenario for building good family relationships.

A friend wrote me the following:

> Your approach helped us prepare our son for the teenage years. He was fairly immature and tended to be a follower. Just thinking about approaching the teen years was terrifying to us. How were we going to keep our son safe? The answer was in your approach. The key element was self-reflection. It was through this process

that he learned to assess the choices he made and their impact on himself and others. Once we began to use the *Raise Responsibility System* and he was required to actually think about possible solutions and consequences, he became aware of the poor choices he was making. He was beginning to make better choices. Instead of reacting to "imposed" punishments, he was now actually learning the very skills he needed to be safe throughout the teen years. In the traditional model, the child is so busy being angry at the punishment and the punisher that there is no possibility of self-reflection. Without self-reflection, there is no possibility of learning from one's mistakes!

PROBLEMS WITH IMPOSED PUNISHMENTS

A major problem with *imposed* punishments is that their effect is only *temporary*. Fear and force produce only short-run changes. Once an imposed punishment ends, the youngster has "served his time" and feels "free and clear" from further responsibility. A coercive approach that works in the short run is rarely effective in the long run. Threatening a youngster with punishment may force compliance—but only as long as the threat is present. It does nothing to encourage responsible behavior or decision-making once the coercion is gone. The threat of punishment may pressure a child to act appropriately at home but have no effect on the way the child interacts with others outside the home—with a grandparent, daycare giver, or other children.

For example, a 10-year-old is placed in a situation where he is tempted to shoplift. All of his friends have been doing it and no one in the store is watching. The child whose parent uses imposed punishments has an easier time of it. If the youngster believes he won't get caught, why not go ahead? In contrast, the young person whose parents have encouraged the development of self-discipline will have a more difficult time. *For that young person, getting caught—getting punished—is not the issue. Using good judgment is.*

For this child, the thought of how his behavior affects others—the owner who has to pay for the merchandise, an innocent victim who might get accused of the theft, parents who may feel they have failed, and others involved in the young person's growth will be hurt by the breach of trust.

What a child will do when adults are not around—when there seems that there will be no consequences—is the measure of parental effectiveness.

Imposed Punishments Are Adult-Dependent

Rather than leading a child to responsibility and self-directed improvement, punishments rely on an adult to initiate any change. The paradox here is that the goal should be for the young person to take the initiative to be responsible. Yet punishments rely on the use of an external agent—someone who is not always around. Young people may learn to control themselves when an authority figure is present (often because they are afraid of the consequences if they do not) but *external motivation* does not promote a *desire* for better decisions or more socially acceptable behavior in the future.

Imposed Punishments Are Often Inconsistently Applied

An irresponsible behavior may be punished at one time but not at another. It is almost impossible to be consistent because the act for which the individual is being punished is only observable in the presence of the adult. In the case where an act is reported by someone else, there is no certainty that the act occurred as the other person reported it. The youngster may have an entirely different viewpoint of the situation.

Imposed Punishments Are Based on Avoidance, a Negative Response

Coercion triggers primal feelings of fear, fleeing, or fighting. Such emotions are counterproductive to learning (including learning to make more responsible choices) as well as to building close, loving relationships. Punishments automatically put the child and parent in adversarial roles, usually with predictable results: (1) The child tests the parent to see what he or she can get away with, and/or (2) the motivation to learn what the parent is trying to teach is diminished. Punishments are negative in that they kill motivation to act in positive ways, which is the very thing we are attempting to nurture.

Imposed Punishments Often Do Little to Modify Irresponsible Behavior

Imposed punishments often do nothing *to help* a young person learn to modify irresponsible behavior. Bad habits are best replaced with good ones, but punishments do nothing to teach young people *how* to make better choices. Instead, imposed punishments prompt youngsters to figure out how *not to get caught* the next time. Additionally, rather than focusing on improving behavior, the focus often becomes one of making excuses and covering one's tracks. Evasiveness increases rapidly under punishments—a sad situation in any family.

Imposed Punishments Foster Victimhood Thinking

Since punishments are based on the idea that a person needs to be hurt in order to learn, the person being punished often feels like a victim. Victims bear little accountability for their behavior, which is not the mindset for promoting personal and social responsibility.

Imposed Punishments Often Promote Aggressive Behavior

Imposed punishments can promote a vicious cycle. Aggressive behavior brings on punishment, which then promotes more aggressive behavior, bringing on more punishments, and so on. Children learn from models; they are great imitators. They learn by watching what their parents do. When punishments are inflicted on young people, they learn some things that perhaps parents may not intend their offspring to learn, such as:

- Might makes right.

- Using coercion and violence on those we love is legitimate.

- Physical force is acceptable to resolve problems.

Imposed Punishments Often Lead to Further Escalation

When punishments fail to work, inevitably more punishments are prescribed and the problems grow worse—with increasing stress for both adult and youngster. Such escalation is a common occurrence in schools, where, by the time some young people reach high school age, they have been talked to, lectured at, sent out of class, kept after school, referred to the office, referred to Saturday school, suspended in school, suspended from school—until they simply no longer care. In some homes, when parents find that a mild punishment does not bring the expected obedience they want, they allow themselves to become so frustrated and angry that they impulsively reach deeper into their arsenal for stronger approaches, sometimes tragically sinking to the level of violence.

Imposed Punishments Lose their Effectiveness

When youngsters are not afraid of punishments, the punishments lose their effectiveness to deter irresponsible behavior. A case in point is school detention. Often, students who are assigned detention as a punishment and who fail to serve it are punished with *more* detention. Yet, in the thousands of presentations I have conducted around the world, teachers who use detention rarely state that it is effective in changing behavior; the same students are repeatedly assigned to the detention room.

Imposed Punishments Can Trigger Low Self-Esteem

Imposed punishments can trigger very sensitive children to retreat into feelings of low self-esteem; they may actually begin to believe that they are "bad." This can lead to "self-punishment"—the worst and most severe type of punishment. In many cases, punishment is too often used with those who don't need it. Kahlil Gibran makes this point in *The Prophet* when he asks, "And how shall you punish those whose remorse is already greater than their misdeeds?"

Imposed Punishments Have Some Very Nasty Side Effects

Imposed or repeated punishments can generate anxiety, depression, unnecessary guilt, shame, self-pity, self-hatred, fear, anger, resentment, resistance, defiance, and even retaliation.

FINAL THOUGHTS ABOUT IMPOSED PUNISHMENTS

The real power, the real influence of parents is measured best *not* by what children do when a parent is *with* them—but rather by what children do when a parent is *not*.

The reality of imposed punishments is that *they bring feelings of satisfaction to the punisher but have little lasting effect on the punished.* This sad truth is expressed in a cartoon where a father is chasing after his son, strap in hand. The mother calls to her husband, "Give him another chance!" The husband yells back, "But what if he doesn't do it again?" If the youngster has learned *not* to do it again, why punish him? The fact is that punishments satisfy the emotions of the one inflicting the punishment. Punishments are reinforcing for the punisher because they seem to validate his or her dominance. Until the day a child is big enough to retaliate, the adult is dominant. At a subconscious level, this may be the primary motivation behind the parent's tendency to punish. *The punisher may be more interested in proving higher status than in improving behavior.* In essence, with punishments, the parent and child are engaged in a power struggle. The paradox of this situation is that the youngster knows which "button" to push to stimulate anger in the more powerful adult; when the adult demonstrates anger, the power desires of the youngster become satisfied.

When I was an assistant principal in charge of discipline at a large high school (3,200 students)—and as an elementary, middle, and high school administrator—I never once had a faculty member say to me or even insinuate that the goal was for the student in question to become more responsible. The underlying goal was always one of revenge or obedience. That's what imposed punishments do—*they satisfy the punisher much more than prompt any responsibility in the punished.*

The only time imposed punishments may be effective is when the person being punished (1) respects and cares for the person doing the punishing and (2) understands that the punishment is in his or her own best interest. But in the vast majority of cases, imposed punishments bring about enmity—not responsibility. They promote victimhood thinking and adversarial relationships. They create stress for both the punisher and the punished, and they rob parents of the joys of parenthood.

An important truth about many young people is that they dislike disappointing their parents—so much so that they would rather be punished than have their parents become disappointed in them. You can prove this to yourself by visualizing for a moment that, as a youngster, you did something you knew was wrong. You also knew that your parents found out about what you did. Which would have a more lasting effect on your future behavior: (1) being punished and thereby getting it over with and forgetting about it, or (2) not being punished and living with the feeling that you disappointed someone important in your life? When I ask this question in my seminars, an overwhelming number of participants choose the first option. The reason is that the feeling of disappointing someone we care about stays with us and prompts a negative feeling every time the thought arises.

POINTS TO REMEMBER

◆ A common myth is that imposed punishments are necessary to change young people's behavior.

◆ Imposed punishment comes out of our desire to control. Out of our desire to raise responsible citizens comes teaching and guidance.

◆ Despite succeeding in stopping irresponsible behavior in some cases, imposed punishments are ineffective with far too many young people as a method for helping them make lasting changes in their behavior.

◆ Imposed punishments have major problems. They:

- Are temporary

- Are adult-dependent rather than self-dependent

- Are inconsistently applied

- Are based on avoidance

- Lose their effectiveness over time

- Do nothing to help a young person learn to modify irresponsible behavior

- Foster victimhood thinking

- Promote aggressive behavior

- Often lead to further escalation

- Often trigger very sensitive children to retreat into feelings of low self-esteem and self-punishment

- Deprive the youngster of an opportunity to become more responsible

12
Telling

*If telling worked, children would do exactly what
you tell them to do the first time you tell them,
and you would not have to repeat yourself.*

We would like our children to gain from our experiences and our wisdom. Therefore, it seems only natural for us to *tell* our children what to do and what not to do since we want them to avoid negative experiences and to engage in appropriate activities. A misconception with this approach is that young people will learn from what we tell them. The truth is, they learn much more from what they see us *do. Modeling responsible behavior* is far more effective than telling as a strategy.

THE INEFFECTIVENESS OF TELLING

You can prove to yourself how ineffective and *stress-inducing* telling can be by reflecting on the statement, *"If I've told you once, I've told you…!"*

Telling and lecturing are generally ineffective with young people who are trying to assert their independence. Besides, when young people become adolescents, they become "experts" in everything. Just try telling a teenager something and see how far you get. This phenomenon is captured in a quotation attributed to Mark Twain:

> *When I was a boy of fourteen, my father was so ignorant that
> I could hardly stand to have him around. But when I got to
> be twenty-one, I was astonished how much he had learned in
> seven years.*

You can visualize the scene. You are talking to your teenage son and attempting to inform him of the disadvantages of what he wants to do. You make your case rather successfully. However, your youngster perceives the situation quite differently. Did you notice the glaze in his eyes? The youngster's self-talk is: "I'm being lectured again; my parent is trying to control me."

Trying to persuade adolescents by *telling them what to do or what not to do* is too often not only ineffective but it can actually become counterproductive if the advice is not followed. The following bears repeating and is considered a universal truth: When young people are *told* they *have* to do something, they *don't want* to do it. Using reason often has little effect; teenagers are, despite all of their insecurities, so sure that they know better and are always right!

I recall a friend sharing with me that he felt his mother was constantly telling him to do something. He hated it! Even when it was something he *wanted* to do, such as playing outside, simply because she *told* him to do it, he invariably found an excuse for not doing it. Think of how *you* feel when someone tells you that you *have* to do something; it prompts a negative feeling. In situations like this, our immediate self-talk often sounds like, "I don't like this" or "I'm *not* going to do that." The term for this *automatic reaction to perceived coercion* is known as "counterwill" (discussed in Chapter 3), and you should be continually aware of it.

PROBLEMS WITH TELLING

Telling has many negative effects. When you tell someone to do something, the inference is that what the person is doing is wrong or not good enough and that the person has to change. People often don't mind changing as much as they dislike attempts to *be* changed or controlled by others. Remember this key point: A change in behavior is as much *emotional* as it is intellectual. Negative emotions do not bring about positive changes.

Because telling is received as criticism, it often creates defensiveness and an immediate tendency to resist or engage in acts of doing the *exact opposite* of what one has been told to do. Even when a parent has an excellent relationship with a child, and even when the young person feels that the parent has the child's best interests at heart, well-intentioned lectures convey a subtle, negative message that often results in hard feelings.

When the parent does the telling, who does the *thinking*? If we want to be effective in promoting a change, the youngster, rather than the parent, should be doing the reflecting. Telling sends the message that we do not have faith in our children's decisions. Repeated lecturing erodes children's self-confidence in their own inner knowing. If youngsters perceive that their parents do not accept their decisions, they tend to make fewer decisions around the parents—with the result that the parents' faith in their children's abilities decreases even more, the lecturing begins anew, and another opportunity is lost.

The ineffectiveness of telling is well illustrated in *Enlightened Leadership* by Ed Oakley and Doug Krug:

> The employees went through the company's training program and were very successful for about a year and a half. After this period of time, sales dropped off, causing the company to complete a fairly intensive investigation. The training approach taught by the company showed how to ask specific kinds of questions, a process that created a bonding with clients. During the process, the salespeople not only learned about the clients' financial situations and future plans but also something about the people as individuals.
>
> After about 18 months, the salespeople began to anticipate the clients' responses and decided they could save some time by asking fewer questions and talking more themselves. Sales dropped off; the salespeople no longer bonded to the same degree with their prospective customers. When sales plummeted, the salespeople began talking even more. They began focusing on the fear of losing sales, became discouraged, and the downward spiral of performance went into full gear.
>
> Time that telling saved came at the expense of success.

SHARE INSTEAD OF TELL

Take a moment to think about a time when you were successful in getting something you really wanted from someone. Did you *tell* the person you wanted it, or did you *ask*? When we want something that is really important to us, we know better than to tell; it sounds too demanding.

Limiting your telling requires constant attention. The tendency to tell is most easily changed by replacing it with some other approach. Because young people are sensitive about being told what to do and because parental help is perfectly appropriate, focus on *sharing information*. Think of your advice as something to *inform*, to have the young person become aware of other possibilities or the consequences of their choices. The following are effective examples: "You may want to think about...." "Have you considered...." "I wonder what effect that will have on others!" Sharing does not carry the negative baggage of telling. Sharing ideas and information is not *coercive*. You may want to review Chapter 3 to hone the skill of asking reflective questions.

CONCLUDING THOUGHTS ABOUT TELLING

Telling—like punishing and rewarding—fails the critical test: *How effective is this approach when you are not around?* When you have told your youngster what to do or what not to do and you are not around, how will your child behave?

Also, remember that responsibility is always taken, never told. You will accomplish what you want more effectively and with less stress by sharing and by asking reflective questions. These approaches avoid negative side effects such as stimulating a natural desire to show independence.

POINTS TO REMEMBER

◆ Telling is perceived as an attempt to control, and people do not want to be controlled.

◆ Telling creates defensiveness and a tendency to resist.

◆ Telling implies that something has to be changed. People don't mind change as much as they mind *being* changed.

◆ Telling aims at obedience, not inspiration.

◆ Sharing information and *asking* reflective questions are more effective than telling.

PART IV
Parenting Pitfalls
Summary and Conclusion

*To reduce your stress and have the young become
what you would like them to become,
communicate with them as if they were already adults.*

SUMMARY

Human beings, especially of the male gender, are competitive. Competition is a natural part of our culture. Newspapers, magazines, and other media are full of information on business and sports, both based on competition and highlighting "winners" who receive rewards in some form. No one can doubt the importance of rewards as motivators. However, as with anything in life, *context is critical.* Because competition and rewards spur performance, does that mean that competition is also best within a family? Is it wise for husbands and wives or siblings to compete? Or should they collaborate for the benefit of the family team?

As was earlier explained, rewards can serve as effective incentives and wonderful acknowledgments. However, when rewards are used as manipulators to change young people's behaviors, there are some very real and unintended drawbacks.

Although rewards and punishments are often considered opposites, the two approaches share a similar focus: obedience. One can also see the similarity between the reward out front and the punishment behind by the questions they ask. To review, rewards ask, "What do they want me to do and what do I get for doing it?" Punishments ask, "What do they want me to do and what happens to me if I don't do it?" Neither encourages reflection for personal growth.

Among the disadvantages of using rewards to change behavior is that they change motivation from what is expected to "What will I get?" They can serve as an effective incentive only if the person is interested in the reward. Rewards do not help children become more moral or ethical because rewards do not change attitudes or commitments. Rewards foster competition rather than cooperation and are counterproductive to the establishment and maintenance of a friendly and kind home atmosphere. When you use rewards and punishments as motivational strategies, you are teaching people to make their decisions based on someone else's reaction. We reinforce the practice of people making their decisions based on how the other person is going to respond. The message tells people, "It's not what is best for you but how the *other person* reacts."

There are many reasons for *not imposing* punishment to promote responsibility with young people. Among them are: (1) a young person is not an adult with just a younger body, (2) hurting a child in order to instruct or harming a young person in order to teach is contrary to all we know about the brain and learning, (3) an imposed punishment satisfies the punisher more than it changes the behavior of the person being punished, (4) an imposed punishment promotes adversarial relationships and resistance, and perhaps most importantly, (5) imposing a punishment is not nearly as effective as *eliciting* a consequence or a procedure to change behavior.

In almost all cases, rewards and punishments need to be intensified over time in order to maintain the same level of results. More and more treats must be offered—or conversely, more threats or sanctions must be applied—to induce young people to continue to act in the way the manipulator desires. Not only does this reward-punishment mentality become progressively more objectionable as the child grows older, but it also inevitably delivers fewer and fewer successes as well. Anyone who works with adolescents, in particular, knows that it gets tougher and tougher to manipulate teens as they become less enamored with small treats and as they shift their reference group—and their desire for approval—from parents to peers.

Most young children can be enticed easily into compliance by an attractive reward, and there are youth who would prefer to take the pain of punishment rather than take the time to make difficult decisions and exert self-control. However, by using rewards and punishments, we unintentionally give children *an easy way out*—at the expense of their development and maturation. Rather than empowering our youngsters with responsibility, we are teaching them that temporary compliance will get them off the hook.

Although rewards and punishments might give children direction, they all too often have serious repercussions as children grow into young adults with less decision-making experiences under their belt. Parents are not around when peer pressure influences young people to take up tobacco, experiment with drugs, or do a whole host of other things that are unsafe or destructive. Such behavior induces stress on parents and, in the long term, on the young person as well.

CONCLUSION

No philosophy is more rooted in parenting (and education) than behaviorism—the idea that all motivation occurs only from external sources—that thinking has no bearing on behavior. Therefore, behaviorism, by definition, relies solely on external approaches. If these motivational approaches—offering rewards, threatening, imposing punishments, or telling people what they should do—were effective, then discipline problems would be only a minor concern of parenting (and teaching). External approaches are too often ineffective and are counterproductive for fostering self-discipline and responsibility. In addition, they have little lasting effect on the person whose behaviors require change.

The Swiss psychologist Jean Piaget believed that adults undermine the development of autonomy in children when they rely on the use of rewards and punishments to influence a child's behavior. Punishment, according to Piaget, is an externally controlled behavior-management technique that often leads to blind conformity, deceit, and rebellion in those being controlled. Children who choose to become conformists need not make decisions; all they need to do is obey. Some children practice deceit to avoid punishment. When parents say, "Don't let me catch you doing that again!" children may respond by exerting every effort *not to get caught*, rather than focusing on appropriate behavior.

Kurt Lewin, the first to write in the area of social psychology, intentionally used the word "manipulation" when referring to external approaches. Rewards and punishments amount to just that. The adult plays a game of power and control in which only the adult wins; both rewards and punishments are unilaterally imposed. The long-term use of this manipulative tactic requires raising the stakes. The adult must keep these incentives ever present because children learn to depend upon these types of motivators. The approach becomes self-perpetuating and needs to be intensified to remain effective.

There is an old Greek myth about a gentleman who was looking for Mt. Olympus. On his journey, he asked directions of an elderly man who turned out to be Socrates. When the traveler asked how to get to Mt. Olympus, the old sage responded in his reflective tradition: "Be sure every step you take is in that direction." Rewarding expected standards of behavior and punishing do not take us in the direction of fostering responsibility.

Although we often think we can *give* responsibility, the truth is that responsibility can only be *taken*; therefore, desire is essential for developing this characteristic. Desire comes only through internal motivation. Responsible behavior is a *chosen* behavior. Remember the paradox: Our goal is to assist young people to become responsible, self-reliant, independent problem solvers; yet, external approaches set up young people to be dependent upon an external agent. The *ultimate* goal should *not* be to have the child obey and keep parents happy. The ultimate goal is that young people act in a responsible way because it *pays off for them*; *it is in their own and others' best interests.* If you have this vision, it is going to reduce your stress because it doesn't box you into coercive, manipulative, and punitive modes.

Practicing positivity, using the empowerment of choice, honing the skill of asking reflective questions (Part I); teaching the difference between internal and external motivation—the foundation of the *Raise Responsibility System* (Part II); and reviewing some suggestions for additional assistance (Part III) will lead you to Mt. Olympus. These strategies will give your children both roots and wings. You will find yourself on the parenting journey of raising responsible kids while keeping a life of your own.

BIBLIOGRAPHY

Alessandra, Tony, and Michael O'Connor. *The Platinum Rule.* New York: Warner Books, 1996.

Allard, Harry G., and James Marshall. *Miss Nelson is Missing.* New York: Houghton Mifflin, 1977.

Alston, John W. *Story Power: Talking with Teens in Turbulent Times.* Stamford, CT: Longmeadow, 1981.

Bluestein, Jane. *21st Century Discipline: Teaching Students Responsibility and Self-Control.* Jefferson City, MO: Scholastic, 1988.

Brooks, B. David, and Patricia Freedman. *Implementing Character Education.* San Diego, CA: Education Assessment Publishing, 2002.

Bruner, Jerome. *The Process of Education.* Cambridge, MA: Harvard University Press, 1961.

Canfield, Jack, and Mark Victor Hansen. *The Aladdin Factor.* New York: Berkley Books, 1995.

Carnegie, Dale. *How to Win Friends & Influence People.* New York: HarperCollins, 1999.

Cathcart, Jim. *The Acorn Principle.* New York: St. Martin's Griffin, 1999.

Clark, Ron. *The Essential 55: An Award-Winning Educator's Rules for Discovering the Successful Student in Every Child.* New York: Hyperion, 2003.

Cline, Foster, and Jim Fey. *Parenting with Love and Logic: Teaching Children Responsibility.* Colorado Springs, CO: Pinon, 1990.

Cooper, Harris. *The Battle Over Homework.* 2nd ed. Thousand Oaks, CA: Corwin Press, 2001.

Cosby, William H., Jr. *Fatherhood.* Garden City, NJ: Doubleday, 1986.

Costa, Arthur, and Bena Kallick. *Habits of the Mind* (Series). Arlington, VA: Association for Supervision and Curriculum Development, 2000.

Covey, Stephen R. *The 7 Habits of Highly Effective Families.* New York: Golden Books, 1997.

_____. *The 7 Habits of Highly Effective People.* New York: Simon & Schuster, 1990.

_____. *The 8th Habit: From Effectiveness to Greatness.* New York: Free Press, 2004.

Crudele, John, and Richard Erickson. *Making Sense of Adolescence: How to Parent from the Heart.* Liguori, MO: Triumph, 1995.

Damasio, Antonio. *Descartes' Error: Emotion, Reason, and the Human Brain.* New York: Quil, HarperCollins, 2000.

Davidson, Jay. *Teach Your Children Well: A First-Grade Teacher's Advice for Parents.* Palo Alto, CA: Tojabrel, 2000.

Deci, Edward L., and Richard Flaste. *Why We Do What We Do: Understanding Self-Motivation.* New York: Penguin, 1995.

Doidge, Norman. *The Brain That Changes Itself.* New York: Penguin, 2007.

Dorn, Michael. *Weakfish: Bullying Through the Eyes of a Child.* Macon, GA: Safe Havens International, 2003.

Ellis, Albert, and Catherine MacLaren. *Rational Emotive Behavior Therapy: A Therapist's Guide.* San Luis Obispo, CA: Impact Publishers, 1998.

Frankl, Viktor. *Man's Search for Meaning.* New York: Washington Square Press, 1968.

Fredrickson, Barbara. *Positivity.* New York: Crown, 2009.

Gelb, Michael. *Thinking for a Change.* New York: Harmony Books, 1995.

Gibran, Kahlil. *The Prophet.* New York: Alfred A. Knopf, 1996.

Gladwell, Malcolm. *Blink: The Power of Thinking Without Thinking.* New York: Little, Brown and Company, 2005.

_____. *Outliers: The Story of Success.* New York: Little, Brown and Company, 2008.

Glasser, William. *Choice Theory: A New Psychology of Personal Freedom.* New York: HarperCollins, 1998.

_____. *Unhappy Teenagers.* New York: HarperCollins, 2002.

Glenn, H. Stephen, and Jane Nelsen. *Raising Self-Reliant Children in a Self-Indulgent World.* Rocklin, CA: Prima, 1989.

Goleman, Daniel. *Emotional Intelligence.* New York: Bantam, 1995.

_____. *Social Intelligence: The New Science of Human Relationship.* New York: Bantam Dell, 2007.

_____. *Working with Emotional Intelligence.* London: Bloomsbury, 1999.

Gordon, Thomas. *Discipline That Works: Promoting Self-Discipline in Children.* New York: Plume, 1991.

_____. *Parent Effectiveness Training: The Tested New Way to Raise Responsible Children.* New York: Plume, 1975.

Gray, John. *Men Are from Mars, Women Are from Venus.* New York: HarperCollins, 1992.

Grote, Richard. *Discipline Without Punishment.* Kansas City, MO: American Management Association, 1995.

Harris, Judith Rich. *The Nurture Assumption: Why Children Turn Out the Way They Do.* New York: The Free Press, 1998.

Helmstetter, Shad. *Choices.* New York: Simon & Schuster, 1989.

Howatt, William. *A Parent's Survival Guide for the Twenty-First Century.* Kentville, Nova Scotia, Canada: A Way with Words, 1999.

Kennedy, John F. *Profiles in Courage.* New York: Black Dog & Leventhal, 1984.

Kohn, Alfie. *Punished by Rewards.* Boston: Houghton Mifflin, 1993.

_____. *Unconditional Parenting: Moving from Rewards and Punishments to Love and Reason.* New York: Atria, 2005.

Laiken, Deidre S., and Alan J. Schneider. *Listen to Me, I'm Angry.* New York: William Morrow, 1995.

Levine, Mel. *A Mind at a Time.* New York: Simon & Schuster, 2002.

Marshall, Marvin. "Discipline without Stress® Punishments or Rewards." *The Clearing House* (September/October 2005).

_____. *Discipline without Stress® Punishments, or Rewards: How Teachers and Parents Promote Responsibility & Learning.* 2nd ed. Los Alamitos, CA: Piper Press, 2007.

_____. "Ensuring Social Responsibility," *Thrust for Educational Leadership.* Burlingame, CA: The Association of California School Administrators, January 1994.

_____. *Fostering Social Responsibility.* Bloomington, IN: Phi Delta Kappa Educational Foundation, 1998.

_____. "Rethinking Our Thinking on Discipline: Empower— Rather Than Overpower." *Education Week* (May 27, 1998).

_____, and Kerry Weisner. "Using a Discipline System to Promote Learning." *Phi Delta Kappan* (March 2004).

Maslow, Abraham H. *Motivation and Personality.* 3rd ed. New York: Addison Wesley Longman, 1987.

Maurer, Robert. *One Small Step Can Change Your Life: The Kaizen Way.* New York: Workman Publishing, 2004.

McGregor, Douglas. *The Human Side of Enterprise.* New York: McGraw-Hill, 1960.

McIntire, Roger. *Raising Good Kids in Tough Times: 7 Crucial Habits for Parent Success.* Berkeley Springs, WV: Summit Crossroads, 1999.

_____. *Teenagers and Parents: 10 Steps for a Better Relationship.* Berkeley Springs, WV: Summit Crossroads, 2000.

Morris, Steve, and Jill Morris. *Leadership Simple: Leading People to Lead Themselves.* Santa Barbara, CA: Imporex, 2003.

National PTA. *Discipline: A Parent's Guide.* Chicago: National Congress of Parents and Teachers, 1993.

Oakley, Ed, and Doug Krug. *Enlightened Leadership: Getting to the Heart of Change.* New York: Simon & Schuster, 1993.

Payne, Ruby K. *A Framework for Understanding Poverty.* Highlands, TX: Aha Press, 2001.

Peale, Norman Vincent. *The Power of Positive Thinking.* Pawling, NY: Peale Center for Christian Living, 1978.

Peck, M. Scott. *The Road Less Traveled: A New Psychology of Love, Traditional Values and Spiritual Growth.* 25th Anniversary ed. New York: Touchstone, 2003.

Polland, Barbara K. *No Directions on the Package: Questions and Answers for Parents with Children from Birth to Age Twelve.* Berkeley, CA: Celestial Arts, 2000.

Popkin, Michael. *Parenting Your 1- to 4 -Year-Olds.* Kennesaw, GA: Active Parenting, 1998.

Prager, Dennis. *Happiness Is a Serious Problem.* New York: Regan HarperCollins, 1998.

Reynolds, Peter H. *The Dot.* Cambridge, MA: Candlewick, 2003.

Robert, Cavett. *Success with People.* Wise, VA: The Napoleon Hill Foundation, 1969.

Roberts, Monty. *Horse Sense for People.* New York: Viking, 2001.

Rosemond, John. *John Rosemond's Six-Point Plan for Raising Happy, Healthy Children.* Kansas City, MO: Andrews and McMeel, 1989.

Salk, Lee. *Familyhood: Nurturing the Values that Matter.* New York: Simon & Schuster, 1992.

Scoresby, A. Lynn. *Teaching Moral Development.* Oram, UT: Knowledge Gain Publications, 1996.

Seifert, Kathryn. *How Children Become Violent: Keeping Your Kids Out of Gangs, Terrorist Organizations, and Cults.* Boston: Acanthus, 2006.

Shore, Penny. *How to Achieve Joyful and Competent Parenting.* Toronto, Ontario, Canada: The Parent Kit, 2006.

Simmons, Rachel. *Odd Girl Out: The Hidden Culture of Aggression in Girls.* New York: Harcourt, 2002.

Sosin, David, and Myra Sosin. *Attention Deficit Disorder: A Professional's Guide.* Westminster, CA: Teacher Created Materials, 2001.

Steinberg, Laurence. *The Ten Basic Principles of Good Parenting.* New York: Simon & Schuster, 2004.

Stone, Douglas, Bruce Patton, and Sheila Heen. *Difficult Conversations: How to Discuss What Matters Most.* New York: Penguin, 2000.

Sutton, James D. *If My Kid's So Nice...Why's He Driving ME Crazy?* Pleasanton, TX: Friendly Oaks Publications, 1997.

Tracy, Louise Felton. *Grounded for Life: Stop Blowing Your Fuse and Start Communicating with Your Teenager.* Seattle, WA: Parenting Press, 1994.

Urban, Hal. *Life's Greatest Lessons or 20 Things I Want My Kids to Know.* Redwood City, CA: Great Lessons Press, 2000.

_____. *Positive Words, Powerful Results.* New York: Simon & Schuster, 2004.

Van Leuven, Dean. *Life Without Anger.* Camarillo, CA: DeVorss, 2003.

Voors, William. *The Parent's Book About Bullying.* Center City, MN: Hazeldon, 2000.

Wubbolding, Robert. *Reality Therapy for the 21st Century.* Philadelphia, PA: Brunner-Routledge, 2000.

INDEX

For additional copies of *Parenting without Stress*
visit the website at *www.ParentingWithoutStress.org*,
e-mail to Order@ParentingWithoutStress.org,
or call the Piper Press distributor at 800.606.6105.

Substantial discounts are available.